Understanding white collar crime

CRIME AND JUSTICE
Series editor: Mike Maguire
Cardiff University

Crime and Justice is a series of short introductory texts on central topics in criminology. The books in this series are written for students by internationally renowned authors. Each book tackles a key area within criminology, providing a concise and up-to-date overview of the principal concepts, theories, methods and findings relating to the area. Taken as a whole, the *Crime and Justice* series will cover all the core components of an undergraduate criminology course.

Published titles

Understanding youth and crime
Sheila Brown

Understanding crime data
Clive Coleman and Jenny Moynihan

Understanding white collar crime
Hazel Croall

Understanding justice
An introduction to ideas, perspectives and controversies in modern penal theory
Barbara A. Hudson

Understanding crime prevention
Gordon Hughes

Understanding violent crime
Stephen Jones

Understanding criminology
Sandra Walklate

Understanding white collar crime

Hazel Croall

Open University Press
Buckingham · Philadelphia

Open University Press
Celtic Court
22 Ballmoor
Buckingham
MK18 1XW

email: enquiries@openup.co.uk
world wide web: www.openup.co.uk

and

325 Chestnut Street
Philadelphia, PA 19106, USA

First Published 2001

A catalogue record of this book is available from the British Library

ISBN   0 335 20427 9 (pb)   0 335 20428 7 (hb)

Library of Congress Cataloging-in-Publication Data
Croall, Hazel, 1947–
    Understanding white collar crime / Hazel Croall.
       p. cm. — (Crime and justice)
    Includes bibliographical references and index.
    ISBN 0–335–20428–7 — ISBN 0–335–20427–9 (pbk.)
       1. White collar crimes. I. Title. II. Crime and justice (Buckingham, England)

    HV6768 .C755 2001
    364.16′8 — dc21

                                                                    00–050174

Typeset by Type Study, Scarborough
Printed in Great Britain by Biddles Limited, Guildford and Kings Lynn

Contents

Series editor's foreword

Hazel Croall's book is the latest contribution to the Open University Press Crime and Justice series, which provides relatively short but challenging introductory textbooks on important areas of debate within the fields of criminology, criminal justice and penology. All the books are written by experienced lecturers and researchers, and the aim is to give undergraduates and graduates both a solid grounding in the relevant area and a taste to explore it further. Although aimed primarily at students new to the field, and written as far as possible in plain language, the books are not oversimplified. On the contrary, the authors set out to 'stretch' readers and to encourage them to approach criminological knowledge and theory in a critical and questioning frame of mind.

Croall's focus is upon 'white collar' crime. As she points out, this is far from a clear category of crime – indeed, some authors prefer not to use the term at all, finding it ambiguous and outdated. However, she argues that alternatives are no less problematic and that it is the term best understood by both academics and the public to describe what she is primarily interested in: as she defines it, crime involving an 'abuse of a legitimate occupational role which is regulated by law'. This includes both occupational and organizational (or corporate) crime, that is, crimes by employees (particularly those with medium or high status) as well as crimes by companies or other organizations. While her primary focus is on British research, she emphasizes that such crime has to be seen in a global context and illustrates her arguments with examples from all over the world.

Croall examines a number of distinct categories under the overall umbrella of white collar crime, including theft at work, fraud, corruption, consumer crime and environmental crime. She looks at how such crimes come to light (or, more often, do not) and at the kinds of offenders involved. She examines alternative explanations for these kinds of behaviour, ranging from individual greed to the nature of capitalism itself. She also (unusually in this subject area) takes a close look at the victims of white collar crime and the impact it has on them. Her closing chapters are concerned with the difficult question of how to regulate and prevent white collar crime, including the balance between criminalization, regulation and self-regulation. She points out major discrepancies between white collar and 'ordinary' offenders in their treatment by legislators, police and courts, and raises fundamental questions about the relationships between social class, power and the role of the criminal law.

Other books already published in the Crime and Justice series – all of whose titles begin with the word 'Understanding' – have covered penological theory (Barbara A. Hudson), criminological theory (Sandra Walklate), criminal statistics (Clive Coleman and Jenny Moynihan), youth crime (Sheila Brown), crime prevention (Gordon Hughes) and violent crime (Stephen Jones). Others in the pipeline include texts on criminal justice (Mike Maguire), prisons (Kathryn Chadwick, Margaret Malloch and Phil Scraton), policing (Simon Holdaway), crime and social exclusion (Loraine Gelsthorpe), community penalties (Peter Raynor and Maurice Vanstone) and drugs and crime (Karen Duke). All are major topics in university degree courses on crime and criminal justice, and each book should make an ideal foundation text for a relevant module. As an aid to understanding, clear summaries are provided at regular intervals, and a glossary of key terms and concepts is a feature of every book. In addition, to help students expand their knowledge, recommendations for further reading are given at the end of each chapter.

Mike Maguire
Professor of Criminology and Criminal Justice, Cardiff University

Acknowledgements

Many people have helped during the preparation of this book. Academically, colleagues at the many conferences and discussions I have participated in have been encouraging and have considerably enhanced my knowledge and appreciation of many aspects of white collar crime. Special thanks are due to Jenifer Ross for her collaboration and helpful suggestions on the draft. Socially, my friends and colleagues have been always ready to provide the opportunity for much-needed breaks and my daughter Ailsa has also played her part. The staff at Open University Press have been of great help and thanks are also due to the series editor for his supportive and helpful comments. All errors, of course, remain mine.

chapter one

Conceptualizing white collar crime

White collar crime affects key areas of contemporary life. Financial 'scandals' such as the collapse of major banks and pension frauds question the legitimacy of the financial world, and the climate of 'sleaze' has become a political issue. Tax and public sector fraud reduces government resources for health, education and welfare. The harmful activities of corporations endanger the safety of workers, consumers and passengers, and have a wider impact on public health and the environment. For example, in the United Kingdom, following widespread concern about the failure to prosecute rail companies following rail crashes, the government has recently announced its intention to introduce a law dealing with '*corporate killing*' (*Guardian* 10 May 2000: 4). Although these activities are subject to criminal law and criminal justice, they are not regarded as crime in the same way as burglary, robbery or assault, and they are less likely to prompt calls for tougher policing and punishment. It is not common, for example, to hear demands for 'zero tolerance' of fraudsters or antisocial behaviour orders for companies.

These are some of the issues raised by the study of white collar crime. The existence of white collar crime questions the way in which crime is defined, counted and treated by criminal justice agencies. It encompasses a wide range of harmful activities which are not all widely regarded as criminal, raising questions of how it can be compared with other crimes. The analysis of white collar crime moves beyond the traditional concerns of criminology into wider areas of financial regulation, the environment, occupational health and safety, consumer affairs and food regulation. Can it therefore be incorporated into the study of crime? These and many other questions will be tackled in this book. This first chapter will start by briefly exploring the development of the concept of white collar crime and its status in criminology before turning to questions of how it can be defined, whether it is distinct from other crimes and whether it can be conceptualized as 'crime'. The chapter will then explore some of the problems involved in researching white collar crime.

White collar crime and criminology

The harmful nature of the activities associated with white collar crime have long been recognized. Chaucer's *The Pardoner's Tale* contains a sermon against avarice (Ruggiero 1996a), and in the Middle Ages traders caught using false scales or adulterating food were excommunicated, pilloried, put in the stocks or banished from towns (O'Keefe 1966; Harvey 1982). The morality of emergent capitalism is discussed in the work of Daniel Defoe, and 'entrepreneurship' has often been associated with 'deviant' business activities (Ruggiero 1996a). During the nineteenth century laws sought to protect the safety of workers and passengers and the economic interests of 'honest' traders and consumers, and to prevent the widespread adulteration of food (Croall 1992). Developments in finance and commerce have continually produced new opportunities for fraud, from the formation of joint stock companies to contemporary frauds using electronic technology and cyberspace. Capitalism itself has been seen as criminogenic – the Dutch criminologist, Bonger, linked crime among the bourgeoisie to the motivating ideologies of capitalism (Bonger 1905, cited in Slapper and Tombs 1999), and Sutherland's (1949) original identification of white collar crime followed a long tradition of 'muckraking' which exposed the harmful activities of US capitalism.

To early criminologists, however, crime was associated with the activities of the lower class offenders who populated courts and prisons. Theory and research sought to identify the 'causes' of crime that were assumed to lie in the pathologies of individual offenders and in poverty and deprivation. This was challenged in 1939 by the US criminologist Edwin Sutherland who advanced an alternative thesis:

> that persons of the upper socio-economic class engage in much criminal behaviour; that this criminal behaviour differs from the criminal

behaviour of the lower socio-economic class principally in the administrative procedures which are used in dealing with the offenders and that
variations in administrative procedures are not significant from the
point of view of causation of crime.

(Sutherland 1949: 9)

He thereby drew attention to crimes not 'ordinarily included within the
scope of criminology' and 'approximately' defined white collar crime as 'a
crime committed by a person of respectability and high social status in the
course of his occupation' (Sutherland 1949: 9). He specifically associated the
term 'white collar' with business managers and executives to distinguish
their offences from the confidence games of the underworld. His research
established that many prominent corporations had been found guilty of
multiple violations of civil and criminal statutes. This made them recidivist
offenders who should, he argued, be included in general theories of crime.
This attracted considerable criticism, particularly on the grounds that criminology should look only at activities covered by criminal law (Tappan
1977). Otherwise, argued Tappan, criminologists could define any behaviour they disapproved of as crime and undermine the 'scientific objectivity'
of the discipline. The definition itself raised many problems and this, along
with discussions of whether white collar crime was, indeed, crime, led to
what were characterized as 'sterile definitional disputes' (Aubert 1977).

Controversial though the concept was, it challenged many aspects of
criminology. Its existence questioned the use of official statistics, which
largely excluded it, as objective indicators of crime, and questioned the definition of crime by drawing attention to equally harmful activities subject to
different laws and procedures. The high status of offenders questioned the
long-standing preoccupation with lower-class offenders and raised important issues about bias in criminal law, prosecution and punishment. This pre-
ceded the emergence of critical perspectives in criminology from the 1960s
which posed similar questions. To **labelling perspectives**, no activities were
intrinsically deviant or criminal and the processes that led to activities being
criminalized and to offenders being processed and labelled were themselves
worthy of research. To Marxist perspectives criminal law and its enforcement reflected the interests of the powerful and were a means of controlling
the activities of powerless lower-class offenders; and the harmful activities
of business groups lay largely outside their scope (Pearce 1976). Criminal
law and crime came therefore to be represented as contested categories. This
rendered the concept of white collar crime less problematic and made the
study of how different kinds of crime were subjected to law and the criminal justice process a valid concern for criminology and an emergent sociology of law (Pearce and Tombs 1998).

These theoretical advances had a considerable impact on the study of
white collar crime. In Britain, where the critical tradition was strongest

(Punch 1996), research explored the developing use of criminal law against business activities and the respective roles of business groups, enforcers and government (Carson 1971; Paulus 1974 and see Chapter 6). Out of this emerged a distinction between some forms of white collar crime and 'real' crime and a different process of law enforcement, which was itself subjected to a considerable volume of research (see Chapter 6). In the USA, research on white collar crime also looked at enforcement decisions and continued Sutherland's tradition of exposing its extent, particularly following the growth of consumerism and the Watergate scandal. Despite this, however, the subject remained marginal to criminology, and the promise of the critical tradition was not fulfilled. With some exceptions such as Pearce's (1976) work on the 'crimes of the powerful', studies in labelling and critical perspectives focused largely on how the activities of criminal justice agencies adversely affected lower-class young offenders rather than 'looking upwards' at white collar offenders (Punch 1996). As Weisburd and Schlegel (1992: 352) argue, the concept of white collar crime became somewhat of an ideological or theoretical 'gadfly', invoked, often in simplistic terms, to debunk stereotypes about criminality, and it was not translated into 'substantial theoretical or empirical concern among criminologists about the problem of white collar crime'.

What is often described as 'mainstream', '**administrative**' or 'establishment' **criminology** itself changed focus. The 'failure' of rehabilitative methods and strategies associated with the '**criminological project**' to reduce the volume of crime substantially was recognized by academic criminologists and policy makers as official crime rates continued to rise. Attention turned from the search for the 'causes' of or 'cures' for crime towards what were argued to be more realistic ways of preventing it and dealing with convicted offenders. An increasing number of **victim surveys** provided more accurate measures of the incidence and impact of offences on victims along with valuable information about the circumstances in which offences took place. Techniques of situational crime prevention, which targeted these circumstances, came to be seen as a more useful way to reduce crime than attempting to change offenders' motivations. The focus remained on lower-class crime, with white collar crime and victimization being almost entirely excluded from the growing number of victim surveys and crime prevention initiatives (Croall 1999a, 1999c).

Critical criminology was in turn criticized by the '**left realist**' perspective for what was seen as a preoccupation with the **crimes of the powerful** and with criminal law and its enforcement at the expense of the lived 'reality' of crime (Lea and Young 1993; Young 1997). Analyses of crime, it was argued, should take account of the 'square of crime', which stresses interrelationships between victims, offenders, the public and state agencies. Explanations should recognize the specificity of different kinds of crime, and relative, rather than absolute, deprivation was seen as a contributing factor. This approach, it was argued, could encompass white collar and conventional crime, although the work of left realists has in turn been criticized for a focus on 'street crime' (Croall 1992). Left realism was also seen to be ill adapted to analysing the more complex problems posed by crimes associated with impersonal organizations and fewer individual victims (Ruggiero 1992; Pearce and Tombs 1998). Other critical strands also questioned the construction of crime and the activities of criminal justice agencies. **Feminist perspectives** questioned the marginalization of domestic violence in constructions of violent crime and in police priorities, and they also criticized the 'gender blind' nature of criminology, which had failed to account for the gender gap in criminal convictions and the different treatment of women in the criminal justice process. Attention was also drawn to the way in which different racial and minority ethnic groups were subject to **criminalization** and institutional racism in respect of policing, courts and prisons. Although these approaches did not incorporate analyses of white collar crime, they raised comparable issues.

The relative lack of attention to white collar crime has continued, despite what can be seen as its increasing significance (Croall 1999a). The 1980s and 1990s saw a series of major financial scandals such as the collapse of the Bank of Credit and Commerce International (BCCI), and, in the UK, revelations of the massive frauds on the pensions funds of the Maxwell organization and the collapse of Barings Bank following the activities of the 'rogue trader', Nick Leeson. The advent of electronic banking has increased opportunities for fraud, some of them on a global scale, with it being possible to move money around the world in seconds. Major disasters and incidents such as the death of between 3000 and 5000 people in Bhopal in India following the release of methyl isocyanate into the atmosphere, and the disaster at the Chernobyl nuclear power plant, which caused widespread radiation across Europe, drew attention to the significance of corporate responsibility for safety. In the UK, a spate of 'disasters', subsequently attributed to faults in organizations, such as the sinking of the *Herald of Free Enterprise*, and the Clapham and later the Southall and Paddington rail crashes, led to public debate about the prioritization of profits over safety and to the emergence of groups campaigning for the criminal prosecution and punishment of those responsible. There have also been calls for those responsible for crimes perpetrated on behalf of states or political causes, such as the activities of General Pinochet or the 'ethnic cleansing' in former Yugoslavia, to be subject to criminal trials. Yet, as Slapper and Tombs (1999: 9) comment in relation to **corporate crime**:

> in what is best understood as a self-perpetuating cycle of omission and ignorance, most standard texts on criminology pay little or no attention to it; most theoretical criminology does not attempt to explain it; most undergraduate courses in criminology or criminal justice marginalise it.

Often repeated criticisms are that the *Oxford Handbook of Criminology* (Maguire *et al.* 1997), which is generally regarded as representing the current state of British criminology, devotes only one out of 32 chapters to white collar crime, and white collar crime has not featured strongly in theoretical texts, major journals such as *The British Journal of Criminology*, or in the British Criminology Conference until 1999, when a stream was devoted to the 'Crimes of the Powerful'. White collar crime is not associated with an identifiable 'school' of thought, and relatively few British scholars, described by Punch as 'lone rangers', have pursued its study (Punch 1996). Although there is more work in the United States, this is still small in comparison to work on other crimes. Nonetheless, as will be seen throughout this book, its critical role is considerable although it remains a highly contested concept. The remainder of this chapter will focus on how to conceptualize white collar crime, starting with problems surrounding its definition.

What is white collar crime?

Sutherland's 'approximate' definition (see p. 2) and the debates surrounding it led to much conceptual and linguistic confusion – as Nelken (1997a: 896) comments, 'if Sutherland merited a Nobel prize, as Mannheim thought, for pioneering this field of study, he certainly did not deserve it for the clarity or serviceableness of his definition'. The key words and phrases '*crime*', committed by '*persons of respectability and high social status*', '*in the course of*' an '*occupation*' all lead to problems in determining which activities are to be included. The contentious issue of crime will be dealt with below, and this section will focus on social status and occupation.

One major problem is whether the occupational nature of the activities or the social characteristics of offenders should be the major defining feature. By including both, Sutherland sought to distinguish crimes associated with 'respectable' or legitimate occupations from the 'ordinary' crimes such as rape or murder of high-status individuals, and from the crimes of those whose occupation could be said to be 'criminal' – from what is more generally defined as **organized** or **professional crime**. This poses the immediate problem of how 'high social status' or 'respectability' are to be defined. Where is the line to be drawn in the occupational hierarchy? Although white collar crime is often associated with the crimes of senior management and executives, the term white collar is used to describe all non-manual workers, and any specific form of crime associated with occupations is likely to contain offenders from a wide spectrum of employment levels. Customers and employers can be defrauded by junior or senior sales personnel, and corporate executives, secretaries or porters can sell inside information (Levi 1987a), and people lie, cheat or commit sins of 'omission' up and down the occupational hierarchy (Shapiro 1990). Occupational roles can therefore be abused in similar ways, irrespective of status. Although Sutherland talked of major corporations, small businesses can also be responsible for similar offences. Consumers can be 'ripped off' by local corner shops, market stalls or large manufacturers, and environmental pollution or safety offences in the workplace can be associated with 'cowboy' operators or large multinational conglomerates (Croall 1992).

Some have consequently argued that the definition of white collar crime should include all crimes committed in the course of occupations and should be redefined as '**occupational crime**' (Quinney 1977), or it should be based on an abuse of occupational trust (Shapiro 1990). This, however, removes what to many is the major feature of white collar crime – its association with high social status. It also makes the category extremely large, incorporating the 'perks', 'fiddles' and sabotage usually associated with 'blue-collar' occupations; the **insider dealing, embezzlement** and fraud generally associated with higher-level employees; and offences involving the neglect of safety, health, consumer or environmental regulations associated primarily with companies. On the other hand, it could be argued that to draw a line between higher-status and lower-status employees would be somewhat arbitrary and would preclude exploration of the different range of opportunities available to employees at different levels and the different ways in which their offences are perceived and subject to different kinds of sanctions.

A related problem is how to define 'respectable' or 'legitimate' occupations. Here, again, Sutherland confuses the characteristics of offenders with the activities concerned (Ruggiero 1996a). It is difficult in practice, argues Ruggiero, to draw a line between a legitimate and an illegitimate business, where, for example, organized criminals use legitimate businesses as a 'front', or where the extent of crime in an organization renders it 'criminal' – as was the case with the BCCI, which involved legitimate investors, governments and professional criminals (Punch 1996). Many small businesses exist at the margins of legitimacy and illegitimacy – selling legitimate and counterfeit and stolen goods. Looking at examples of activities involving legitimate and illegitimate businesses, often working together, Ruggiero (1996a) argues that corporate, white collar and organized crime are variants of the same form of crime and should be analysed jointly. Although again this would produce an extremely large group of offences, it further illustrates the problems of defining the category by the status of offenders and highlights how the broadly similar activities of different groups of offenders are conceptualized.

A further difficulty of using the status of offenders as a starting point is that it incorporates assumptions that may predetermine research questions and analysis. To academics and general commentators, the key feature of white collar crime is the high status of offenders, which is assumed to lead to its different treatment in the criminal justice process. This can become a circular argument – if class and status are taken to be the defining point, and offenders are treated differently, this is then explained by the class and status of offenders to the exclusion of any other factor. Class and status are not therefore unimportant, but are perhaps better perceived as related to rather than a key part of the definition.

Are white collar crimes distinct from other crimes?

Defining white collar crime implies that it can be distinguished from what are often, for comparative purposes, described as conventional or ordinary crimes. This, in turn, involves exploring which, if any, characteristics are associated with such a comparison. A number of distinctive features of white collar crime have been identified (Clarke 1990; Croall 1992; Langan 1996), some of which are a direct consequence of the location of offences in occupational roles, whereas others have been more often associated with the class and status of offenders. Although these are useful tools for comparison, it will be seen that it is not easy to draw clear dividing lines between different crime categories and that there are also variations between different kinds of white collar crime.

A number of characteristics are closely related to the occupational nature of offences. Because they take place in the private sphere of the workplace they are relatively *invisible* and can be concealed more easily because 'business offenders are legitimately present at the scene' (Clarke 1990: 21). Because they are committed during the course of an occupation, they involve an abuse of the *trust* inherent in an occupational role (Shapiro 1990). Offences are made possible by the use of some form of *technical* or '*insider*' *knowledge*, which may be an awareness of how to use organizational routines to conceal offending or may involve the abuse of professional, scientific or financial '*expertise*'. This makes many offences *complex*, and the extent, duration and details of offending are difficult to determine. Offences may be sins of 'omission' or 'commission', with a long 'paper trail' and cover-ups often being involved. Many are highly *organized* and involve several participants with differing degrees of responsibility. In many cases, determining who is responsible is difficult because of the *diffusion of responsibility* in organizations, where responsibility for particular tasks is delegated, enabling participants to 'blame' others up or down the hierarchy.

Offences also involve different patterns of *victimization*, and many offences are characterized as victimless. Some offences, such as the sale of short weight goods or abstracting small amounts of money from a large number of customers', investors', or clients' accounts, lead to small losses to individual victims. Victims may not be aware of any harm, which is also the case with offences such as food adulteration or safety offences. Other kinds of crime affect the 'public health' or 'the environment' rather than individual victims and, in other cases, effects are immeasurable and indirect. **Corruption**, for example, involves exchanges of money or favours, in which the 'criminal' element is the abuse of trust and the effect is on the legitimacy of institutions such as business, public service or political organizations. This can be contrasted with the immediate, direct and measurable victimization involved in, for example, an assault or robbery.

The *ambiguous legal and criminal status* of white collar crimes is a further characteristic, which is also related to their treatment in the criminal justice process. In many offences there is an apparent *lack of intent*, particularly where a diffusion of responsibility is involved, and where, although a regulation may have been broken, the consequences of that violation, such as injury, were not intended. This means that the moral element so important to the definition of crime is absent. Victims' lack of awareness and the invisibility and complexity of offences make them difficult to detect, and difficulties of attributing responsibility and obtaining evidence also make offences difficult to prosecute. This leads to a relatively *low rate of detection and prosecution*. In addition, many offenders receive what are seen as *lenient sentences*, which are also related to the absence of intent, lack of direct victimization and the ambivalent criminal status of offences. Differences in the legal processing of white collar crimes are therefore related to their particular characteristics, although a major issue is how much they are also related to the class and status of offenders.

These features are most often used routinely to compare white collar crimes with other crimes. As will be seen in subsequent chapters, however, such generalized comparisons can be misleading because many of these features are not unique to or shared by all white collar crimes. Some conventional crimes are also invisible, particularly those that take place in the private sphere of the family. Some, like burglary or robbery, involve considerable expertise and can also be highly organized and complex, which makes them similarly difficult to detect. Moreover, successful professional criminals delegate responsibility to minimize the risk of being detected and prosecuted (Ruggiero and South 1995). Not all conventional crime involves immediately harmed victims and those crimes that involve willing exchanges between consenting adults, such as gambling, prostitution or drug offences, are also represented as 'victimless' and pose particular problems for detection and prosecution. These and other conventional crimes are also characterized by an ambivalent criminal status and perceptions of the 'criminality' of activities vary over time. Intent, so often seen as a major element in criminal liability, is problematic in other forms of crime – those who drive while drunk may not intend to harm others and can see themselves as 'unlucky' (Slapper and Tombs 1999). Other, more unambiguously criminal offences are also perceived to be treated leniently – rape cases, for example, have a high rate of attrition leading to low prosecution rates (Lees 1996) – and many sentences are criticized as lenient.

A further problem with broad contrasts is that not all white collar crimes share all these characteristics. Not all offences are equally invisible – some frauds, safety or food offences are immediately detectable. Their location in occupational roles means that most white collar crimes do involve an abuse of occupational trust, but occupational roles vary in the extent to which employees are trusted and offences involve varying degrees of knowledge and expertise. Not all white collar crimes involve complex organization – employees may simply steal money or goods and neglect of regulations may arise from ignorance or incompetence. Patterns of victimization vary, with some having a direct and severe impact, including death, injury and heavy financial losses. Some white collar offences are more unambiguously criminal than others – few would dispute, for example, that serious frauds are crimes, and some offences more clearly involve intent than others. And as will be seen in subsequent chapters, not all white collar crimes enjoy lenient treatment.

No clear dividing line can therefore be drawn between white collar and other crimes, and many of these characteristics would be better seen as representing a series of continua (Nelken 1997a). Nelken, for example, points out that organized crime involves cases of cold-blooded calculation and those cases where it is difficult to distinguish malevolence from incompetence, and also points to a continuum between accidental and deliberate, although for other crimes the criminal sanction is less problematic. Were different kinds of crime to be plotted along a series of continua, it is likely that many white collar crimes would cluster at one end, with many conventional crimes at the other. Broad comparisons often draw on extreme examples – thus the invisibility, lack of intent, diffuse victimization and complexity of a major pollution incident may be compared with the visibility, intent, direct victimization and simplicity of a mugging.

These kinds of considerations also suggest that different characteristics are in themselves subject to social construction. Although a drunken driver does not necessarily intend to kill or injure, most would now accept that taking such a risk is morally wrong, and the law incorporates notions of recklessness and negligence. Although neglecting safety regulations similarly involves recklessness about the consequences, it is not generally regarded as morally wrong (Slapper and Tombs 1999). The complexity of offences can also be overstated – many, argue Slapper and Tombs, are simple acts of omission or commission but are made more complex by legal procedures (Slapper and Tombs 1999). Categories of crime are also socially constructed – it has been seen, for example, that the distinction between organized and white collar crime rests in part on a conception of the 'respectableness' of offenders. Although some white collar crime involves death and injury, it is not normally related to violent crime, which is more often constructed around public, interpersonal violence. This is, in turn, distinguished from the legitimate 'force' of state agencies, although the dividing line between this and an abuse of the occupational roles of police or military personnel is a narrow one. Constructions of violence also omit the physical harms associated with the neglect of safety or health regulations, which could well be defined as **institutional violence** (Wells 1993; Levi 1997) in the same way as is 'institutional racism'. The above discussion also indicates that there are many variations in the category of white collar crime, which will be explored below.

Varieties of white collar crime

The enormous range of activities encompassed by the category of white collar crime has inevitably led to attempts to divide it into subcategories, to provide researchers with a manageable group of offences and enable comparisons between offences. In practice, research has tended to focus on specific groups of activities, often legally defined, such as fraud or safety, environmental or consumer offences. The status of offenders continues to be an important feature of these definitions, with some referring to **elite crime** or crimes of the powerful, and to corporate and **state crime**. Some activities can be seen as largely motivated by financial gain, whereas others intentionally or otherwise cause physical harms. Thus, some people distinguish financial white collar crimes from others. Some studies have focused on specific industries such as the chemicals (Pearce and Tombs 1998) or pharmaceutical industry (Braithwaite 1984), or on particular occupational groups such as specific professions. This can lead to a proliferation of overlapping and often confusing definitions and categorizations. Many people now accept that a broad distinction can be drawn between offences primarily motivated by individual monetary gain and those that are more directly related to the survival or profitability of organizations, although in this respect, as in so many other respects, the characteristics of offenders are also important.

The distinction between occupational and **organizational crime** points to some major contrasts. Broadly speaking, occupational crime, a typical example of which is embezzlement, involves offenders, either individually or in groups, engaging in illegal or rule-breaking activities for personal gain at the expense of consumers, clients or employers. Organizational crime, on the other hand, a typical example of which is the neglect of safety regulations, does not involve personal gain, but may be seen as being 'for the good of' the organization by enhancing profitability or efficiency. Whereas occupational crime more obviously involves intent and individual responsibility, organizational crime illustrates the diffusion of responsibility. Where an employee neglects or violates a regulation they can claim that it is ultimately the organization's responsibility to ensure that regulations are complied with. This distinction parallels others. As will be seen in later chapters, there are particular legal problems associated with corporate liability and, in general terms, organizational crime fits less easily within a construction of crime centred on notions of individual guilt and responsibility (Wells 1993; Slapper and Tombs 1999). Organizational crimes are therefore often perceived to be less 'criminal' than those of individuals, and patterns of victimization are less direct, whereas individual offences may attract stronger public reaction and heavier sentences. This can be further related to differences in the interests threatened by offences – Pearce (1976), for example, distinguishes between crimes that threaten the interests of capital, such as fraud, and those that can be interpreted as being in the course of capitalist activity.

This distinction, while useful, cannot be overdrawn (Slapper and Tombs 1999) and cross-cuts other commonly used categories. Organizational crime is often equated with corporate crime, although the former term is arguably more appropriate because regulations can be violated in public and voluntary organizations as well as in corporations. The term 'state crime' is often used to describe offences in state organizations, although some of these may be carried out for individual gratification – police officers may, for example, accept favours or break the rules to benefit themselves. Where such activities are for the perceived benefit of the state or one of its agencies, however, they can be seen as **state organized**. **Political crime** similarly involves politicians accepting favours for their individual economic benefit or career advancement, or can be perceived to be in the interests of the party or government. **Crimes of professional occupations** such as doctors, lawyers or accountants can also be motivated by personal gain, such as embezzlement or prescriptions frauds, or can be for the benefit of the organization which employs the professionals. Financial crimes such as frauds are often seen as individual but can also be organizational – in the recent cases of pensions 'misselling' in the United Kingdom, company policies lay behind the actions of individual sales personnel. In addition, many individual offences could be seen as organizationally induced (Punch 1996; Pearce and Tombs 1998). Perks, fiddles and neglecting regulations that can be seen as cumbersome and slowing down the pace of work may be undertaken to keep up with production schedules or to secure a 'fair day's pay' (Ditton 1977; Mars 1982). As Punch (1996: 57) points out, 'organisations may create climates where collective deviance is an acceptable answer to perceived institutional dilemmas, and where organisational culture, resources and facilities are intrinsic to the development of the deviance'.

Some attempts to categorize offences retain elements of the status of offenders and many argue that the term white collar crime is intrinsically related to the characteristics of offenders and should therefore be restricted to occupational crime. Slapper and Tombs (1999: 14), for example, argue that the phrase white collar crime should be restricted to crimes by the 'individually rich or powerful which are committed in the furtherance of their own interests often against corporations or organisations for or within which they are working'. Punch directs his attention to 'organizational deviance', encompassing both organizational and occupational offences, which he associates with 'influential people who utilize their power or resources for ends which some other people define as illicit, and then, not infrequently, employ that power or those resources to protect themselves from the consequences of social control' (Punch 1996: 57). Many different definitions are therefore used in practice.

Is white collar crime, crime?

A final and crucial question to be addressed in relation to the definition of white collar crime is whether or not it should include only legally defined 'crimes' and legally convicted offenders. Sutherland's original inclusion of activities subject to civil and administrative laws raised the question of how the harmful activities of different groups of offenders were treated differently by law and criminal justice, but was widely criticized as threatening the objectivity of criminology. This led to many debates centred around the theme 'is white collar crime, crime?' Although this question becomes less problematic once the socially constructed nature of crime is acknowledged, any consideration of which activities are to be included must nonetheless take into account the significance of law and criminal law. Adopting a legal definition of crime may be seen as overly restrictive, but including activities not subject to criminal law continues to attract criticisms of political and moral subjectivity (Slapper and Tombs 1999).

Debates about whether white collar crime is crime reflect a conflict between legal and social representations of crime (Nelken 1997a; Slapper and Tombs 1999). Criticisms from writers such as Tappan (1977) represented a strictly legal approach in which the criminal law is the starting point for criminological analysis. Sutherland (1949), however, argued that non-criminal forms of law also result in judgements of fault and liability and are followed by the imposition of a penalty; thus the difference lies in procedures rather than in the 'wrongful' nature of activities. Later critical approaches to criminal law have also pointed to the absence of any clear-cut criteria distinguishing 'crimes' from other 'wrongs' or criminal from public law (Lacey 1995). In criminal law a distinction is made between activities that are regarded as *mala in se*, wrong in themselves, and those that are regarded as *mala prohibita*, subject to prohibition. For the latter, the criminal law is justified as being the most efficient way of securing compliance with protective regulations, and violations are often seen as 'technical' rather than 'criminal' offences. As argued above, however, such violations could be constructed as morally wrong and perceptions of activities as 'criminal' may change over time. As Nelken (1997a: 901) points out, 'the topic of white collar crime thus illustrates the possibility of divergence between legal, social and political definitions of criminality – but in so doing it reminds us of the artificiality of all definitions of crime'.

If criminal law need not be the starting point for the definition of white collar crime, what should be? Including a long list of harms inevitably leads to accusations of bias, such as those attracted by attempts by early critical criminologists to include activities such as economic exploitation (Schwendinger and Schwendinger 1970) or the manufacture and sale of tobacco products (Simon and Eitzen 1993). One way of overcoming this problem is to restrict the category to all violations of law but to include non-criminal violations. This recognizes that there is a difference between activities proscribed by some form of law and a wider range of harms not yet subject to law (Pearce and Tombs 1998). It also allows the inclusion of cases involving clearly 'wrongful' activities, which have not been subject to criminal prosecution but have involved legal judgements of fault and responsibility. In these cases the failure to use the criminal law against evident and legally established 'wrongdoing' becomes an issue for exploration. Such an approach also recognizes the potential significance of criminalization – as Slapper and Tombs (1999: 4) argue, there are 'persuasive arguments that it *matters* both practically and ideologically whether something is defined as a crime or a civil offence'. Although such an approach nevertheless leads to accusations of bias, these can be mitigated by presenting sufficient information about activities from widely credited sources and not relying on unsubstantiated allegations (Pearce and Tombs 1998). Before reaching a conclusion on this, and other definitional issues, some of the difficulties of researching white collar crime will be outlined.

Researching white collar crime

In part, the relative neglect of research into areas of white collar crime is related to its exclusion from those offences most readily associated with the 'crime problem' for which research funding is easier to obtain. It is also a difficult area to investigate. The invisibility and complexity that make it difficult to detect also make it difficult to research. The low rate of prosecutions means that there are fewer and more unrepresentative cases to study, and the absence of direct victimization renders victim surveys less appropriate. This leads to a tendency to rely on disparate and often less reliable forms of data and to go beyond the kinds of studies most often associated with criminology.

The starting point for much research on crime, for example, is data such as official statistics, crime surveys and court records, most of which exclude white collar crime. Official statistics are largely based on police records, but many white collar crimes are not dealt with by the police. Details about specific offences such as fraud are often not sufficient to determine which offences are white collar, and details of many organizational offences, often counted as summary offences, are sparse. Statistics from the enforcement agencies that do deal with white collar crime are less widely available, do not always provide detailed information on prosecutions, convictions or sentences and may not distinguish between what are described as 'incidents' or 'complaints' and offences. In Britain, as in many other countries, white collar crimes are not part of victim surveys such as the British Crime Survey (BCS), and few victim surveys have covered this area (Croall 1999a).

Other criminological research relies on interviews or ethnographic work with offenders, which is particularly difficult for white collar crime. This is largely because of problems of gaining access to offenders which, although also a problem with ordinary crimes, is exacerbated in the case of white collar offenders. As Slapper and Tombs (1999) point out, the 'powerless' are less able to resist research than the 'powerful'. Managers or business executives may also find it easier to obfuscate and conceal the 'truth' from researchers (Punch 1996). These points are well illustrated by Punch (1996: 43), who asks: 'do you approach senior executives of major corporations and say you are interested in bribery, corruption, industrial espionage, fraud and manipulation of accounts to hoodwink external auditors, and would be quite willing to undertake research for them within their companies?' He goes on to point out that:

> even if one could get inside, then the practical dilemmas of researching these issues may be almost intractable because managerial 'deviants' are likely to be clever, conspiratorial, and secretive, their activities will be concealed behind walls or locked doors and they will not only be unwilling to co-operate . . . but will simply deny that any nefarious practices take place at all.

Although covert research could overcome some of these difficulties, this too is limited because of the private and concealed nature of activities (Punch 1996). Difficulties of obtaining access to higher levels of management have meant that much research on occupational deviance has been restricted to lower level employees (Davies and Jupp 1999). Moreover, as Nelken (1997a: 901) points out, because of the political distaste felt for 'crimes of the powerful', there are few attempts to 'appreciate' their activities.

Despite these difficulties, some useful research has been carried out in companies (Braithwaite 1984; Tombs 1995). It is also easier to gain access to enforcers, and studies of their policies, practices and attitudes have formed a major stream of research, particularly in Britain (see Chapter 6). These may also yield useful details of offences and offenders and, although the length of court hearings can prohibit research, so too can observation of cases in court and work with court records (Croall 1988; Levi and Pithouse 1992). Interviews with judges and sentencers have also been a valuable source of information about the sentencing process (Wheeler *et al.* 1988).

Major scandals and incidents lead to the formation of victim groups, official reports and independent investigations and serious investigative journalism – all of which can provide valuable insights if used with caution (Nelken 1997a).

A further difficulty is that many areas of white collar crime involve moving away from fields of study usually associated with criminology, such as criminal law, sociology or psychology, into areas as diverse as financial management, industrial relations, management and business studies, the environment, food policy, environmental health and consumer protection, disasters and crisis management or studies of social movements (Slapper and Tombs 1999). Apart from the problem that criminologists may not be experts in these fields, these fields are characterized by their own discourses, which do not include a focus on 'crime'. As Punch (1996: 43) comments in relation to management and business studies in the USA, issues of business ethics are seen as 'soft' – 'the social organization of management studies does not usually lend itself to critical, penetrating, cross-disciplinary studies of business practice that might also illuminate the darker side of that practice. The dirty side is largely ignored'.

The absence of widely available material and accessible sources has led to a reliance on secondary rather than primary sources of information, on mass media reports and case studies involving major 'scandals'. Other sources include the autobiographies of major offenders, the production of which can provide, as Levi (1987a) comments, a lucrative pastime or alternative employment. They are, however, like the autobiographies of organized criminals, necessarily subjective and can be read as justifications for the offenders' activities. Moreover, newspaper accounts may be of dubious accuracy (Nelken 1997a) and information may not be verifiable. They cannot give information about trends – an apparent increase in media reports may be a response to a 'moral panic' and signify increased concern and reporting rather than an increasing incidence of offending (Nelken 1997a). It may be difficult to generalize from case studies, which may not be typical – cases involving major 'scandals' or large companies may divert attention from the mundane cases that are more typical (Croall 1988; Slapper and Tombs 1999). This is particularly the case because so many examples of and research on white collar crime originate from North America rather than Europe.

Despite all these problems, considerable innovative research has been carried out and subsequent chapters will refer to this. Moreover, some information is now more widely available – the growth of the Internet has made newspaper archives easier to access and many enforcement and government agencies include enforcement information on websites. However, full use of these sources requires a knowledge of where to look and an initial definition of interest. There is also still a need to develop more innovative research methods for the study of white collar crime (Davies and Jupp 1999).

Concluding comments

White collar crime is therefore a complex area to conceptualize. It remains on the sidelines of criminology and poses analytical, definitional and research problems. Many of the issues surrounding its definition and its relationship to other crimes remain unresolved and affect estimates of its extent, explorations of its nature and impact and approaches to its analysis. White collar crime asks major questions about the definition of crime, the role of class status and power in criminalization and law enforcement and the scope of criminology. All of these issues will recur throughout subsequent chapters of this book. Indeed, these problems are seen as intrinsic to the analysis of white collar crime and its status in criminology. Nelken (1997a), for example, organizes his contribution to the *Oxford Handbook* around seven kinds of ambiguity, drawing on Aubert's comment that:

> for purposes of theoretical analysis it is of prime importance to develop and apply concepts which preserve and emphasise the ambiguous nature of white collar crimes and not to solve the problem by classifying them as either crimes or not crimes. Their controversial nature is exactly what makes them so interesting from a sociological point of view.
>
> (Aubert 1977: 93)

The many difficulties surrounding the concept of white collar crime have nonetheless led to arguments that it is outdated and redundant and that its study should be disaggregated into the separate spheres of occupational or corporate crime or some other category. There are, however, persuasive arguments for retaining the term white collar crime, which forms the title and focus of this book. In part this is because it is widely recognized and has a public and academic resonance. In arguing, for example, that white collar, corporate and organizational crime are variants of the same kind of crime, Ruggiero asks whether one definition should encompass them all. He resists this temptation and chooses to 'utilise the traditional definitions, both because they make these forms of offending more easily identifiable by readers and to avoid adding to the existing terminological confusion' (Ruggiero 1996a: x). This echoes Braithwaite's earlier argument that 'the concept is shared and understood by ordinary folk as more meaningful than occupational crime, corporate deviance, commercial offences, economic crime or any competing concept' (Braithwaite 1985a: 3).

For the purposes of this book, it is intended to adopt an inclusive definition in which white collar crime is conceptualized as an 'abuse of a legitimate occupational role which is regulated by law' (Croall 1992: 9). White collar crime is used as an umbrella term encompassing both occupational and organizational crime, although the distinction will form a major part of subsequent chapters. It is intended to be inclusive, including activities of employees across the occupational hierarchy along with many harmful and illegal activities that are not at present regulated by criminal law, although this remains an important reference point. This avoids the narrowness of referring only to criminal law at the same time as avoiding the subjectivity of ignoring law entirely. Although the class and status of offenders are not part of this definition, analysis will seek to establish their significance. The notion of a legitimate occupational role is retained while recognizing the blurred boundaries with illegitimate occupations.

Adopting an inclusive definition of the subject means that its scope is extremely broad, and that it includes activities ranging from the crimes of individual employees and small businesses, through those of managers, executives and owners of companies, to corporate crime and crimes of governments and states, such as war crimes or the state-organized terrorism alleged to have been involved in the bombing of the Pan American airliner over Lockerbie, recently subject to a criminal trial. As will be seen in Chapter 2, some offences are global and transnational, spanning territorial and jurisdictional boundaries, whereas others are primarily local, taking place in a variety of different markets. Some lie on the borderline between what are more generally seen as professional or organized crimes. A text of this length cannot hope to fully detail and analyse all these forms of crime and, accordingly, the focus of this book is selective. As its primary focus is British, the focus will be on British research. However, this must be seen in an increasingly global context and, where relevant, material and analyses from other countries will be drawn on. In common with much of the literature on white collar and corporate crime, the book will largely restrict itself to financial and commercial crimes and those of private corporations and businesses, although reference will be made to offences in public sector organizations and the importance of the growing area of state and state-organized crime, which raise very similar issues, is also recognized.

The book will cover many of the key issues identified in this chapter. Chapter 2 will look at the problems of 'counting' and rendering more visible the extent and nature of white collar crime and will look at some of its major forms. Chapters 3 and 4 will explore issues surrounding offenders and patterns of victimization, and Chapter 5 will look at the different ways in which white collar crime has been explained and analysed. Chapters 6 and 7 will explore how white collar crimes are regulated and subjected to law and the criminal justice process and to the role of class, status and power. Chapter 8 will return to some of the questions posed in this chapter in relation to the utility of the concept and its continuing significance for criminology.

Further reading

The concept of white collar crime has been extensively written about and a good collection of classic and contemporary writings can be found in

D. Nelken (ed.) (1994a) *White Collar Crime*. Nelken's (1997a) chapter in the *Oxford Handbook of Criminology* provides a good and comprehensive introduction and discussions of definitional and conceptual issues can also be found in Slapper and Tombs' (1999) recent text on *Corporate Crime*, in Punch's (1996) text *Dirty Business: Exploring Corporate Misconduct* and in Croall's (1999a) recent overview. Ruggiero's (1996a) linking of white collar, corporate and organizational crime also provides an interesting approach to the subject.

chapter two

Exposing white collar crime

Exposing the considerable extent of white collar crime has, since St
been a major feature of work on the subject and it has often been a
the amount of white collar crime exceeds that of conventional
that it has more serious effects. Although its invisibility makes these claims
difficult to substantiate, its incidence and impact are considerable. It is found
in most occupations and organizations and has both economic and physical
costs, although a large proportion of it is not counted as 'crime'. Offences
range from the relatively trivial cons and scams perpetrated against consumers or investors to global financial frauds and major transport or
environmental disasters, often linked to managerial policies. This chapter
will start by exploring the issues involved in quantifying the extent and costs
associated with white collar crime and will then look at some of its major
forms, outlining their nature and providing selected examples.

'Counting' the uncountable: quantifying white collar crime

It is difficult to reach reliable estimates of any form of crime, and the limits
of official criminal statistics are well recognized (Coleman and Moynihan
1996; Maguire 1997). Many crimes are not reported, leading to a large
'dark' or 'hidden' figure, and, in what has been described as a process of
attrition, only a small proportion of reports are investigated by the police,
'counted' as offences and result in a conviction. These are supplemented by
a large number of alternative sources – victim surveys and crime 'audits' cast
some light on the hidden figure, although they too leave out some offences.
Nonetheless, along with official statistics, they do, at the very least, indicate
how many offences in specific categories are reported by victims, investigated by the police and appear in criminal courts. They provide some information about the 'costs' associated with these offences, the sex and age of
offenders, and they are readily available through published digests (Barclay
and Tavares 1999), statistical bulletins (Povey and Prime 1999) and on the
Home Office website. There are, however, no equivalent sources for white
collar crime and the problems of defining the subject make it difficult to
determine what should be counted. Its ambiguous criminal status means
that many activities are not conceived of as, let alone counted as, 'crimes'
and its invisibility and lack of direct victimization mean that it has a large
hidden figure.

Even if, for example, attention is restricted to activities subject to criminal
law, legal categories of crime do not specify whether or not crimes take place
in the course of an occupation. The most relevant categories in official statistics are theft by an employee and fraud. The latter, however, includes
fraud by a company director and false accounting, both of which could be
counted as white collar, and cheque and credit card fraud, which largely are
not (Levi 1995), and 'other frauds', which probably includes many white

collar frauds (Slapper and Tombs 1999). Many organizational crimes, such as those under trade descriptions, health and safety, food and public health legislation, are categorized as summary offences, for which only minimal details are provided. More information about these can be obtained in the records of individual enforcement agencies but these are less widely available and do not provide systematic information. A vast number of agencies are involved and compiling a comprehensive list would in itself be an enormous task. As Slapper and Tombs (1999) point out, attempting to reach an overall figure for fraud in the United Kingdom would mean examining, dissecting and recategorizing data from bodies as diverse as the police, the Serious Fraud Office, the European Commission, the British Retail Consortium, the Association of British Insurers, the Association of Payment Clearing Systems, the Credit Industry Fraud Avoidance Scheme, the Audit Commission, the Charity Commission, the Inland Revenue and HM Treasury. Broadening the category to include all violations of law or disciplinary codes exacerbates these problems because many activities are not subject to publicly recorded proceedings. Many employees are dismissed or subject to internal disciplinary proceedings, professional employees are dealt with by the largely private procedures of professional bodies and a wide range of other bodies regulate aspects of trade and financial services. Sources of information are therefore extremely diverse and a comprehensive survey would be extremely costly and time consuming.

Any such survey would have to take the large hidden figure into account. As seen in Chapter 1, many white collar crimes are undetected and unreported, few are prosecuted and victim surveys are necessarily limited. Even where victims are aware of some harm, it may be too trivial to consider reporting and they may complain not to agencies but to the organization concerned. Where the onus of detection lies with enforcement agencies, they may uncover only a small proportion of offences. Even where victims or members of the public make a complaint or where enforcers uncover irregularities, many are dealt with informally and are therefore not 'counted'.

It is nonetheless important to look at some quantitative evidence about white collar crime because this is often the basis for establishing its serious and widespread impact (Slapper and Tombs 1999). Some attempts to quantify white collar crime have been made, although they have relied on disparate information. Statistics of some enforcement agencies can be used, although these often need what Tombs (1999) describes as further social scientific work, which can in turn lead to accusations of manipulating statistics. Some victim surveys have been carried out with businesses (Levi 1988) and in respect of consumer and workplace safety crimes (Pearce 1992). In the United Kingdom, business groups and the Audit Commission have also carried out surveys attempting to look at the costs, impact and extent of specific activities. These, added to the considerable amount of information in the public domain, can be used to explore assertions that white collar crime is widespread and that its net costs are likely to exceed those associated with conventional crimes.

Often cited in this respect is Conklin's (1977) attempt to compare the total costs of selected conventional and white collar crimes in the USA. While the total cost of robbery, theft, larceny and car theft was estimated at $3–4bn, selected white collar crimes such as consumer fraud, illegal competition and deceptive practices cost an estimated $40bn. These kinds of 'guesstimates', however, suffer from many of the problems outlined above, and in addition the hidden figure of white collar crime makes it likely that they are under-estimates (Slapper and Tombs 1999). An alternative approach is to contrast the costs associated with different kinds of offences. The enormous sums of money involved in serious frauds can, for example, be compared with the total and average costs of property crimes. Levi (1995) points out that in the United Kingdom in 1994, at the same time as a report prepared for Crime Concern calculated the total cost of burglaries at £1bn (Crime Concern 1994), the Serious Fraud Office was dealing with cases involving an aggregate value of more than £5bn. The Maxwell pensions case alone involved a sum equal to the financial losses from car crime. In the USA, what is known as the Savings and Loan débâcle, in which large numbers of savings and loan or 'thrift' institutions collapsed amid allegations of fraud, embezzlement, false accounting, bribery and corruption (Calavita and Pontell 1995; Punch 1996), was estimated to have involved total losses of up to $1.5 trillion, which at the time, according to Slapper and Tombs (1999: 67) 'exceeded the Gross Domestic Product of any national economy outside the G-7', G-7 being the group of countries representing the world's largest economies. Even less serious frauds involve much higher amounts of money than conventional property crimes – while the theft or burglary of goods valued at more than a few thousand pounds would be regarded as serious, fraud occupies a different perceptual category, as if, 'once one passes a certain figure, the number of additional "zeros" becomes irrelevant' (Levi 1995: 184).

White collar crime also causes injury, illness and death – as Box (1983) pointed out, 'corporate crime kills'. Major cases include the disabilities suffered by the children of mothers who took the drug thalidomide, and arguably, the worst industrial 'accident' was at Bhopal in India in 1984, where between 3000 and 5000 people were killed and more than 200,000 were affected following the release of methyl isocyanate into the atmosphere (Punch 1996). In Britain, a series of major 'disasters' highlighted the safety issues involved in corporate activities. These included the drowning of 192 passengers following the sinking of the *Herald of Free Enterprise* off the coast at Zeebrugge, when the ferry set sail with its bow doors open, and the deaths of 51 people in the pleasure boat *Marchioness* in 1989 (Wells 1993). More recently, a series of rail crashes, including those at Clapham in 1987 which led to 34 deaths and at Southall in 1997 in which seven people died, have led to prosecutions, and there has been public discussion of the difficulties of prosecution in relation to the crash at Paddington in October 1999 in which 31 people died on the same stretch of track as the Southall crash (*Guardian* 10 May 2000: 4). To these 'disasters' could be added the numbers of workers killed annually as a result of violations of safety legislation, which, as will be seen below, exceeds the numbers killed in homicides (Tombs 1999); tenants killed and injured as a result of landlords' neglect of safety; and illnesses and deaths from food poisoning caused by bacteria such as *E.coli* (Croall 1998a, 1998b). Injuries can also result from dangerous consumer products, particularly cars. Psychological and physical harms are also associated with bullying, harassment and intimidation at work and sexual and physical abuse in institutions, which also involve abuses of occupational roles. The case of Dr Harold Shipman, recently found guilty of murdering 15 elderly patients but said to be responsible for the deaths of as many as many as 150 (*Guardian Unlimited* 1 February 2000), could also be considered to be a white collar crime, as he abused his position as a doctor to administer lethal doses of drugs to patients and was able to cover up evidence of his offences. If white collar crime is defined such that it includes state crimes such as state-organized terror, torture, mass killings, 'ethnic cleansing' and genocide, the total number of deaths and physical harms becomes staggering – so much so that, as Cohen (1996a: 493) argues, it becomes an 'insult to the intelligence' to add up the total and compare it to conventional crime.

Despite the difficulties of making precise estimates, arguments that the prevalence and impact of white collar crime exceed that of conventional crime therefore have some basis. To more fully explore its nature and extent, the following sections will look at selected offences, drawing on a range of sources. Those wishing to draw comparisons with conventional crime should bear in mind that, in England and Wales in 1998, the average value of property stolen in burglaries with a loss was £1416, and the average cost of damage was £245 (Barclay and Tavares 1999). The risk of being a victim of a burglary in inner-city areas is 8.5 per cent. In 1997, 739 offences of homicide were recorded, and the 'risk' of being a victim of violence is 6.1 per cent for men and 3.6 per cent for women (Barclay and Tavares 1999).

Patterns of white collar crime

The difficulties of developing meaningful categories of white collar crime were outlined in Chapter 1, where it was seen that no single set of criteria produce a clear-cut classification. Legally defined offences such as fraud incorporate both white collar and non-white collar offences, and popular and legal descriptions do not indicate the organizational or occupational nature of offences. They also encompass activities involving financial and physical harms committed by employees at all levels of the occupational hierarchy. The following sections will, in common with other approaches, use a combination of legal classifications and widely recognized descriptions such as theft, fraud and corruption, and will move on to selected **regulatory offences** involved in employment, consumer protection, food and the environment (Slapper and Tombs 1999). The use of primarily legal categories is justifiable on the grounds of expediency – they provide a basis for collecting information about offences, offenders, prosecutions and sanctions which may be contained in reports of specific enforcement agencies. Their limitations need nonetheless to be recognized along with the often blurred boundaries between different offence groups. In addition to revealing the considerable extent of white collar crime, this exploration also reveals its diversity and illustrates some of the major characteristics of offences, such as their often ambiguous criminal status and the narrow line between 'deviant', 'criminal' and 'normal' activities. The examples, drawn from a wide range of sources, are selective and do not in any way represent a comprehensive survey.

Theft at work

Theft by an employee is one of the clearest occupational offences in the criminal statistics. This now, according to the *Oxford Legal Dictionary* (CD Rom version 1994), incorporates embezzlement, defined as 'the dishonest appropriation by an employee of any money or property given to him on behalf of his employer'. Between April 1998 and March 1999, a total of 17,900 cases of theft by an employee were reported, of which 71.3 per cent were cleared up (Povey and Prime 1999). In a survey of retail outlets by the British Retail Consortium, theft by staff accounted for losses of £364m, 26 per cent of the total losses from crime. Theft by customers accounted for 43 per cent (Barclay and Tavares 1999). Large though these figures are, this form of crime is likely to have a large hidden figure. Many cases are never taken to court (Clarke 1990) and employers may choose to dismiss employees rather than risk the embarrassment that revelations of widespread theft might cause.

Few details are given about the nature of offences or the status of the employees involved. The large hidden figure is largely confirmed in studies of theft at work, in which many activities legally definable as 'theft' are described as 'fiddles' and 'perks' (Mars 1982), which further illustrates the narrow dividing line between 'normal' and 'deviant' activities. Although theft is most often associated with money or goods, it can also involve less identifiable rewards such as the use of employers' computers and time to carry out personal business (Mars 1982), to play computer games or to make long-distance phone calls. Perks and fiddles are often widely tolerated in workplace subcultures, and can also be tacitly tolerated by management, who may consider that to take action might disrupt the fine balance of industrial relations. Most British studies of theft at work have been carried out with lower-level employees, leaving a gap in knowledge about expense and other 'fiddles' among higher-level employees (Davies and Jupp 1999). Although often relatively simple, thefts can be highly organized, such as those in the catering or building trades (Mars 1982). Although generally regarded as an individual's crime, theft can also be organizationally induced, particularly where accounting systems enable and indeed encourage it in order to 'balance' the books, or where low rates of pay make activities justifiable to ensure a 'fair day's pay' (Ditton 1977). There may also be a narrow borderline between theft at work and some forms of organized or enterprise crime – many goods stolen from work, or which fall off proverbial lorries, are sold through the 'hidden economy' along with stolen or counterfeit goods.

Fraud

Fraud is not easy to define precisely – as Weait (1995) points out, it is a 'fudgy' word. A simple legal definition from the *Oxford Legal Dictionary* is that it is 'a false representation by means of a statement or conduct made in order to gain a material advantage'. It is difficult, however, to determine at what point 'false representations' such as advertising or descriptions of goods or services are considered as 'criminal'. Indeed, it has been said that 'fraud is a difficult thing to define in the ethics of trading, which are essentially the ethics of deceiving the other side' (Arnold 1937: 232, cited in Weait 1995). Although often characterized as an occupational crime, fraud may also be perpetrated by organizations or, like employee theft, be organizationally induced (Punch 1996). To Weait (1995: 88), fraud is like a virus which 'thrives parasitically within the organization'. It is found across the financial world, the public sector and in relation to taxation and pensions, and it is also increasingly global, as illustrated in the cases of Barings bank and the BCCI.

Some indication has been given of the large figures involved in major frauds and the scope of fraud and the large amounts involved in individual cases, is further indicated in a British victim survey which included different groups of victims (Levi 1995). Banks reported losses of £3.2m, only £170,000 of which was attributed to blue collar fraudsters, the remainder to 23 white collar ones. Clients or customers lost £1.8m to 11 white collar fraudsters; employers £1.7m to 28 employees; suppliers of goods and services £1.1m to 10 white collar offenders and insurance companies £230,000 to 9 white collar compared with £60,000 to 16 blue collar offenders. The former head of the SFO estimated the cost of City fraud at £5bn a year, a figure said to be increasing (*Guardian* 13 May 1999), and a 'fraud barometer' devised by the accountancy firm KPMG found that a total of £190m was involved in cases going before the courts in the first half of 1999. This compared with a mere £28m the previous year, the rise being attributable to two major investigations into money laundering and the £25m black market in alcohol (*Guardian* 28 October 1999). While it is impossible in this chapter to explore all kinds of fraud, the following selected examples indicate its ubiquity and some of its complexities.

Fraud in the public sector

While often associated with the private sector, fraud is prevalent in public sector organizations such as Local Authorities and the National Health Service (NHS). A series of reports in the early 1990s drew attention to its increasing significance and the Audit Commission (1993) called for the development of an 'anti fraud' culture. While much public attention centres on benefit fraud, other frauds are clearly associated with white collar employees. In 1993, the Audit Commission carried out a study of Local Authorities and external auditors in England and Wales to explore the extent of fraud and corruption resulting in either criminal proceedings or internal action. While the commission acknowledged that the difficulties of detecting fraud mean that 'in truth no-one can ever know' (Audit Commission 1993: 1) its full extent, and that much of the fraud, about 80 per cent, it uncovered was not white collar, it found that fraudulent claims for expenses and allowances, and frauds in relation to cash income, payroll and creditor payments had increased, amounting in 1992/3 to 1600 cases involving losses of £4.8m. Fraudsters could be well organized, quick to exploit weaknesses in controls and quick to discover new opportunities for fraud. Examples included a Local Authority officer defrauding £16,000 by amending accounts and signed minutes, submitting false invoices and destroying evidence, and a housing officer bypassing official waiting lists and selling keys to more than 100 council properties. In another case, an administrator continued to send cheques to staff who had left, intercepted the cheques and misappropriated £13,000.

Most authorities reported fraud, but they argue that standards of probity were high and suggest that fraud is less prevalent in the public sector than in the private sector. Compared with Levi's (1988) survey, in which 30 per cent of private sector companies had reported at least one fraud of more than £50,000 in two years, less than 10 per cent of local authorities had detected a fraud of this magnitude over three years. The Audit Commission also link an apparently increasing incidence of reported fraud with changes in public service organizations brought about by the introduction of internal markets, pointing to the 'altered' priorities of local government given an increasing workload, changes in the management of colleges, housing and schools along with compulsory competition, all in a period of financial stringency (Audit Commission 1993).

Fraud in the NHS

Considerable publicity has surrounded revelations of prescription and other frauds in the NHS, and another Audit Commission (1994) report detailed a wide range of frauds on the part of healthcare professions who are involved in a large number of financial transactions, and whose claims are dealt with largely on the basis of trust. Over a three-year period the commission uncovered 960 known cases of fraud and corruption which had led to resignation, dismissal or prosecution, involving losses of about £5.9m. Other surveys have also found high rates of fraud. One survey of 82 health authorities by the Healthcare Financial Management Association found 96 cases of known or suspected fraud in a two-year period, with false claims for payment for ophthalmic services amounting to 36 per cent of the total (*Guardian* 24 June 1997: 8). In May 1998, the UK government appointed a 'fraudbuster' to tackle what were said to be £115m losses from 'prescription crime'. Although much of this is attributed to patients, a substantial but unknown amount can be attributed to dentists, general practitioners (GPs), opticians and pharmacists (*BBC news* 28 May 1998). Examples from these surveys and the media include offences on the part of:

- general practitioners: including false claims in relation to practice staff, numbers of patients, night visits and vaccinations. One GP was said to have 'siphoned off' £700,000 in five years by writing bogus prescriptions for residents in old people's homes (*Herald* 8 January 1998).
- opticians: including false claims in relation to dispensing glasses, sight tests and tinted lenses.
- pharmacists: including false claims for emergency opening, colluding in prescription frauds, processing bogus prescriptions and collecting prescription charges for drugs costing less than the prescription charge.
- dentists: including false claims for non-existent patients.

Frauds in NHS trusts involved payroll and expenses, procurement, stock, income, employment, travelling expenses, including consultants' claims for private work, misappropriation of patients' money and social security benefits. Some of these frauds were highly organized. As with other forms of primarily occupational crime, these may also be organizationally induced, with the systems of control for regulating the large number of payments in the health service being characterized as inadequate (Audit Commission 1994). The high levels of trust accorded to professional groups also means that many can escape detection, a feature also noted in relation to Medicaid and prescription fraud in the USA (Jesilow *et al.* 1993).

'Euro frauds'

In 1999, attention was drawn dramatically to the extent of fraud in the European Union (EU) with the resignation of members of the European

Commission (EC). Like most frauds, the extent of 'euro fraud' is notoriously difficult to measure, with the hidden figure being 'virtually impossible to assess with any degree of precision' (Passas and Nelken 1993: 223). Nonetheless, estimates all indicate substantial losses to the EU budget. UCLAF (Unité de Co-ordination de la Lutte Anti-Fraude), which is responsible to the European Commission for all aspects of the fight against fraud on the EU budget, estimated in 1995 that 1–2 per cent of the budget is subject to fraud and irregularities, representing about 1.5bn ECUs (Doig 1995). This is 'realistically' assumed to be an underestimate, with some estimates amounting to 10 per cent of the EU budget (Clarke 1994). A 1996 report to the EC by financial auditors catalogued about 7000 'preventable' frauds and swindles, largely by farmers, in the Common Agricultural Policy (CAP), and a 1997 report from a House of Commons Committee in the United Kingdom estimated the costs of the exploitation of loopholes in VAT and customs duties in relation to cigarette smuggling at about £10bn (Taylor 1997).

The CAP, which makes arrangements for intervention in relation to pricing, dealing with surplus produce and providing subsidies to farmers, provides the opportunity for many of these frauds, and major areas affected include wine, olive oil, beef and cereals (Clarke 1994). Imports from non-EU countries also provide considerable opportunities for fraud (Doig 1995). Many of these frauds are extremely complex and involve 'transnational' or 'cross-border' crimes which exploit loopholes between the laws of different jurisdictions. These also illustrate the close relationship between white collar and organized crime, with some major frauds involving partnerships between legitimate and illegitimate businesses (Passas and Nelken 1993; Ruggiero 1996a). Some frauds also require the collusion of government officials, which may depend on the political and fraud 'cultures' typical in different countries. Passas and Nelken comment, for example, that in some cases there need be no corruption because the activities are seen as the usual way that 'things are done'. The study of EU fraud also reveals the fragmented form of control which involves agencies in all countries for whom detection of EU fraud may not be a major priority (Passas and Nelken 1993; Clarke 1994).

Tax fraud

Taxation frauds have been said to cost five or six times as much as all conventional crimes put together (Levi 1987a). One 'conservative' estimate by accountant Deloitte and Touche suggests that the cost of 'tax dodging' between 1976 and 1996 was £2000bn – the equivalent of six years of government expenditure (*Guardian* 4 February 1999). Not all of this is strictly white collar crime because individuals may provide false information about their income and many cases involve builders and other workers 'moonlighting' (Cook 1989). Tax fraud can also be occupational and organizational and involves major corporations and organized crime – as illustrated by the vast sums to be made by evading taxes on cigarettes and 'bootleg' alcohol. Tax fraud also illustrates the narrow borderline between the legal and illegal. McBarnet (1988) points to many practices that comply with the letter of the law but quite clearly contravene its spirit, with lawyers and accountants being employed to advise clients on how to reduce their tax liability. Like occupational theft, many forms of tax fraud are widely tolerated in a culture in which 'beating the taxman' is a legitimate activity (Cook 1989).

Despite this, there are few prosecutions for tax frauds. Like many other regulatory agencies, the Inland Revenue prosecutes only a small proportion of detected offenders, being more concerned with recovering lost income. Cases that are prosecuted involve large sums. Inland Revenue press releases, available on the Revenue's website (http://www.inlandrevenue.gov.UK), contained details of 13 cases resulting in successful prosecutions in 1999, of which three involved losses of more than £1m each, and all losses amounted to five-figure sums. A number of subcontracting frauds in the construction industry were included, along with cases involving accountants. In one case, an accountant was sent to prison after being found guilty of submitting false accounts, tax returns and SC60 forms on behalf of, but without the knowledge of, his clients, with losses to the taxpayer estimated at more than £92,000. In another press release the Inland Revenue estimates a £50m saving from changes in regulations to prevent avoidance of capital gains tax (Inland Revenue press release 9 November 1999).

Pensions 'misselling'

In what has been described in Britain as the 'worst financial scandal this century' (*Guardian* 8 November 1997), two million or more people were sold pensions on the basis of false or misleading information. This was related to government policies to withdraw from pension provision and to encourage employees, often public servants, to purchase pensions in the private sector. In addition, many major financial service providers advised employees to change to new private schemes. One survey found that only 9 per cent of pensions companies complied with legal requirements in the 'hard sell' that ensued (Black 1997; Slapper and Tombs 1999). In one case Lloyds bank was fined a record £325,000 following a failure to warn employees that its policies could produce a much smaller pension than the company scheme they were leaving (*Guardian* 9 January 1997: 3). The bank gave no explanation of the value of the benefits or their links with inflation, which precluded a true comparison. It was also said that sales personnel had failed to investigate customers' overall financial position. The same report indicates that four national insurance brokers had been fined a total of £405,000. By 1998 it was estimated that the costs amounted to £11bn and fines had been imposed on 49 companies including many 'household names' (Slapper and Tombs 1999; *Herald* 13 March 1998). Despite this, and attempts by the new labour government to 'name and shame' companies, the 'scandal' received relatively little publicity, although, as Slapper and Tombs (1999) point out, its costs dwarf almost all estimates of all forms of street crime put together. It also provides an illustration of how fraud can be organizational – although the attention of regulators has focused on individual sales personnel, senior management, who may have exhorted salespersons to sell products aggressively regardless of their suitability for customers, may also be prosecuted (*Guardian* 5 August 1999). It also provides an interesting example of the close relationship between what are regarded as 'normal' and deceptive sales practices.

Corruption

In common with other white collar crimes, bribery and corruption are difficult to define, although in general terms they involve an employee using his or her position to gain monetary advantage in return for some favour. The Audit Commission defines corruption as the 'offering, giving, soliciting or acceptance of an inducement or reward which may influence the action of any person' (Audit Commission 1993: 12), and in Britain the criminal offence of bribery involves 'the transaction of soliciting or receiving inducements or rewards to local government politicians (but not to MPs) and all public officials for decisions or actions – or, conversely, the failure to act or to make a decision – that favours the donor or their organization' (Doig 1996: 36). To Mars (1982), occupations involving 'gatekeeping' or broking, where an employee introduces a buyer to a seller of services, are 'fiddle prone' because sellers may wish to secure an advantage by rewarding the gatekeeper. The line between corrupt and acceptable activities is a particularly hard one to draw – at what point, for example, does receiving gifts or hospitality become unacceptable? This may also vary considerably between different organizations – public sector organizations are often seen as having higher standards than private ones. As seen above, in some countries rewarding officials and other agents may be regarded as normal and cultural standards vary considerably and change over time (Levi and Nelken 1996). Indeed, allegations of corruption or 'anti-corruption' campaigns are often politically motivated and representations of corruption are linked to different political persuasions – left-wing parties tend to link corruption to the power of the business elite to 'buy' political and commercial favours, whereas right-wing parties link it to the public sector and local authorities (Levi and Nelken 1996).

The extent of corruption is particularly difficult to explore. It is often characterized as 'victimless', as few direct losses are involved although it may indirectly disadvantage competitors who lose the chance to bid for contracts and it also affects confidence in the institutions in which it is found (Ruggiero 1994). Because it involves a private agreement between individuals it is largely invisible, often being detected only when individuals are seen to have a suspiciously large income or to engage in conspicuous consumption. The Audit Commission (1993) points out that investigations of corruption are notoriously time consuming, complex and are often unresolved. Corruption may be occupational, where it is motivated by personal gain, or organizational, where, for example, agents of companies bribe officials to gain valuable contracts. It may also extend to governments, which may 'turn a blind eye' to the bribery of overseas officials to secure contracts or exports. It is found in many different sectors, and some examples are outlined below.

Corruption in local authorities

Corruption may involve local authority officers accepting rewards in relation to tenders for works – in a major 'scandal' in the 1970s, the architect John Poulson was implicated in corrupt activities in relation to building contracts (Doig 1996). The Audit Commission (1993) survey found 143 cases of corruption in a three-year period that were sufficiently proven to justify some form of action. Although it acknowledged that corruption is difficult to quantify, it estimated a total loss of £1.2m. Only a small number of cases (38 per cent) where corruption was alleged resulted in prosecution, resignation, dismissal or recovery action. Tenders and the award and settlement of contracts were involved in 47 cases; permissions, planning consents, licences, allocations, grants and loans were involved in 22; disposal of assets accounted for 10; and the remainder included canvassing, pressure selling and non-disclosure of interests. One case involved a 'gift' of golf clubs worth £500 from a shopping centre manager to offset rent arrears, another involved the offering of a bribe of £30,000 to a councillor in relation to a planning application and yet another involved a photocopier supplier and administrative officer amending the terms of a supply contract involving excess payments of more than £100,000.

Public sector corruption

It was seen above that government officials may become involved in frauds, some associated with organized crime and there have been recurrent scandals and allegations concerning police corruption, particularly in relation to the drugs industry and organized crime. In 1997 a tax inspector was sentenced to five years' imprisonment after taking bribes totalling £150,000, accepting excessive hospitality on overseas visits to investigate taxpayers, and withholding information from the police (*Guardian* 19 February 1997:

1). Universities and colleges of higher education have also been associated with corruption involving franchises for overseas degree programmes (*Guardian* 31 January 1997).

Political corruption

Recent years have seen recurrent allegations of corruption and 'sleaze' on the part of politicians in Britain and a series of major scandals have involved allegations which led to extensive litigaton of money being paid to MPs in brown paper envelopes and politicians receiving lavish hospitality. In some ways the political process itself can be seen as 'criminogenic'. Political parties, if elected, are in a position to grant favours and positions and require funds to fight elections. This provides the basis for 'buying' influence (Levi and Nelken 1996). Political parties' need for finance was linked to allegations of corruption in Europe in the 1980s and, in the USA, the 'political machine', which involves elected politicians appointing non-elected officials, has long been associated with corruption (Simon and Eitzen 1993). In Britain, allegations of corruption were associated with the rise of professional lobbying firms that specialize in introducing clients to politicians. In this respect a balance has to be sought between the need, in a democracy, for interest groups to gain access to politicians and a situation in which such representation is perceived to be unfair and involves any kind of payment. In Britain, it was revealed that MPs were paid retainers, some not declared to the Inland Revenue or to Parliament, by lobbying firms. The clients of one of these firms included the Serbian government and a tobacco company seeking to market carcinogenic tobacco products aimed at young people, and other allegations involved links with arms exports (Leigh and Vulliamy 1997). Although the extent of such wrongdoing is difficult to estimate, the Nolan Committee report of 1995 referred to cultures of 'slackness' and 'moral vagueness' and the Downey report found 'compelling evidence' that politicians had misrepresented payments and favours (Doig 1996).

Corruption in commercial organizations

Corruption also involves commercial organizations, often colluding with state officials, securing contracts with foreign governments or obtaining licences to export goods. Bribery is often justified as being necessary to win contracts in countries where it is widely tolerated (Braithwaite 1979) and, until recently, it was possible for British firms to claim tax relief on bribes offered to public officials (*Guardian* 23 September 1997: 20). In 1997, this was challenged by Clare Short, who pointed to the high price paid by the poor for this global problem, as money intended for aid is diverted by crooked officials and corruption and weak governance undermine economic stability and sustainable development objectives. Bribery and corruption exist across many sectors including sport and, in one recent case, two defendants were charged with taking £1m bribes each in relation to contracts for the Co-operative Wholesale Society's 'own label' food products (*Guardian* 22 September 1999).

Offences of theft, fraud and corruption are generally seen as occupational although, as has been seen, fraud and corruption can also be organizational and all can be organizationally induced. They are often distinguished from the next group of offences in that they are more unambiguously regarded as criminal even though their criminal elements may be difficult to define. Other offences are normally depicted as organizational and corporate and are covered by **regulatory law** because they involve the violation of regulations that protect employees, consumers, the public health and the environment. They also involve both economic and physical harms along with different kinds of fraud.

Employment offences

Many laws and regulations surround aspects of employment including safety in the workplace and wages legislation, which protects workers from being exploited by very low wages. An inclusive definition of white collar crime encompassing administrative law also extends this category to anti-discrimination laws (Szockyj and Fox 1996) and breaches of laws dealing with unionization, conditions of work and the right to strike (Tombs 1999). It can also, as seen above, cover abuses of occupational positions where, for example, employees or clients are bullied or intimidated, activities which may also have a racial or sexual component. Employment offences involve physical and economic harms and can also be perpetrated by small and large businesses, from 'sweatshops' employing workers with very low wages and poor conditions, to major corporations failing to ensure compliance with safety or environmental regulations, risking disastrous consequences. Some may have a primarily local effect whereas others can be global and 'transnational', as in cases where production is sited in third world countries with less stringent labour and safety regulations. This can involve the exploitation of child or immigrant labour and, in one recently reported example, it was revealed that British companies were paying third world labourers as little as 81 pence an hour to work illegal hours in harsh conditions on North Sea oil rigs. Although illegal under European and British law, the companies were exempt as they were operating more than 12 miles off the Scottish shore (*Observer* 7 February 1999). In some cases, legitimate companies collude with organized criminals, who arrange for the illegal 'trafficking' of workers destined to work for low wages, providing another example of the close relationship between white collar and organized crime (Ruggiero 1996a, 1997). The death of 58 illegal Chinese immigrants in a lorry en route to Dover dramatically drew attention to this problem – although their 'trafficking' is widely attributed to 'criminal' gangs, many such immigrants are employed in primarily legitimate restaurants and other businesses (*Guardian* 20 June 2000; 21 June 2000). The extent of employment offences is therefore considerable, as revealed in attempts, outlined below, to estimate the number of one group of these offences.

Occupational health and safety

Recent attempts to calculate the scope and extent of health and safety offences provide a good example of the 'counting' difficulties outlined above. Figures on prosecutions released by the United Kingdom's Health and Safety Executive (HSE) are likely to represent a small proportion of known offences and an even smaller proportion of total breaches of regulations because many are dealt with by informal warnings (Carson 1971; Tombs 1999). Reduced resources for the HSE have also led to fewer inspections and investigations. Giving evidence to the House of Commons Select Committee, David Bergman of the Centre for Corporate Accountability stated that the HSE failed to investigate 90 per cent of major injuries reported to it and that only 10 per cent of those investigated resulted in prosecution (*Guardian* 3 November 1999). Not all accidents or deaths, however, result from offences and using these statistics can be criticized on the grounds of political bias. Tombs, however, argues that much can be extrapolated from them (Tombs 1999).

He starts his analysis with published figures for 1994–5, which revealed a total of 376 fatal injuries reported under the Reporting of Injuries, Diseases and Dangerous Occurrences Regulations (RIDDOR). Although the HSE claims that these figures, a record low, are virtually complete, they exclude several categories of deaths and injuries. Thirty-six fatalities arose from the supply or use of flammable liquids, 27 occurred in the course of sea fishing, transport and communications work and, most significantly, 877 deaths were associated with driving in the course of employment. This brings the total number to 1316 to which, he argues, could be added deaths arising from occupationally caused fatal illnesses, which are difficult to calculate as they are not always recorded by coroners. The clearest cases of such diseases, asbestosis and occupationally caused lung disease, provided a further 1702 occupationally caused deaths – producing a total that exceeds the 834 homicides in England, Wales and Scotland. These are deaths not offences, but he argues that assumptions can be made about offending on the basis of evidence rather than 'mere' moralizing. During the 1980s a series of investigations and official inquiries attempted to attribute responsibility for fatalities. Although they are not legal judgements, a series of reports consistently attributed about 70 per cent of fatalities to managerial responsibility and provided evidence that regulations had been violated even where no formal action was taken (Slapper 1993). In most workplace fatalities there is therefore at least a criminal case to answer. Such conclusions are less applicable to occupational illness, although Tombs argues that employers are also responsible for much of this. On the basis of these considerations he concludes that the scale of unlawful workplace deaths 'vastly outweighs the numbers of recorded homicides' (Tombs 1999: 77). To this could be added the large numbers of non-fatal injuries at work caused by similar failings. Some industries are particularly dangerous – in the construction industry, for example, it has been claimed that two builders are killed and 85 suffer major injuries each week, with a further 200 sustaining accidents serious enough to keep them off work for more than three days (*Guardian* 9 February 1999).

Consumer offences

The vast area of **consumer crime** involves violations of the laws and regulations surrounding the production, distribution and sale of goods and services. In the United Kingdom, for example, criminal offences are included in the Trade Descriptions and Weights and Measures Acts and also in food legislation. An inclusive definition would also include violations of competition and other legislation. Like many other offences in regulatory categories, consumer crime can be occupational and organizational and committed by large manufacturers and retailers along with 'cowboy' businesses and organized criminals involved in the counterfeiting industry. Although often seen as involving relatively trivial offences of goods sold with a lower weight than indicated, it can also be global and transnational with, for example, counterfeit and cheap, shoddy and, on occasion, unsafe goods being manufactured in third world countries with less stringent regulations and sold in retail outlets, markets and car boot sales in Britain. A fine line divides fraud from the 'misleading descriptions' covered by the Trade Descriptions Act and from normal retailing practices (Croall 1987). At what point, for example, can consumers claim that they have been deceived by descriptions of goods and by what is declared, or not declared, on labels? Although generally associated with primarily economic harms, consumer offences may also endanger health and safety.

The total number of prosecutions recorded in the United Kingdom by the Office of Fair Trading (OFT) represent only a small proportion of detected or total offences, as is the case with other regulatory offences. Many consumers cannot check the contents of goods themselves and even if they are dissatisfied they rarely complain to relevant agencies. Statistics of 'complaints' cannot be taken as an indication of offences and, even where offences are detected, many are dealt with by formal and informal cautions rather than prosecution (Cranston 1979; Croall 1992). The following examples illustrate selected aspects of this enormous area of offending.

Car safety

The most notorious case involving the safety of cars involved the decision, by senior executives, to market the Ford Pinto car in the USA while knowing that it had several design faults. The decision was based on a cost-benefit analysis in which potential insurance claims were balanced against the cost of changing the design, and the car was withdrawn only after several deaths and severe burn injuries led to class action suits (Punch 1996). More common are the fraudulent and unsafe practices involved in the second-hand motor trade. The 'clocking' (turning back) of odometers was estimated to have cost consumers £100m in 1990 (Automobile Association 1994), and the rebuilding and selling of insurance 'write-offs' can create potential 'death traps' known in the trade as 'cut and shuts' (*Independent* 29 June 1994). Trading standards officers have estimated that one in every three used cars sold would fail an MOT test and the Automobile Association (AA) has found that one in five has defective steering, inadequate wipers or an illegal spare tyre (*Guardian* 11 October 1999). Repair frauds, where motorists are charged for unnecessary repairs or receive unsafe cars, have also been reported.

'Cowboy' builders

Considerable publicity has been attracted recently by so-called 'cowboy' builders, whose victims are abandoned with unfinished work which has been paid for, lost deposits and shoddy work. Trading standards organizations receive more than 100,000 complaints each year about the activities of such builders and it is estimated that only one in five victims complains (*Guardian* 18 September 1999). A study by the Norwich Union insurance company found that only 21 per cent of customers reported offences because they are too embarrassed to do so and estimated that up to three million home owners have been victims of traders (*Guardian* 1 December 1999). Apart from the economic cost, these offences also have safety implications.

Pricing offences

A major feature of consumer protection legislation is the regulation of prices. In the United Kingdom, recent, non-criminal investigations into 'price fixing' have questioned the prices charged for cars by major manufacturers, which are higher in Britain than in other European countries. Another major problem lies in the marketing practices of large and small retailers, who use 'bogus bargain offers' in which 'sale prices' do not represent genuine reductions (Croall 1992). This is extremely widespread and the prices of some goods may also rise before sales, only to fall during sale periods (*Guardian* 14 January 1998: 19).

Marketing malpractice

A good illustration of the fine borderline between legal and illegal sales techniques is provided by 'marketing malpractice', which involves misleading descriptions and high-pressure sales techniques and may also include an increasing number of sales via the Internet. In the United Kingdom, it has also been reported in the recently privatized utility companies, where suppliers have deliberately misled customers and used improper sales practices including doorstep selling (Croall 1999b; *Guardian* 13 March 1999: 21)

Deceptive packaging

A 'classic' form of white collar crime is the deceptive practice of selling goods in containers that far exceed the size of their contents – which may mislead consumers and which amounts to the sale of 'fresh air' (Croall 1992). Common examples are containers of vitamin pills that contain very few pills and cosmetics that are sold in double-skinned containers *(Daily Telegraph* 2 August 1990). A recent report by the Edinburgh Trading Standards Department gave examples of washing powder sold in the same size carton with different quantities of the product in each, and toys and computer games in large boxes (*Scotsman* 4 June 1999). Although seemingly trivial, and lying on the margins of legality, such tactics are inherently deceptive. Losses are not directly measurable, but large excess profits are generated. Other indications on labels may routinely deceive – recent concerns have surrounded claims that goods are 'green' or 'environmentally friendly', which may have little basis. Indeed, a further problem with deceptive packaging is that its disposal exacerbates environmental problems.

Counterfeit goods

The manufacture and sale of counterfeit goods is now said to be a major industry costing legitimate businesses over £1bn a year in the UK alone and it also leads to the loss of legitimate employment (Crime Concern 1994; *Scotsman* 8 December 1994). There are major trades in audio and video tapes, computer software, designer goods and everyday products such as soap powder and even tea bags (Croall 1998a). Counterfeiting provides a further example of the involvement of organized crime with semi-legitimate and legitimate businesses. Goods may be manufactured abroad or in 'cottage industries' by largely illegitimate industries and sold in a variety of outlets. Counterfeiting is also a vehicle for laundering the proceeds of drugs money, and terrorist groups have also been said to be involved. Although legitimate business is often seen as the major victim, as Ruggiero points out, it may benefit by the proliferation of 'brand name' products and has been known to collude with counterfeiters (Ruggiero 1996a).

Food offences

A major part of legislation for consumer protection involves the quality and safety of food, recently highlighted in the United Kingdom by concerns over the spread of bovine spongiform encephalopathy (BSE), major cases of food poisoning and the production of genetically modified food. Like consumer crime in general, food offences involve large manufacturers and retailers along with a host of small traders and can be local and global: food was involved in many of the euro frauds discussed above, which also involve organized crime. Food offences involve fraud and issues of safety and marketing malpractices – food adulteration is one of the oldest forms of food fraud. The rise of mass-produced convenience foods has also provided many opportunities for manufacturers to 'add value' to basic ingredients by using a variety of additives and food substitutes of which consumers are often unaware, which amounts, according to some commentators, to 'legalized adulteration' (Cannon and Walker 1985). The main offences involve the adulteration of food, the sale of 'unfit food' and the sale of food 'not of the nature, quality or substance demanded by the consumer'. These include many fraudulent and unsafe practices ranging from the sale of mouldy food to major frauds in which horse, kangaroo or other meat, some of it intended for pet food, is included in meat products such as burgers (Croall 1992). Lists of prosecutions reveal a host of 'foreign bodies' in food, which are not only extremely unpleasant, such as the presence of sticking plasters or ball-point pens, but can also injure consumers. Improperly or illegally slaughtered meat also presents health risks over and above the spread of BSE – recently revealed, for example, was a trade in illegally slaughtered sheep and goats whose hides were burnt for sale as 'smokies', which carried risks of food poisoning. In the United Kingdom, the Ministry of Agriculture estimates that hundreds of animals are slaughtered each week, with illegal carcasses fetching up to £200 (*Guardian* 4 April 1999). Some selected examples of food offences are outlined below.

Food frauds

Some food frauds are linked to subsidies frauds on the EU, which include illegal imports of meat (Van Duyne 1993) and the substitution of different and cheaper meats in meat products. Contaminated cooking oil killed 259 Spanish consumers during the 1980s and wine was also contaminated with anti-freeze (Croall 1992; Clarke 1994). Regulations preventing the spread of BSE also produced frauds, with prosecutions involving evasion of regulations by forging certificates and cattle tags and dealing in cheap cattle sold from herds infected with BSE (*Observer* 17 March 1996). During the export ban on British beef, Dutch customs officers found British beef, transported under false papers claiming it was Belgian, in a consignment of frozen beef.

It was stored in the Netherlands, sold to a French company and later exported from the EU with the help of subsidies worth more than £700,000 (*Herald* 7 May 1998).

Food labelling offences

There has been much recent public discussion about the declaration, on labels, of the presence of genetically modified foods. Other concerns about food labelling have included the omission of food additives and the misleading nature of labels and pictorial images portraying farmyards and 'natural' ingredients such as fruit on foods that are essentially 'chemical cocktails' and contain few of the products indicated by descriptions (Croall 1992). The labelling of 'diet' foods has also been contentious, with many being little different from other products. Many of these practices, like deceptive packaging, lie on the fringes of the law.

Food poisoning

Food safety also involves hygiene and the dangers of food poisoning, which have been said to have increased along with the spread of convenience foods, take-aways and precooked foods. Here, again, published figures are difficult to relate to offences. Many consumers do not report illnesses to their doctors and, even if they do, establishing the chain of evidence necessary to link illness to the food consumed is difficult. Those that are linked often involve several victims, where detecting the source may be easier – cases prosecuted often involve large groups of people such as wedding guests or residents in homes and hospitals (Croall 1987, 1992). By far the most serious case of food poisoning in Britain in recent years was the outbreak of *E. coli* 0157 in Wishaw in 1997, which led to the deaths of 21 elderly victims. One butcher's shop, which provided cooked meats for functions, to nursing homes and to a large number of local outlets, was found to be the source of contamination. The butcher's lax attitude to regulations, to which he was said to pay 'lip service', was criticized in a subsequent Fatal Accident Inquiry, and his failure to cooperate with early investigations by withholding a list of outlets is said to have contributed directly to six of the deaths (Cox 1998; *Herald* 20 August 1998: 5).

Environmental crime

Environmental crime encompasses a wide range of offences including pollution of the atmosphere, rivers, beaches and water, along with the illegal dumping of toxic waste. South (1998a, 1998b) points to the global, regional and local elements of this kind of crime, from the major cases of

Chernobyl and Bhopal, the pollution of the rivers of Europe, particularly the Rhine, as a result of corporate negligence, to the many local cases of the pollution of rivers and other local amenities. Environmental crime also involves the noise pollution from local companies which may exceed that produced by 'noisy neighbours' (Croall 1998a). Offenders may be local 'cowboy' operators or multinational corporations and environmental crime also involves organized crime and the bribery of state officials to ignore illegal exports and imports. It can also include governments – South (1998b) points to the impact of wars on the environment, as seen in the use of Agent Orange in Vietnam and the burning of the oil fields in Kuwait at the end of the Gulf War. Some selected examples of environmental crime are outlined below.

Waste dumping

Increasing requirements for companies to obtain permits for disposing of waste or to process it have increased costs and created a market for illegal waste 'dumping' (South 1998a). These offences may be global – Block (1993) describes one case in which toxic waste was moved from the USA to northern Europe with false papers, and then shipped to the impoverished West African nation of Benin. Like European and food frauds illegal waste dumping may also involve cross-border crime. Van Duyne (1993) recounts a case in which a corrupt manager in a Belgian dumping site allowed the daily dumping of Dutch toxic waste, including one instance in which the dangerous chemical PCB was not declared at customs and was simply covered with earth. Waste 'dumping' may involve the disposal of waste containing ingredients which are not included in the licence for a local site, and which are also more dangerous. Fears have been expressed by Friends of the Earth that Scotland may become a 'dumping ground' owing to regulations that differ from those in England and Wales (Croall 1999b).

Pollution

The contamination of rivers and tap water features strongly in environmental offences and since the privatization of water companies, several have amassed large numbers of prosecutions. In 1996, Severn Trent Water received its 34th conviction for an incident that killed 33,000 salmon, with the judge commenting on its poor record and 'very slack' management (*Herald* 6 August 1996). In May 1998, the Environment Agency for England and Wales reported that every water company had been found guilty of pollution in the previous year (BBC news online 29 May 1998). The Scottish Environmental Protection Association (SEPA) provides some details of prosecutions on its website. The 37 prosecutions for water pollution and waste offences listed for 1998–9 include farmers (one prosecuted for allowing blood and gut contents to enter land and controlled waters), companies and water and local authorities (one of which was prosecuted for allowing diesel fuel to enter controlled waters). For England and Wales, the Environment Agency website (http://www.environment-agency.gov.UK) similarly lists prosecutions of farms and large companies. This also contains a 'Hall of Shame' which details the total fines received by companies during 1998. The list was topped by ICI, which was convicted three times on a total of seven charges – one for the accidental release of 56 tonnes of trichloroethylene into the Western Canal. Water companies are also included. Following the classic tradition of Sutherland, these companies could be regarded as recidivist offenders. It also has to be borne in mind that, in common with other regulatory areas, many companies are not prosecuted (Hawkins 1984).

Concluding comments

Many more examples could be added to those detailed above. White collar crime takes place in virtually all occupations and organizations and could include state crimes, which have not been discussed in depth. Many more serious frauds could also have been detailed. The above examples do, however, illustrate the vast range, amount and impact of white collar crime as well as showing its distinctive characteristics and diversity. The wide variety of sources used also indicates the wealth of information that is available, although it is more disparate and diverse than that used in relation to other crimes.

   As is the case with all crime, it is difficult to reach any conclusive estimates of its total extent, whether its prevalence or impact exceeds that of conventional crime or whether it is increasing: apparent increases in prosecutions or press reports of 'scandals' and 'disasters' may indicate increasing concern rather than increasing offending and, as the extent of white collar crime is not known, it is impossible to assess whether or not it is rising (Nelken 1997a). Nonetheless, it can be argued that, if known, its total cost could well exceed those associated with conventional crime. The average or total costs of other crimes pale into insignificance when compared with the sums involved in even individual cases of serious financial or tax frauds and the costs attributed to other categories adds considerably to this total. The above examples also show that the physical toll of white collar crime is extensive. Some activities, such as selling underweight foods, misdescribing goods or allowing effluent into a stream, seem more trivial. Nonetheless, the aggregate profits made at the expense of consumers may be enormous and, as South comments in relation to local 'small-scale' pollution incidents, 'the *adding up* and *accumulation* of such localized examples provides a global picture of millions of other "little" events which bring with them modest to devastating changes in people's experience of the environment and conditions of life' (South 1998b: 444). This underlines the considerable impact of offences not only on individual victims, but on public health, the environment and on standards of trading, commerce and public service. The examples indicate the impact of white collar crime on key areas of everyday life such as safety, shopping, eating, investing or saving (Croall 1998b). White collar crime, therefore, involves major areas of contemporary concern, such as food and transport safety, the environment and consumption.

Attention has also been drawn to the way in which offences reflect the major characteristics and diversity of white collar crime. Many specific forms of white collar crime are both occupational and organizational and involve a range of offenders, from major corporations to local traders, senior executives and officials and lower-level employees. This diversity of offenders will be discussed in the next chapter. The impact of white collar crime is global and local and many crimes involve what some people see as an increasing tendency for the 'upperworld' to be involved with the 'underworld', because many activities involve partnerships between organized crime, legitimate organizations and government officials (Ruggiero 1996a). The ambiguous criminal status of offences was seen throughout the chapter. Many activities are not generally regarded as 'crime' and the issues that they involve go well beyond the boundaries of criminology into areas of food and workplace safety or consumer and investor protection. For most activities there is also a fine line dividing 'normal' trading, business or manufacturing practices from those that are considered to constitute 'wrongdoing' or crime.

A final question that should be addressed is why, given their immense impact, so little systematic information is collected about white collar crimes. Information, for example, on the costs of tax evasion, or frauds perpetrated on the NHS by professional groups, is not readily available. Indeed, despite the costs of white collar crime in these spheres much political and media discourse focuses on the non-white collar offences of patients, claimants or individual tax payers rather than on the professional groups whose offences might well be regarded as more serious. This indicates that 'exposing' white collar crime continues to attract accusations of political bias, and that describing the activities of powerful or respectable groups as 'crime' remains inherently problematic (Davies and Jupp 1999; Tombs 1999).

Further reading

This chapter has drawn on diverse sources. Useful examples and case studies of corporate and organizational crime can be found in Punch (1996),

Ruggiero (1996a) and Slapper and Tombs (1999). Levi (1995; 1999a) provides a review of different aspects of fraud in Britain which updates his previous comprehensive work (Levi 1987a). Other case studies and material from the USA can be found in edited collections by Schlegel and Weisburd (1992) and Nelken (1994a). Statistics and other details of offences and prosecutions can also be accessed through the websites of many of the government departments and agencies responsible for specific groups of offences.

chapter three

White collar offenders

It was seen in Chapters 1 and 2 that white collar crime involves a diversity of offenders, although popular and academic representations of white collar criminals play on their high status and assumed wealth. Class and status are not the only characteristics attributed to offenders – they are often explicitly or implicitly assumed to be white, middle-aged men in contrast to the young, lower-class men, many from ethnic minorities, so often identified with the 'crime problem'. Women, who are in any event not associated with elite and powerful groups, have also been assumed to have a negligible involvement. Exploring these stereotypes involves looking further at the social characteristics of offenders. It is also important to look beyond the characteristics of convicted offenders to the law enforcement process in which offences are detected and offenders selected for prosecution: since Sutherland's research, a major question asked about white collar crime has been the extent to which high-status offenders can avoid prosecution. This chapter will start by outlining some of the difficulties of obtaining information about offenders and will briefly explore how they are academically and popularly represented. It will then look at their social characteristics and at how these are affected by law enforcement strategies.

Although the class and status of offenders have been so central to the concept of white collar crime, they have not featured strongly in research, and high status is often assumed rather than established. Some writers and researchers continue to define the subject by the high status of offenders, whereas others use more inclusive definitions thus producing variations depending on which definition is used in any particular research (Nelken 1997a). The relative neglect of offenders is further related to the difficulty of obtaining details about their characteristics. Official crime statistics, whose limitations have already been outlined, do not indicate social class or status, nor do they feature in the statistics compiled by enforcement agencies. In any event, the low rate of prosecutions means that statistics on convicted offenders are unrepresentative, particularly as class bias on the part of enforcers is so often alleged.

More extensive research is therefore needed to obtain details of offenders. This can involve looking at total numbers prosecuted in particular courts over a period of time (Levi and Pithouse 1992), observing court proceedings (Croall 1988) or obtaining information prepared for the court such as pre-sentence reports (Weisburd *et al.* 1991). Although this provides useful information, it is time consuming and necessarily limited to those prosecuted for selected offences in one particular locality. Records of enforcement agencies are a further source of information that can additionally be used to ascertain which offences and offenders are more likely to be prosecuted (Hawkins 1984; Hutter 1988; Cook 1989). This kind of work tends, however, to be focused on enforcement decisions rather than on the social characteristics of offenders, which may not be fully recorded in enforcement files. It is also limited to specific agencies dealing with one group of offences, often in one administrative area. Fuller information about offenders can also be gained from case studies, investigative journalism and media reports, but, as already seen, this is highly unrepresentative. The media are likely to focus on 'big' cases, 'scandals' and disasters (Levi 1999c) and neglect the more typical everyday cases – one British study found that one-third of cases dealt with by the Serious Fraud Office (SFO), which deals with the most serious frauds, were not reported in the period studied (Stephenson-Burton 1995). Cases involving prominent individuals who have 'fallen from grace' or those involving major companies are also likely to receive greater attention. Conclusions about the distribution of offenders therefore remain somewhat tentative.

Representations of the white collar offender

The pervasive identification of white collar crime with high-status offenders is illustrated in the terms often used to describe it, such as 'elite crime' or the 'crimes of the powerful', and in contrasts between 'suite crime' and 'street crime' or the 'crimes of the powerless'. As the authors of a major study carried out in the USA comment:

> both in rhetoric and research, the white collar offender has been pictured as the polar opposite of the common criminal . . . as much as we have come to see street crime primarily as the work of disadvantaged young men from broken families and decaying neighbourhoods, white collar crime has been linked to advantaged older men from stable homes living in well-kept communities.
>
> (Weisburd *et al.* 1991: 47)

These stereotypes are further related to the assumption that high-status offenders are treated differently by law enforcers, which is often crudely characterized as representing a situation of 'one law for rich and one for the poor'. A similar stereotypy surrounds organizational crime, which is often depicted as 'corporate crime', which focuses attention on major, multinational corporations and businesses. It is also widely assumed that the ambiguous criminal status of offences is related to the ability of powerful groups and business interests to prevent their activities being fully criminalized.

It will be seen below, however, that many offenders do not conform to these stereotypes and, furthermore, the association of business groups with high status and power can be qualified. Ruggiero (1996a) points out, for example, that, historically, 'entrepreneurs' have not enjoyed a universally respectable status, having been seen as 'mavericks', and that business and commercial groups were not previously regarded as part of the upper-class establishment. Entrepreneurship has often been associated with 'innovative' business and financial operations and individual entrepreneurs characterized as 'outsiders' rather than insiders. Moreover, as seen in Chapter 2, there is often a blurred boundary between the crimes associated with 'non-respectable', professional criminals and those involving legitimate businesses. Issues of class, status and respectability are therefore more complex than is often assumed.

Popular imagery also reflects the stereotype of the high-status white collar offender, although a closer examination reveals a preoccupation with polar extremes and the use of a variety of class images (Levi 1999c). Maximum publicity is attracted, argues Levi (1999c), by cases in which the 'extravagant lifestyle' of offenders can be contrasted with the suffering they have imposed on their innocent victims. Major themes in the media are the 'fall from grace' of wealthy and powerful pillars of the community, seen, for example, in the extensive coverage given in the UK media to politicians such as Jonathan Aitken or Neil Hamilton, and those involving major corporate institutions whose names are immediately recognizable. The celebrated 'Guinness' case, for example, may have received such extended publicity because of an immediate identification with the product (Levi 1999c). More complex class messages are also possible, as indicated by the extensive coverage in the UK media of the less high-status 'rogue trader', Nick Leeson, which, argues Levi, generated greater fascination among the press than other major frauds. Coverage of this case, he suggests, played on the high status of the victims, who included senior executives of the bank and high-status investors such as the royal family. It also involved the failings of regulators who noticed nothing wrong. Leeson was seen as a 'scapegoat' and characterized as a 'rogue trader' – he was, for example, described in *the Independent* as 'the last oik of the British Empire' (Levi 1999c).

Popular imagery also includes stereotypes of offenders at the lower end of the status scale, who are often presented as 'villains', more akin to conventional criminals. Recent UK press coverage, for example, has been attracted by the activities of 'cowboy' builders, 'rogue' landlords and the 'car cowboys' who sell cars made up from insurance 'write-offs'. This may reflect the selective criminalization of offenders at the lower end of the status hierarchy – there is, for example, less coverage of the deceptive practices of major manufacturers or retailers. Although the local press may give considerable coverage to cases involving individual traders, this may be very unsystematic (Croall 1988). Nonetheless, it does illustrate the variety of stereotypes associated with different forms of white collar crime and underlines the importance of looking more closely at the diversity of offenders.

The examples outlined in Chapter 2 confirm the involvement of a variety of offenders drawn from different status groups and including large and small businesses. This not only questions any simple association between high status individuals and white collar crime, but suggests the potential of exploring the extent to which offences are linked to the range of criminal opportunities available to employees at different status levels and to organizations and businesses in different economic situations. It also suggests that within categories of white collar crime the status of offenders may affect how offences are perceived and subjected to the criminal justice process. The relative respectability of offenders, for example, may affect how likely their activities are to be seen as 'criminal' and prosecuted. The lack of respectability of offenders regarded more readily as 'rogues' may, for example, make them more vulnerable to attention from law enforcement agencies and to prosecution. Recognizing and accounting for the diversity of offenders is therefore important and, in addition, although class, status and respectability have tended to receive more attention, it is also interesting to look at gender, age and race.

Crimes of the powerless and powerful? Social status and respectability

Research has largely confirmed the involvement of a wide variety of offenders across the spectrum of white collar crime. In a British survey of companies (Levi 1988), it was found that about one-third of frauds attributed to employees were associated with managers, one-fifth with accounting personnel and one-tenth with directors or partners. The remainder were attributed to lower-level employees such as sales or shopfloor personnel (12.9 per cent), computer operatives (3.2 per cent) and distributors and drivers (6.5 per cent). Levi (1999a) further points out that the general category of fraud includes embezzlements by staff with 'modest status' along with frauds involving 'respectable' and illegitimate businesses. Even in major cases where a higher proportion of the elite might be expected, many offenders can be characterized as 'mavericks' rather than 'establishment' figures (Levi 1987a). North American research also confirms this picture. In a Canadian study of offenders convicted of securities violations, Hagan (1988) found that 27.9 per cent were employers, 19 per cent were managers, 9 per cent were attributable to the petty bourgeoisie who owned a business but had no employees, and 43 per cent were workers in both legitimate and illegitimate businesses. In a major study in the USA, which looked at pre-sentence reports for offenders convicted in federal courts for a range of white collar offences (Weisburd *et al.* 1991), it was found that offenders were much closer in background to average Americans than to those occupying positions of great power and prestige.

It is more difficult to attribute class or status to organizational offenders – what social status, for example, could be associated with a 'company'? Size is clearly important, as is the legitimacy of the company's activities. It was seen in Chapter 2 for example, that many so-called corporate offences are attributable to a host of small businesses, many operating on the fringes of the legitimate market. Indeed, corporations or large businesses may form a minority of those prosecuted. In one study, in the UK, of food and consumer offences, smaller businesses outnumbered larger ones in prosecutions, with only nine out of 50 cases involving large, 'household name' corporations. Convicted companies were more typically small concerns owned and run by one individual, including butchers, bakeries, bars, small food stores and take-aways (Croall 1989). Other offenders, such as those involved in manufacturing or selling counterfeit goods or in food frauds, operated very much on the margins of legitimacy. Similarly, a study of tax offences found large numbers of small concerns such as video stores (Cook 1989), and Nelken (1983) found that landlords with a small number of residential properties were more likely to be prosecuted for illegal eviction.

Similar findings have been reported in other countries. In the USA criminal consumer fraud has been depicted as a product of 'fly by night' operations and 'shaky businesses' (Rothschild and Throne 1976) and car repair frauds were found to be more prevalent among smaller operators (Leonard and Weber 1977). In Australia, Sutton and Wild (1985) indicate that large corporations form a minority of offenders for environmental and consumer complaints, with smaller and medium-sized firms predominating. 'Typical' European fraudsters are said to include small producers facing financial difficulties, large agricultural concerns defrauding the subsidy system on a consistent and methodical basis and 'organized white collar gangs' whose main purpose is fraud, such as those involved in the smuggling and sale of contraband cigarettes (Doig 1995).

A tentative classification of white collar offenders could therefore be suggested. Individual offenders can be grouped according to broad approximations of occupational status, from senior management and executives, through middle-level, middle-class offenders, to those of a lower, clerical status. Organizational offenders can be grouped according to size, from large corporate offenders or state organizations to the 'petty bourgeoisie' incorporating small but primarily legitimate businesses. These groups can both be distinguished from the 'maverick' and not wholly legitimate occupations and businesses, ranging from more sophisticated 'entrepreneurs' engaging in serious and widespread illegal activities or semi-legitimate businesses to the smaller 'rogues' and 'cowboys' involved in more trivial offending. Although it is difficult to quantify each group, it could be suggested that the distribution of offending is related to the overall distribution of occupational groups, with elite or corporate offenders forming a relatively small minority outnumbered by those from lower levels. The problems of estimating such a distribution are exacerbated when account is taken of the assumption that those of higher status might be less likely to be prosecuted, which will be discussed below. Such a distribution can also be related to the seriousness and impact of offences. Weisburd and his colleagues (1991), for example, suggest a hierarchy of offences and offenders, with those of higher status, who enjoy greater trust, being able to commit more complex offences with higher levels of victimization in comparison with the simpler offences, such as embezzlement, of lower-level employees.

Elite offenders

Descriptions of offenders as elite and, in Britain, as 'establishment' figures (Levi 1987a) clearly reflect elements of status and respectability. Although these terms are difficult to define precisely, they could be assumed to include offenders in the highest socioeconomic status group, such as owners of large firms, senior executives, high-status civil servants or government ministers. Prosecutions in Britain have, however, included relatively few such offenders. Levi (1987a) claimed that no elite insiders have been prosecuted for fraud since the Second World War. In the USA, one major study found that only one-third of the sample came from the highest-status group, most having been convicted of securities and antitrust offences (Weisburd *et al.* 1991). These offenders were described as white, middle-aged males, who had well above average socioeconomic status, with stable employment in white collar jobs and who were more often than not owners of, or officers in, companies. This group, Weisburd *et al.* suggest, are closest to the traditional white collar criminal stereotype. Among the 'elite' could also be counted senior politicians involved in bribery and corruption, often in collusion with wealthy individuals seeking influence. British examples are also rare, although they could include the celebrated case of Jonathan Aitken along with those involved in the illegal arms trade, which includes arms manufacturers, senior army officers and state inspectors. In the Matrix Churchill case, which involved the export of defence-related equipment to Iraq, the prosecution of company executives was halted following revelations that government ministers had known about and encouraged the exports and had misled Parliament (Ruggiero 1996b).

Crimes of the middle classes

Far more typical are likely to be the 'crimes of the middle classes' (Weisburd *et al.* 1991), which would include offences committed by middle managers, civil servants, professional practitioners and employees and politicians whose offences tend to reflect their positions and their opportunities for crime. In the major study in the USA, most tax offenders were the sole proprietors or owners of larger businesses and professional groups such as lawyers and doctors who also had a history of other offences (Weisburd *et al.* 1991). Professional groups in general were also involved in bribery, with attorneys being reported to have been involved in credit and mail fraud, trust violations concerning clients' funds, making false claims and political corruption or 'influence peddling'. Although such detailed information is less available for England and Wales, middle-class offenders would include a number of those involved in tax frauds, many of whom are accountants, and the local authority officers and healthcare professions involved in the fraud and corruption outlined in Chapter 2, along with managers associated with frauds.

Crimes of white collar workers

Other white collar offenders are drawn from clerical workers lower down the occupational hierarchy, but who are nonetheless distinguishable from blue collar workers. These include the thefts and embezzlements of clerks, bank tellers and relatively junior employees. Among the frauds of 'modest status' staff referred to by Levi (1999a) are thefts of incoming and outgoing company cheques and conversion into cash. In the study by Weisburd *et al.*

(1991), bank embezzlers were found to be younger than other offenders, more likely to be female and to come from stable working families. Although the offences of those higher up the occupational ladder had a more serious impact, Weisburd *et al.* point out that those of relatively junior staff can nonetheless involve considerable organization and sums of money, which is also the case with forms of blue collar occupational crime.

The corporate offender

Large multinational corporations and 'household' names clearly lie at the top of any hierarchy of organizational offenders. These would include the large companies named in the UK Environment Agency's 'Hall of Shame', the major chemical companies identified by Pearce and Tombs (1998), the supermarkets and food manufacturers prosecuted for food labelling, pricing and other trade descriptions offences (Croall 1989), and the large rail and shipping companies prosecuted for safety offences involving workers and passengers. Were full details of prosecutions across a range of offences available, it is also likely that some of these would be recidivist offenders. State organizations such as the police or army may also be implicated although individual employees may also be 'scapegoated' for offences, and local authorities have been prosecuted following the deaths of tenants as a result of faulty heating appliances (Croall 1998a).

'Petty bourgeois' and small business offenders

Another group includes the offences of smaller companies that operate at a more regional or local level, along with clearly respectable and legitimate small businesses such as smaller manufacturing companies, farmers and individual retail outlets. This category could be split to reflect the size of business, whether it operates regionally or just locally, and the number of staff that it employs. It may be useful, for example, to distinguish between businesses which employ several staff and who, like the butcher's business prosecuted following the outbreak of *E. coli* in central Scotland, distribute goods to a number of outlets, and smaller individual retail outlets and corner shops, employing few staff, where less diffusion of responsibility is involved. Breaches of safety regulations may also be prevalent in small, non-unionized companies (Tombs 1999), and landlords operating on a relatively small scale have been implicated in failing to maintain the safety of residences and appliances (Croall 1998a). One of the very few convictions in the United Kingdom for **corporate manslaughter** involved the owner of a small leisure company, OLL, and, as will be seen below, smaller companies, where the owner can more clearly be identified as the responsible person, may be more vulnerable to prosecution for offences requiring criminal intent (Slapper and Tombs 1999).

'Entrepreneurs and mavericks'

Alongside these groups lie the large number of offenders found in most categories of white collar crime who are involved in less clearly legitimate occupations and whose status is problematic. Some offenders, for example, although working in apparently legitimate, high-status sectors such as the financial services industry, may not be considered to be 'insiders' or part of the establishment, being regarded as 'maverick' – a depiction often, as seen above, associated with many 'entrepreneurs'. These offenders may indeed be more typical of those prosecuted and convicted, although this may be associated with law enforcement. As Levi (1991) points out, even in the case of the notorious 'Guinness four', which clearly involved senior executives and wealthy men, two of the defendants were described as 'classic self-made entrepreneurs', representing 'new money' and the 'much-vaunted Thatcherite enterprise culture'. Robert Maxwell, said to have 'plundered' his companies' pension fund, could also arguably be portrayed as a 'maverick' rather than an establishment figure, and the BCCI case included bankers whose 'third world' origins may also have precluded them from being seen as 'establishment' figures. Also in this category lie serious fraudsters from a mixture of backgrounds whose businesses are primarily illegitimate although presented as legitimate. One example is the case of Peter Clowes, a 'self-made' entrepreneur whose business in investments and trade in gilts, although extensive and allowing him to live a 'lavish lifestyle', was based largely on fraudulent products (Lever 1992). In this group would also be found the many examples of 'enterprise' crime where firms use legitimate businesses as a front to assist illegal activities and which may aim to consolidate their activities in legitimate businesses that carry fewer risks than wholly illegitimate enterprises (Ruggiero 1996a).

'Rogue' and 'cowboy' businesses

The size of their operations and the seriousness of their offences divides the above category from the smaller concerns, which are often operating at the margins of legitimacy and illegitimacy, and which are found across the spectrum of white collar crime categories and have been described as 'shady operators' (Sutton and Wild 1985), rogues and 'cowboys'. This category includes small traders, often in car boot sales and markets, selling counterfeit, short weight and sometimes stolen goods, and the 'cowboy' businesses breaking consumer, health and safety and other regulations. It also includes the many small businesses such as subcontracting builders and moonlighting tradespeople associated with tax prosecutions (Cook 1989). Many of these smaller enterprises are involved in a mixture of legitimate and illegitimate activities, and their proliferation may also be related to the rise of unemployment and the post-industrial economy. They provide niches for alternative business activities and employment opportunities and are ideo-logically supported by the culture of 'enterprise' (Hobbs 1995; Taylor 1999). They can also be closely related to the more illegitimate activities of those at the lower levels of organized crime (Ruggiero 1996a).

It could, of course, be objected that these categories include much that is not considered as 'real' white collar crime, although this goes back to defin-itional issues. Yet most of these offenders work in white collar jobs, with the exception of those whose activities border on the illegitimate. In addition, they are distinguishable from typical offenders in conventional crime cat-egories, although those at the top of the hierarchy could be considered to be 'pure' white collar offenders (Weisburd *et al.* 1991). Levi comments that 'involvement in sophisticated financial swindles is far from being the pre-serve of a social elite, although, with the exception of extortion, it is by defi-nition outside the range of the routine criminal lumpenproletariat who constitute the majority of prisoners' (Levi 1999a: 144). Occupational status may also be related to opportunities for offending (Hagan 1988). Weisburd and his colleagues (1991) found, for example, that more organizationally complex offences – defined as those that show a pattern, last for long peri-ods of time, involve organization and have five or more participants – were positively related to greater degrees of victimization. Social background characteristics are, they argue, important because they enable people to be placed in positions that provide them with the opportunity to commit organizationally complex crimes. This may not, however, be the case with all offences – considerable damage can be done by the small company vio-lating safety or hygiene regulations.

Crimes of white, middle-class older men? Gender, age, race and white collar crime

Gender

Feminist criticisms of the male-centred nature of criminology have had less impact on the study of white collar crime than on violent or property crimes (Levi 1994). The largely stereotypical assumptions that character-ized 'malestream' criminology (Gelsthorpe and Morris 1988) have also permeated white collar criminology in that offenders are assumed to be male. This is further related to women's lower involvement in the high-status or powerful positions associated with white collar crime. Popular representations also reflect the 'maleness' of white collar crime – most major 'scandals' involving serious frauds or political corruption in the United Kingdom have involved men, with the exception of Dame Shirley Porter, who was involved in so-called gerrymandering while at Westminster Council. Popular depictions of entrepreneurs and mavericks are also pri-marily male (Davies and Jupp 1999), reflecting the association of business with men. Punch, for example, points to the gendered language often used in business – takeovers have been likened to rape, with a male aggressor and female victim (Punch 1996). Images of 'rogues' and 'cowboys' are also gendered – where, for example, are the 'cowgirls'? Personal characteristics may be less evident in respect of organizational crime, although much of this is associated with male-dominated businesses – safety offences often involve male-dominated sectors such as construction and much consumer fraud is associated with car dealing and the building or repair work of 'tradesmen'.

Exploring these gendered assumptions is particularly difficult because the sparse information about offenders makes little reference to gender. Although larger numbers of women are found in fraud categories than in other offences, these include non-white collar frauds such as benefit frauds, assumed to include more women, and the major fraud prosecution bodies in England do not keep any statistics on gender (Levi 1994). Statistics for regulatory crime refer largely to 'companies' and most research studies do not refer to gender. Relatively little is also known about women in areas of organized crime, which are also seen as male-dominated but can involve women (Hobbs 1995).

From the limited amount of information available, a mixed picture emerges. Few women have been convicted for elite crime. From the establishment of the SFO until 1993, only 15 out of 200 prosecutions involved women, all of whom were said to be 'junior partners', and no women featured in the 445 exclusions or suspensions for fraud and 'misconduct' by the Institute of Chartered Accountants in England and Wales between 1989 and 1993 – although 14 per cent of its members are women (Levi 1994). Women's share seems to increase lower down the occupational hierarchy, with more women being involved in 'low level clerical fraud in financial services' (Levi 1994: 236). Weisburd et al. (1991) found that women's share was greatest, at 20 per cent, for bank embezzlement, and few women were found at the top of the hierarchy. In the cases of fraud and corruption cited by the Audit Commission, which did not systematically refer to gender, women do feature in their capacity as local authority officers (Audit Commission 1993).

Many interesting questions are raised by a consideration of gender. Has, for example, the wider participation of women in the labour market, albeit restricted by the 'glass ceiling', led to an increasing involvement in white collar crime? If not, the association between crime and masculinity made for many conventional crimes also becomes an issue for white collar crime (Levi 1994). The above figures tend to suggest that women's involvement parallels their employment status, and Weisburd et al. (1991) found contrasting situations, with most male offenders being managers or officers and most female offenders being bank tellers or in other clerical positions. Women were also much less likely to commit complex crimes with large-scale victimization which, as seen above, was related to higher status. Some women did, however, commit serious frauds, suggesting to the researchers that if more women enter powerful positions, their crimes will be very similar to men's. Accordingly, Weisburd *et al.* argue, it is women's structural position rather than socialization or cultural factors that accounts for gender differences. Nonetheless, it is difficult to make clear conclusions on the basis of one study that was restricted to specific kinds of white collar crime.

Women's crime has also been related to poverty and economic need and US writers have tended to suggest that this is also the case for white collar crime because women offenders were found to be motivated by personal problems and family-based needs (Weisburd *et al.* 1991). It has also, however, been argued that women can commit similar crimes to men for similar reasons (Carlen 1992). As they do participate in frauds at all levels, an interesting question is therefore the extent to which they may be involved in crimes assumed to be motivated more by 'greed' than need (Davies and Jupp 1999). This is difficult to answer in view of the absence of work looking at the variety of female white collar crime, which might also reveal rational women 'entrepreneurs' participating in crime because of its attractions and rewards (Davies and Jupp 1999) – examples of which have been found in the drugs industry (Hobbs 1995). Further research is therefore needed on gender issues, although it will be seen that gender is a potentially important feature in relation to victimization and in the analysis of white collar crime, which will be discussed in later chapters.

Age

White collar offenders are further distinguished by their older age. Steffensmeier and Allan (1995), for example, report different 'age curves' for crimes in the USA with a more even spread among age groups for fraud and gambling compared with a younger peak age for burglary. In Britain, tax offenders tend to be older and theft at work increases with age (Coleman and Moynihan 1996). As for gender, this can in part be explained by participation in employment, because younger people are less likely to be employed or in the high-status, trusted positions associated with forms of white collar crime. In the major US study, the mean age of offenders was more than 40, with younger offenders being found lower down the hierarchy, among mail fraud and bank embezzlement offences (Weisburd *et al.* 1991). Very little attention has been paid to this significant factor. The age of offenders challenges the long-standing and pervasive association of 'crime' with younger offenders and it would also be interesting to explore the extent to which some forms of white collar crime might involve 'criminal careers' similar to those found in respect of organized crime (Ruggiero 1996a), with, for example, former property offenders or young criminals moving into areas of white collar crime.

Race

Race, ethnicity or religion have also been little explored in studies of white collar crime, in sharp contrast to research on conventional crime. This is also assumed to be related to the employment status of different groups, with higher-status occupations being dominated by majority rather than minority groups. Weisburd *et al.* (1991), for example, found that the racial characteristics of offenders was similar to those of the general population, with white offenders being involved more in the upper ranges and in the 'crimes of greatest consequence' whereas more black people were involved lower down the hierarchy. This, they argue, is linked to discrimination in employment, citing a black New York politician's comments during a municipal bribery scandal that it was unlikely that any blacks would be indicted as they 'never got invited to the table when the pie was being divided up' – indeed they 'didn't even know there was a pie' nor were they given an 'equal opportunity to steal' (Weisburd *et al.* 1991: 83). They also found that Jews were over-represented, forming 33 per cent of securities and anti-trust offenders. Although this could be related to stereotypes, disadvantage and discrimination on the part of enforcement agents, they also suggest that it may reflect the higher number of Jews found in the securities industry.

There is very little British information about these factors. Most prosecutions of so-called elite offenders have been of white men, as have convictions of politicians – although this could again reflect participation. Nonetheless, part of the stereotypy associated with 'entrepreneurs' and 'mavericks' may also have racial and ethnic overtones (Ruggiero 1996a), with the origins of 'outsiders' being different from those of 'insiders'. Businesses owned by members of minority ethnic groups are found among the data on small business crimes – one study of food and consumer offences, for example, found equal numbers of Asian and white small businesses, many of the former being small take-aways and grocers (Croall 1989), a feature of food and environmental prosecutions confirmed by other sources (Hutter 1988). As with other features, this could be attributed to a combination of the marginal position of such businesses, their predominance in these retail sectors and the activities of enforcement agents who associate, for example, the spread of food poisoning with the growth of take-away food.

Class bias and law enforcement? Accounting for the distribution of offenders

Most information on the characteristics of offenders is based on studies of convicted offenders, and therefore any conclusions can be criticized for being based on an unrepresentative group of offenders. Findings, for example, that corporate or elite offenders are less common than middle-class or small business ones can readily be interpreted as reflecting the class bias that has been associated with the prosecution process. Law and its enforcement will be the subject of Chapter 6, but some consideration must be given to the extent to which higher-status offenders are advantaged – whether directly, through the attitudes and actions of officers, or indirectly, by virtue of their different legal and structural position. Whether or not law enforcement does affect the distribution of offenders, it must also be asked whether it is possible that elite and corporate offenders have less need to commit offences in the first place.

Since Sutherland's work, it has been assumed that law enforcement agents may be more sympathetic to offenders who are socially and culturally similar to themselves. There has, however, especially in Britain, been relatively little evidence of direct bias on the part of enforcers whose decisions are not based primarily on the grounds of class or status (Hawkins 1984; Hutter 1988; Croall 1989). Nor do they deliberately avoid prosecuting large corporations – indeed, some have been found to welcome the chance to prosecute prominent companies or individuals (Croall 1989). Nonetheless, class is indirectly implicated in other features associated with law enforcement. 'Respectable' companies are often distinguished from 'rogues', who are seen as incorrigible and persistent offenders (Hutter 1988). Consumer protection departments have been found to target secondhand car dealers and market traders (Cranston 1979), health and safety officers may look closely at construction sites (Hutter 1988) and tax inspectors may focus on video shops and builders (Cook 1989). Groups who are seen as less likely to comply may be more likely to be prosecuted. In addition, there is some evidence, particularly from the USA, that large companies and wealthy individuals can and do use their resources to contest prosecution, to negotiate other forms of settlement and, in court, to use skilled representatives in their defence (Mann 1985; Levi 1987a; Croall 1989). This may deter prosecutors from taking a case to court. In addition, some regulatory prosecutions are undertaken by local authorities, and prominent companies and individuals may seek to influence council members although the effect of this is difficult to measure (Croall 1992). Senior employees may be also be protected by organizations' fear of embarrassing publicity, which might be less significant for lower-level employees.

Other features, including those associated with offences, are also related to the different treatment of groups of offenders. Offences vary, for example, in respect of their visibility and ease of detection and it has been seen that those people at the top of the occupational hierarchy may have more opportunity to commit more complex crimes and are subject to less surveillance. The trust accorded to professional employees and practitioners may also lead to their being less likely to be suspected of offences. Visibility is also important for organizational offending. The operations of small businesses are more often carried out in public, on high streets and in markets, and offences are easier to detect by enforcement agents who are passing by. Some may, indeed, be drawn to a business by visual cues, such as displays and price indications for consumer offences, obviously dangerous practices on construction sites for safety offences (Hutter 1988) or, in food hygiene cases, by an unpleasant smell (Croall 1989). Large organizations, on the other hand, do not carry out their businesses in public and inspections are more usually arranged in advance, providing time for preparation (Croall 1989).

Other factors affect decisions to prosecute. It will be seen in Chapter 6 for example, that it is more costly and difficult to gather sufficient evidence for prosecution in more complex cases, particularly where several individuals are involved – again benefiting higher-status individuals and larger organizations. In a small business, on the other hand, proprietors are less able to suggest convincingly that they are not themselves blameworthy, having fewer staff or superiors to blame for neglecting instructions. Where, as is the case with corporate manslaughter, responsibility is particularly difficult to attribute, smaller companies can more easily be convicted (Slapper and Tombs 1999). Less complex offences are also cheaper to investigate – unravelling a serious fraud may take months and years and involve several investigators. Simpler frauds, which are more likely to 'produce a result', are therefore more likely to be prosecuted than complex and international frauds (Levi 1987a), and tax inspectors may choose to prosecute less risky cases involving builders (Cook 1989). On the basis of interviews and observations, Levi (1995) suggests that whereas all prosecution agencies are more cautious when dealing with elite suspects and professional advisers than with middle-status people, the non-prosecution of some top managers and professionals is attributable principally to the difficulty of proving guilt.

Higher-status individuals and large organizations may therefore be protected from prosecution, skewing the distribution of convicted offenders towards those at lower levels. Nonetheless, it must also be asked to what extent the resources of wealthy individuals and corporations can be further used to avoid offending. They may, for example, be able to maximize rewards and profitability while staying within the 'letter' of the law but quite evidently breaching its 'spirit' (McBarnet 1988), or to organize their business in such a way as to maximize profits legitimately. This may be further related to their superior resources and to the expert advice that these resources can purchase. For much regulatory crime, for example, a standard defence is to claim that the organization has instituted systems to check that regulations are complied with. Many of these systems are technically complex and costly to institute, which is easier for the larger concern that can employ expert advisers who can also provide evidence that operations are 'safe'. The smaller concern, on the other hand, cannot afford expert advice, and can less credibly claim the existence of 'systems' to prevent violations, leaving themselves open to allegations of sloppiness or incompetence (Croall 1989, 1992).

A further way in which professional and expert advice can be used is to find ways to supplement income or profits without breaking the law. Experts can, for example, advise on how to avoid paying taxes legally (McBarnet 1988), or, in an organization, about how the law can be 'sidestepped' or what the company can 'get away with' in respect of advertising or compliance with other regulations. In relation to tax evasion, McBarnet (1988) points to the process of 'legal leapfrogging' in which the law has to keep up with ever more elaborate tax avoidance schemes. This may happen in other areas – food labelling laws, for example, are subject to considerable contestation, which has been seen most recently in respect of genetically modified food, and, as seen in Chapter 2, labels that mislead or deceive consumers can be perfectly legal. Other corporate strategies include operating in third world countries with less stringent quality and safety regulations. Finally, as will be seen in Chapter 6, high-status and powerful groups may be able to affect the law itself and prevent the criminalization of their activities. In many ways, therefore, Box's comment that 'corporate crime need not occur' (Box 1987: 55) has some resonance, and high-status individuals or corporate executives may have less need to break the law. They may also have more to lose if caught, thus making the law a greater deterrent. They are nonetheless not necessarily more 'socially responsible'.

Concluding comments

The discussion in this chapter largely confirms the diversity of offenders suggested in previous chapters, and suggests that white collar crime is found, albeit in different forms, throughout the occupational hierarchy. It involves elite and corporate offenders, crime that has been characterized as 'middle-class crime' (Weisburd *et al.* 1991) and crimes of those often associated with the petty bourgeoisie and small businesses. Similar activities may also be engaged in by those whose status is more questionable and who are better perceived of as 'mavericks', along with the rogues and 'cowboys' more typical of many regulatory areas. This has considerable significance for many aspects of white collar crime. It challenges the long-standing association of white collar crime with elite and 'powerful' offenders and the consequent assumption that this alone affects the way in which they are subject to criminal law and enforcement. This will be taken up further in Chapter 6. It also confirms the utility of defining the subject in such a way as to allow analysis of the involvement of different groups and to explore the independent significance of class and status, although it might be objected that the offences of lower-status personnel are not 'really' white collar crime. They are, however, distinguishable from conventional crime, not only in terms of the occupational status of offenders but also in terms of age and race. The involvement of different groups is also, as will be seen in

Chapter 5, significant for the analysis of white collar crime, which must take account of the possibly different motivations of employees at different levels or businesses and organizations in a different economic and market situation. The illegitimate opportunity structures associated with offending may also vary. Exploring the diversity of white collar crime rather than identifying it with specific class or status groups or with corporations is also important when considering patterns of victimization, which will be the subject of the next chapter.

Further reading

Relatively few works have focused specifically on the characteristics of offenders, with the exception of Weisburd *et al.* (1991), used extensively in this chapter. Croall (1989) also contains an account of research and Levi (1995) gives a useful overview for fraud and considers aspects of gender in Levi (1994).

chapter four

White collar crime and victimization

Although white collar crime is often seen as victimless, it was seen in Chapter 2 that it does have direct and indirect effects on individual victims and communities and has global dimensions. The considerable human misery that it causes formed a major part of early attempts to expose its extent. It is said to affect everyone, irrespective of class or status, but it is also important to look in more depth at how it is related to wider social inequalities. Exploring these aspects is far from easy because the crime surveys and other quantitative methods that have attempted to measure victimization are less appropriate as they are based on a conception of crime that excludes white collar offences. The less direct nature of much victimization means that it is also important to look at its structural as well as its individual dimensions. This chapter will start by briefly exploring how victimization from white collar crime is constructed before looking at its scope. It will then outline the different impact of white collar crime on different groups before exploring the growth of victim support groups and responses to white collar crime.

Constructing white collar victimization

The distinctive nature of white collar crime victimization has been previously outlined, although it is important to recognize differences between offences. Some have a serious and relatively direct impact on individuals whereas others, such as corruption, have a much more diffuse effect that is difficult to quantify. Some offences that cause direct harm may lead to only trivial individual losses but to large cumulative gains, especially where they last for long periods of time. The main effect of some offences is not primarily on individuals but on public health or the environment and still others are perceived to adversely affect trust in institutions or standards of manufacturing, trade or commerce. Many offences therefore lack the immediate direct, measurable harm associated with robbery, burglary or assaults. Cases that do involve extensive direct harm such as deaths and injuries also tend to be those in which the apparent lack of intent and interpersonal contact between offender and victim make them less likely to be represented as 'crime' and make victims less likely to be seen as 'crime' victims. There is therefore less of a cause and effect relationship (Slapper and Tombs 1999). In other offences it may be more difficult to identify who benefits and who suffers (Ruggiero 1996a). Where, for example, corruption in relation to government contracts leads to companies undercutting competitors it could be argued that the public benefit by cost savings (Friedrichs 1996), although it could also be argued that such work may be substandard (Levi 1987a). Consumers buying counterfeit goods could be seen to benefit from the chance to buy desirable, albeit fake, designer goods which they could not otherwise afford and the counterfeit industry also provides jobs and advantages manufacturers by confirming the desirability of their products (Ruggiero 1996a). Again, however, it could be argued that many such goods are substandard and even dangerous, and that employment in legitimate industries is threatened (Croall 1998a).

A considerable amount of white collar crime victimization does not therefore fit the social construction of crime victimization, which relies on notions of interpersonal, individual harm. Moreover, much victimization is denied and, as with some forms of conventional crime, a distinction is drawn between 'innocent' victims and those who are seen to have 'asked for it' (Walklate 1989). Feminist writers have pointed to the mythology surrounding offences such as child sexual abuse, rape or domestic violence which blame the victim by, for example, suggesting that women who dress or behave in particular ways are inviting rape, that family violence or sexual abuse happens only in certain 'kinds' of families or that women in violent relationships could leave but choose not to (Kelly 1988; Walklate 1989). These can be contrasted with 'innocent' victims such as the elderly victim of a mugging or the child who is murdered.

Many forms of white collar crime similarly involve victim blaming mythologies, with victims being said to have 'asked for it' and defendants blaming the victim (Croall 1998c). Investors who have willingly placed their money in high-risk financial products are seen to be less innocent than those who have chosen apparently 'safe' pensions or low-risk investment schemes (Levi 1999b). Consumers who willingly purchase cheap products are also seen as undeserving of sympathy as a consequence of the ideology of *caveat emptor,* let the buyer beware, which underlies legal conceptions of consumer protection (Croall 1992). Workers in 'risky' jobs, which are often perceived to carry high rewards, are similarly seen to be inviting danger and as having chosen to work in dangerous environments, and, in many workplace accidents, workers are blamed for being careless or for ignoring safety precautions (Tombs 1999). Female consumers of harmful pharmaceutical products, contraceptives or silicone breast implants are criticized for being sexually active or for having chosen to undergo surgery for non-medical reasons (Finlay 1996). As is the case with conventional crime, many of these representations are accepted by victims and affect their propensity to complain.

The 'mythological' and socially constructed nature of the nature of victimizaton from white collar crime can nonetheless be illustrated. A major justification for the use of the criminal law in regulatory areas is that consumers, workers or the public require protection from dangers that they cannot protect themselves from (Croall 1992). Consumers can less readily 'beware' where they cannot be expected to judge the quality or contents of mass-produced goods or where they possess insufficient information about the possible side effects of pharmaceutical products (information that is often withheld by manufacturers) (Braithwaite 1984; Finlay 1996). Although many so-called 'risky' jobs do carry high short-term rewards, many other jobs with a high risk of injuries are poorly paid and involve casual labour. Like women in violent relationships, therefore, workers may have little option but to remain in dangerous environments. Representing incidents in which workers or passengers are killed and injured as 'accidents' further denies victimization because it makes them seem unavoidable rather than the outcome of a systematic neglect of regulations (Slapper and Tombs 1999).

These kinds of constructions affect reactions to different groups of offences. Pearce and Tombs (1998), for example, suggest that chemical companies are more likely to respond to legislation dealing with the 'environment' than that dealing with worker safety, and that 'accidents' involving passengers provoke a stronger reaction than those involving workers. Passengers taking an everyday journey can be seen as particularly innocent as they have no control over events, whereas workers, as seen above, can be construed as 'careless' (Wells 1995). In 1994, four teenage schoolchildren were drowned in Lyme Regis Bay while attending a leisure centre. It was subsequently revealed that staff were insufficiently trained and that these and other problems were known to the director of the company. The youthfulness of these 'innocent' victims may well have played a role in the strong public reaction and the eventual prosecution of the company (Pearce and Tombs 1998). Such reactions may also be part of an increasing tendency to 'blame' companies and 'experts' when expertise is seen to have failed (Wells 1995).

Exposing the impact of white collar crime

The construction of white collar victimization is also related to its exclusion from what has been described as **conventional victimology**, which relies on a conventional construction of crime based on individual offending and victimization (Mawby and Walklate 1994). As so much white collar crime is relatively invisible, exposing its impact involves an approach similar to that suggested by **critical victimology**, which involves looking at the 'victims we cannot see' (Walklate 1999) by exploring further its diffuse, indirect and structural nature. Attempts, such as those outlined in Chapter 2, to expose the widespread nature of white collar crime indicate some of the ways in which victimization can be conceptualized. Some offences do have a relatively severe and immediate effect on victims and their families and, like conventional crime, white collar crime affects the quality of life in communities and neighbourhoods (Croall 1998a, 1998b). As seen in Chapter 2, its effects can be national and global and its impact on organizations and institutions also, albeit indirectly, affects individuals. Offences against 'the government', for example, indirectly affect taxpayers, who have to pay higher taxes or lose services.

Direct, individual victimization

Far from being victimless, some offences cause considerable financial loss, injury and death and, as with conventional crime, affect victims' families and have an additional emotional and psychological impact. Financial frauds, for example, can have extremely severe effects, particularly where trust has been violated. As Levi (1999b: 7) illustrates,

Not only does fraud lead to broken dreams, it also closes off opportunities which, once passed, are irrecoverable. For older people, vulnerable anyway to loss of confidence in themselves, frauds can destroy happiness permanently, just as readily as any other crime such as mugging or a more serious burglary. Indeed, more so, because victims know that they have supplied funds or goods voluntarily and because the loss of their financial cushion makes meaningless all their lifelong savings and sacrifices.

He also found that an almost universal theme among individual fraud victims was a sense of betrayal and abuse of trust (Levi 1999b) and the experience of fraud has been compared to that of rape in terms of the feeling that trust has been violated (Levi and Pithouse 1992).

The large number of deaths and injuries attributable to corporate and organizational offending outlined in Chapter 2 also has a considerable impact on relatives, friends, survivors who have suffered no immediate injuries, rescuers and witnesses. Deaths in disasters, where the cause may not be clear and where, as is often the case, bodies take some time to be recovered, may additionally involve the death of children, which reverses the 'natural order' of death. All these factors exacerbate grief and make recovery more difficult (Wells 1995). Survivors and those involved in rescues may also experience psychological traumas such as 'survivor guilt' or post-traumatic stress disorder (Wells 1995). Like the victims of major frauds, victims and relatives of those killed by corporate wrongdoing may also feel a sense of betrayed trust, particularly where employers are found to be negligent.

Although these are extreme situations, many other offences cause physical harm and threaten aspects of personal and family safety and economic security. Dangers have been associated with mass-produced foodstuffs and unsafe consumer and counterfeit goods, and white collar equivalents of 'crime in the home' include the dangers of contaminated tap water, which has been responsible for illness and skin irritations, and deaths, injuries and illness attributable to the failure of landlords to ensure safety or maintain appliances (Croall 1998a). Less life threatening are invasive sales practices ranging from 'doorstep' pressure selling to telephone, television and computer selling techniques which may also be fraudulent (Croall 1998a). To this could be added the risks attached to transport and workplace safety and the individual effects of environmental offences, which can have an adverse effect on sufferers of asthma, respiratory diseases and allergies. Although many of these activities may seem relatively trivial, this is also the case with many conventional crimes where victims report only minor effects (Croall 1998c), and food poisoning or other illnesses may have a more severe impact than many less serious conventional crimes. People are not the only victims of organizational offences – wildlife, particularly fish, have been killed in large numbers by the pollution of waterways.

Communities and the quality of life

Other offences, although they have a less direct effect on individuals, affect the 'quality of life' in communities. In extreme cases, disasters affect communities over and above the sense of loss where multiple victims from one community are involved. Some, such as major environmental incidents, devastate the environment, the economic infrastructure or the leisure amenities of communities (Wells 1995). Less dramatically, communities are affected by illegal tipping and other forms of waste disposal, the noise pollution associated with manufacturing or leisure industries such as night clubs, or exhaust fumes from inadequately maintained commercial vehicles (Croall 1998a). The effects of economic white collar crimes may also be felt in local communities and global frauds have local consequences. In Scotland, the Western Isles Council lost about £24m in the BCCI affair, which led to higher council taxes and reductions in budgets for road building, schools and care of elderly people, provoking protests in Stornoway (*Herald* 4 April 1997; Croall 1999b). In local administrations, 'waste', 'mismanagement', fraud and corruption drain resources that could be used for the benefit of local taxpayers and they can also adversely affect local amenities, lead to the construction of unsafe buildings and damage the trust and legitimacy of local government, creating cynicism on the part of the electorate. Revelations of violations on the part of local businesses may threaten local trading in general – magistrates dealing with consumer cases have voiced fears that publicity surrounding the sale of short weight drinks or food hygiene offences might deter tourists and give the area a 'bad name' (Croall 1991). Offences by large employers, which threaten the survival of a business, may also threaten local employment.

Institutional and organizational victimization

Institutions, rather than individuals, are the main victims of some economic offences (Levi 1995; Friedrichs 1996). They are, for example, major victims of embezzlement, employee theft and many other financial frauds. These costs may, however, be 'passed on' – they may keep wages down or lead to higher prices for consumers. Organizations may also commit crimes, such as industrial espionage or violations of competition laws, against each other. Organizations and employers are particularly vulnerable to the abuse of expert knowledge on the part of employees where they may not possess such knowledge themselves (Shapiro 1990) – managers have been found to be particularly concerned about computer crime because so many of their employees have more expertise than they have (Croall 1992). In the Barings bank case, the specialized nature of the financial transactions involved may have contributed to the ease with which Nick Leeson seemed to be able to avoid supervision. The structure of organizations may therefore make them vulnerable, a vulnerability exacerbated by the diffusion of responsibility that also makes offences easier to commit (Friedrichs 1996). Less sympathy is accorded to organizational victims, who can be seen as legitimate targets.

National and global impact

Offences against 'the government' are also impersonal, although, as seen in Chapter 2, their impact can be considerable and they also have an indirect impact on individuals through the reduced resources available for public expenditure. Moreover, as is the case with local authorities, evidence of corruption reduces levels of trust (Ruggiero 1994), as do crimes that are located in state agencies – such as police violence or corruption. The effects of financial scandals may also have national significance, particularly where the legitimacy of financial institutions is concerned. In the United Kingdom, revelations of impropriety in the financial sphere during the 1980s and 1990s were feared as they might discourage smaller investors from investing in the newly privatized industries (Slapper and Tombs 1999). This created, argues Levi (1999a), a 'new class' of victims who posed a political risk.

Finally, as seen in Chapter 2, many forms of white collar crime are global or transnational. These include the euro frauds, which involve enormous losses to the EU budget, and food and waste disposal frauds, which threaten public health and the environment. Levi (1999b) also points to the impact on institutions and indeed countries of frauds committed against developing countries, which can inhibit economic and social development, not least, he argues, through the massive theft of development funds by leaders (Levi 1999b). The effect of some white collar crimes may therefore be experienced globally and nationally in addition to being diffused to individuals. Whether looked at from an individual or collective perspective, therefore, white collar crime has a considerable impact, which is also related to other social inequalities.

Who are the victims of white collar crime? Gender, age, class and victimization

Although these considerations confirm the often made assertion that white collar crime affects everyone (Friedrichs 1996), they say little about how this impact is distributed between different groups. Victims are often characterized as consumers, workers, citizens or residents but it is also important to ask *which* consumers, workers or citizens are more vulnerable to *which* forms of white collar crime (Croall 1999c). The indirect nature of victimization often conceals these aspects and the absence of victim surveys means that there are few figures that highlight the differential effects of offences on groups such as women, elderly people or poor people. It is nonetheless possible to argue that some groups are more susceptible to some offences and the following sections will explore the extent to which victimization reflects wider patterns of gender, age and socioeconomic inequalities along with inequalities of information and expertise.

Victimization and gender

Gender provides a good illustration of these points. As argued previously, the focus on social class has rendered white collar criminology 'gender blind' (Simpson and Elis 1996; Snider 1996) and feminist writers have now begun to explore gendered aspects of victimization. Many of the 'mass harms' associated with pharmaceutical products have affected women (Peppin 1995), and female consumers are harmed by a host of products whose appeal is based on idealized notions of femininity (Claybrook 1996). The gendered division of labour produces different 'risks' for male and female employees, and perceptions of women's relative lack of financial and technical expertise make them particularly vulnerable to different kinds of frauds. Both the economic and physical impact of white collar crime can therefore be gendered and women may be physically victimized in their roles as reproducers, producers and consumers (Simpson and Elis 1996). Women are not necessarily more victimized, as men may also be the specific victims of other offences.

Gender and physical victimization

Starting with physical harms, many major cases of corporate crime have involved attempts to control women's reproduction, particularly with the emergence of forms of contraception requiring medical intervention (Peppin 1995; Simpson and Elis 1996). Typical of many offences in the pharmaceutical industry, these involve producing and marketing products on the basis of inadequate or falsely represented research, even after dangers are evident (Braithwaite 1984). The best-known case was that of thalidomide, a drug given to women during pregnancy, which caused multiple birth defects in thousands of children across the world. Another case involved the Dalkon Shield, an intrauterine device whose design carried a high risk of infection and which caused septic abortions, miscarriages, long-term illness and death and was additionally not an effective contraceptive (Finlay 1996). The company marketing the shield, A H Robins, itself estimated that 5 per cent of users became pregnant and 60 per cent of these suffered miscarriages. There were more than 300 cases of septic abortions in the USA, some of them fatal to the mother (Finlay 1996). In both of these cases, the products were marketed widely in the third world after their dangers were known (Braithwaite 1984; Finlay 1996).

Women can also be harmed by products and services that aim to enhance their appearance (Claybrook 1996). A wide range of health problems have been associated with silicone breast implants, in respect of which, although not the subject of criminal prosecution, the manufacturer was found to have acted with 'fraud, malice and oppression' (Croall 1995; Finlay 1996). Slimming pills, surgery aimed at weight reduction and the products of the 'diet industry' have also been associated with well-established but often unpublicized side effects. At least 35 deaths in the USA during the 1970s and 1980s were associated with diet products and in Britain they have been linked to gallstones, constipation, heart stress, infertility and depression (Croall 1995; Claybrook 1996). A variety of other consumer products also physically harm women – counterfeit perfumes may contain acids that cause burns and cosmetic and common household products are related to a variety of skin disorders and allergies (Croall 1995; Claybrook 1996). This may arise from the use of harmful chemicals or substances often not declared on labels.

Women workers are also physically harmed. Hazards include the higher risks of miscarriage and respiratory ailments associated with the high-tech silicon chip industry (Simpson and Elis 1996), and women workers in the food industry have been found to be at risk of complaints arising from continual exposure to food additives – often not attributed to work but to generalized 'women's problems' (Miller 1985). Pearce and Tombs (1998) cite estimates that as many as 20 million women's jobs entail toxic risks, and women working in modern 'sweat shops' are particularly vulnerable to health and safety violations (Croall 1995). This is not to underestimate the dangers to male workers – indeed, most victims of deaths in the workplace, especially mass deaths such as those involved in the Piper Alpha case, have been men and, in general terms, risky work, such as fishing, building, construction or work in the North Sea oil industry, is male dominated. The reproductive capacities of men may also be affected in the chemical industry (Pearce and Tombs 1998). Women's victimization has, however, often been overlooked – Simpson and Elis (1996) argue, for example, that research on occupational health risks is often carried out with specific reference to men. In addition, legislation protecting women from dangerous jobs may, as in the chemicals industry, be a substitute for ensuring safer workplaces for all (Pearce and Tombs 1998). Although it cannot therefore be argued that women or men are *more* at risk, risks are affected by the gendered division of labour and conceptions of 'women's' and 'men's' work.

Other forms of victimization at work are also gendered. Although much work on women's victimization has focused on the home, a continuum of sexual violence (Kelly 1988) – from mild forms of sexual harassment to bullying and sexual abuse – also occurs in the workplace. Women's working lives may be made uncomfortable, they may be encouraged to keep quiet through fear of losing their jobs or they may feel forced to leave (Stanko 1990). Moreover, although sexual discrimination at work is not widely regarded as 'criminal', it constitutes yet another example of how women may be victimized by corporate neglect of the law (Szockyj and Frank 1996). As consumers, patients or clients, women may also be subject to sexual harassment by 'men at work' (Croall 1995), where doctors, salespersons or other providers of services may use their occupational position, often one with high levels of trust, to sexually harass or abuse women. As these forms of violence are carried out using the opportunities provided by an occupational role, they can be considered to be white collar crime (Croall 1995; Friedrichs 1996).

Gender and economic harms

Frauds and other economic harms may also be gendered. The pharmaceutical, cosmetic and other consumer products aimed at women not only carry physical risks but often make misleading claims. Many dietary and cosmetic products, which are often aggressively marketed with exaggerated claims, fail to produce the desired results, and luxury items aimed at women, such as perfume, designer goods and jewellery, are all subject to counterfeit or cheap imitations and to price fixing (Croall 1995). Such marketing often lies on the borderline between legality and illegality. Many 'diets' make inherently deceptive claims about their effects and little weight loss ensues, and some so-called slimming food products are not very different from other products (Croall 1995). Cosmetics are often used as an example of the misleading packaging referred to in Chapter 2, with perfumes, creams and other cosmetic products often being sold in 'double-walled' containers, giving the impression that they contain far more than they do (Croall 1995).

Gendered assumptions make women attractive targets of other kinds of fraud. In general terms, women are assumed to be less technically or financially knowledgeable, making them potentially vulnerable to sales and investment frauds – 'little old ladies', or 'Aunt Agathas' (Levi 1987a), have long been portrayed as archetypal victims of unscrupulous fraudsters. Peter Clowes identified the 'thousands of little old ladies holding the wrong gilts' as suitable targets for his fraudulent financial products (Lever 1992). Housewives have traditionally been seen as vulnerable to fraudulent doorstep sales and appliance repair frauds (Vaughan and Carlo 1975), and the many activities of 'cowboy' builders may also target women's supposed ignorance, as do the activities of secondhand car dealers or garage repair frauds (Croall 1992).

Again, this should not be taken to suggest that women are *more* likely than men to be victims, because products targeted at men may also have adverse effects, although women are particularly vulnerable to products aimed at 'improving' their bodies (Claybook 1996). It illustrates that victimization can be related to wider gender inequalities and, as feminists argue, to patriarchal culture and capitalism – from a socialist feminist perspective, corporate victimization of women could be taken to represent the 'power of capitalist males to expropriate women's labour and reproductive power for the males' benefit' (Simpson and Elis 1996: 41). The assumed 'need' for women to live up to idealized notions of femininity underlies the appeal of these products and services. Nonetheless, when they do harm, women are 'blamed' for consuming them, as happened in civil litigation involving the Dalkon Shield and silicone breast implants. In cases involving contraceptive products, individual plaintiffs had their sexual history revealed in court and their use of contraceptives to enjoy sexual activity without fear of pregnancy was also used against them. In litigation involving silicone breast implants some plaintiffs were subject to 'character assassination' and women whose implants were the result of cancer surgery were more successful in obtaining compensation than women whose implants were for largely cosmetic reasons (Finlay 1996). Manufacturers, argues Finlay, manipulated the double-edged sword of sexual freedom, the beauty culture and traditional family values:

> their marketing campaigns tantalise women with the promise of a perfect or more healthy baby, or the perfect contraceptive . . . but when these wondrous devices cause cancer, deform their bodies, or erupt inside them, women are impugned for wanting to be sexually attractive and active in the first place.
>
> (Finlay 1996: 94)

Age and victimization

Age is also related to victimization, and, as with gender, to wider patterns of ageism (Braithwaite 1992), with both the old and young being particularly susceptible to some forms of white collar crime. This is related to lifestyles and to the economic and physical dependence of old and young people. As is the case with gender, some products and services are targeted specifically at different age groups, which, coupled with their structural position, makes them vulnerable to different kinds of frauds. Elderly people may also be particularly at risk from the effects of illnesses associated with neglect of food safety regulations, and, like women, may be the target of pharmaceutical and other products – many of which aim to avoid the appearance of ageing, although many, like anti-wrinkle creams, make exaggerated claims and don't work (Croall 1995).

Age and physical victimization

Both children and elderly people are subject to physical and sexual abuse in residential institutions, which is exacerbated by their inability to make credible complaints, particularly where elderly patients are suffering from dementia (Aitken and Griffin 1996) or children are too young to recognize the nature of the harm that is being inflicted on them. Physical abuse may be associated with methods of controlling 'difficult' elderly patients (Aitken and Griffin 1996) or be part of disciplinary methods such as those used in institutions for the young, and drugs may be 'misprescribed' for old people as a measure of control (Peppin 1995). The effects of food poisoning may also be particularly strong on the old and the young. Major cases involving deaths by food poisoning have affected elderly people, particularly residents of old people's homes. One outbreak of *E. coli* in Canada led to the death of 19 residents in 1985 (*Guardian* 20 December 1996), and 19 elderly patients died from food poisoning in the Stanley Royd hospital in Yorkshire, in 1986 (Croall 1992). The previously mentioned outbreak of *E. coli* in Lanarkshire involved about 450 cases, of which 21, all elderly, died – eight as a result of eating contaminated meat pies at a church lunch for pensioners and a further five residents of a nursing home died following the butcher's failure to inform the authorities about the destination of his products (Cox 1998).

Consumer products aimed at children also carry dangers. Around Christmas, reports from trading standards departments regularly warn of the risks of dangerous toys, which have included those with inadequately protected spikes, high levels of toxic paint or cheap electrical Christmas decorations which can explode (Croall 1998a). The active lifestyle and consumption preferences of teenagers, coupled with their limited financial resources, make them another vulnerable group – they are indeed often represented as 'fashion victims'. Already mentioned has been the drowning of teenagers in Lyme Bay while at a leisure centre which took inadequate safety precautions (Slapper and Tombs 1999) and concerns have also been voiced about the safety of fairgrounds, pop concerts, night clubs and other leisure venues (Croall 1998a). Young people, and particularly students, have also featured strongly among the victims of landlords – the Chartered Institute of Environmental Health officers has, for example, claimed that students face living in 'death trap' houses with poorly maintained gas appliances, inadequate fire escapes, inflammable furniture, faulty electrics and pest infestations (Croall 1998a). Their vulnerability lies in their need for short-term, cheap, rented accommodation where landlords have few incentives to improve properties (*Guardian* 14 December 1998). In one case, two students in Glasgow died in a fire in a basement flat rented from a landlord who had failed to register the property, which had unsafe bars on windows (Croall 1999b; *Herald* 19 March 1999).

Age and economic harms

Economic victimization is also related to age. As seen in Chapter 2, many financial frauds have involved pensions. Although the victims of the pensions 'misselling' cases were not elderly, the need to make provision for old age makes pensions and 'safe' investment schemes attractive targets for fraud. The Barlow Clowes case involved the sale of supposedly secure gilts to largely middle-aged and elderly investors, and the Maxwell case involved what Punch describes as the 'plundering' of the company pension fund (Punch 1996). These kinds of offences often attract strong reaction, as victims can be presented as honest and 'innocent'. Elderly consumers are also seen as particularly vulnerable (Burden 1998) and the Director General of Fair Trading has identified 'vulnerable or elderly people' as major victims of deceptive, misleading or oppressive conduct by traders (*Financial Times* 15 December 1994), which included the sale of bogus burglar alarms, preying on old people's heightened fear of crime, and the sale of expensive funeral plans to terminally ill patients in hospitals and nursing homes (*Evening Standard* 17 May 1995). Older children and teenagers are particularly susceptible to counterfeit or cheap copies of goods, including 'pirate' tapes, videos, CDs and computer games. School playgrounds have been reported as being sites for selling counterfeit computer games and computer pornography (Croall 1998b).

As is the case for gender, this does not imply that these groups are more likely to be victimized; indeed, the higher incomes of the 'middle-aged' make them attractive targets. The structural position of the old and the young, however, makes them especially vulnerable to some offences and further illustrates the relationship between victimization and wider structures of inequality. Age also features in the way in which victimization is socially constructed. Elderly victims, as is the case for conventional crime, may be seen as particularly innocent, especially where life savings have been lost in apparently safe investments or pensions funds. Reactions to injuries and deaths, on the other hand, may be stronger when youthful 'innocent' victims are involved. Elderly victims may not, however, always attract such sympathy – for example, it has been argued that a devaluation of aged roles in society may reinforce perceptions of elderly people as 'culturally legitimate victims' (Fattah and Sacco 1989: 158) and deaths of elderly victims may not be seen in the same way as deaths of younger people. A relative of one of the elderly victims of the *E. coli* outbreak in Lanarkshire is reported as saying that 'my mother was old *but* it was her ambition to see the year 2000. She was a lively, healthy woman and I am sure she would have made it, had it not been for this' (*Daily Mail* 20 August 1998; emphasis added). Against this, the economic victimization of teenagers and schoolchildren may be seen as less significant, as is the case with conventional crime, where attention centres on their association with offending rather than victimization (Morgan and Zedner 1992).

Socioeconomic status, cultural capital and victimization

There has been relatively little exploration of the significance of social class and status in relation to victimization, despite their prominence in the conceptualization of white collar crime. Although the assumption that white collar crime 'robs from the poor' to benefit the rich, or that the powerless are victims of the crimes of the powerful, can be read into radical approaches (Van Swaaningen 1997), the view that everyone is at risk implies relatively indiscriminate effects. Many major disasters, such as those involving rail or transport, do seem to have relatively random effects, and wealthy investors are attractive targets for fraudsters. On the other hand, discussions of gender and age also indicate the significance of status. Exploring the relationship between socioeconomic status and victimization therefore involves what Levi (1995) describes as a 'complex moral arena'.

Although the victimization of relatively affluent organizations and employers has been alluded to and is substantial, many white collar crimes adversely affect poorer, more vulnerable groups. Small business offences are more often directed against poorer consumers, who feature more prominently among their clients. More affluent consumers have less need to purchase the cheapest goods or services, to use 'cowboy' builders or to purchase cheap, secondhand cars. Most victims of workplace deaths have been manual labourers, with few having involved managers, and victims are typically casual workers in small, non-unionized companies (Tombs 1999). In addition, it has been found that environmental offences have a greater impact in poorer areas and, in the USA, in black communities (South 1998a; Slapper and Tombs 1999). Developing nations may also become 'dumping' grounds for toxic waste (South 1998a). It was also, argue Slapper and Tombs (1999), those who had less knowledge of financial products who were most likely to be the victims of pensions 'misselling'. Moreover, as for conventional crime, it can be argued that the effects of white collar crime will be felt more severely by poorer victims who have fewer resources to make good their losses or seek compensation.

The vulnerability of lower socioeconomic groups is related to other features of inequality. The more affluent are not only protected by their economic resources but also by their cultural capital. Middle-class consumers are more likely to be aware of the risks of buying cheaper, substandard or dangerous goods, to read consumer advice and to be aware of their 'rights'. Where they do not possess sufficient knowledge or suspect that they have been harmed, they can seek expert advice. Vulnerability to offences also derives from what Shapiro (1990) describes as 'asymmetries of information' – employers are vulnerable to the activities of employees with more expertise, and clients to the providers of professional services. Employers can, however, use 'risk abatement strategies', including financial and legal controls (Shapiro 1990). The information-poor or less well-educated consumer or worker has less knowledge to recognize risks, is less well situated to seek advice or take action, and may have fewer opportunities for risk avoidance – workers in dangerous workplaces may not be able to risk their employment, and residents in areas surrounding polluting factories may have few options for moving. As Tombs (1999) points out in relation to safety offences, victimization is related to wider structures of vulnerability. In the United Kingdom, the Office of Fair Trading considers some groups, among them the elderly, the young and those on low incomes, to be more 'vulnerable' consumers. These groups are less able to obtain or assimilate the information needed to make 'informed' decisions and are exposed to greater 'loss of welfare' through purchasing inappropriate goods or services (Burden 1998). Although not specifically related to offences, this is nonetheless related to victimization.

Inequalities also affect the ability of victims to establish their status as victims and to contest attempts at victim blaming. In 1989, at the Hillsborough football ground in Sheffield, Yorkshire, 96 football supporters of the Liverpool football team were crushed to death as spectators flooded into a section of the football ground after a gate had been opened to relieve pressure at the turnstiles. Initial press reports and police statements alleged that the drunkenness and unruliness of the fans played a major part in the fatal crush. This was fiercely contested by the victim support group, and the crush was later attributed to the decision of police officers to open the gates to that section of the ground (Scraton 1999). Similarly, allegations of worker carelessness are more difficult to contest, as are complaints by workers about unsafe conditions in the face of expert opinions about safety – as Pearce and Tombs (1998) point out in relation to the chemicals industry, chemical engineers determine what is viewed as a 'safe' workplace whereas workers do not constitute 'credible' sources of information.

Victim responses to white collar crime

The exclusion of white collar crime from **victimology** extends to what is often called the 'victim movement'. In addition to its exclusion from victim surveys, white collar crime victimization is not included in the ambit of the Criminal Injuries Compensation Board, victim support schemes or discussions of the victim's role in criminal justice. Although some reference was made to a 'victim movement' against white collar crime in the USA following the growth of the consumer movement (Friedrichs 1996), this was seen as overstated and there has been little evidence of such a movement in Britain. The absence of an organized victim movement is also related to the nature of victimization, which, as seen above, is not constructed as 'criminal' victimization. As many individual victims are harmed little, they take little action, are geographically dispersed and have few avenues for collective action. Sutherland (1949), for example, characterized consumers as disorganized and as unlikely to take action. As many cases are dealt with short of prosecution, victims play only a small role in the criminal justice process and, in regulatory cases, are often not present in court. As so many white collar crimes are not categorized as crime, legal campaigns for criminalization tend to be associated with wider social movements such as environmental groups, trade unions, campaigns for food safety and consumer groups.

Nonetheless, particularly with serious harms, victims can respond and in some circumstances do challenge legal processes. Individual victims may express, sometimes publicly, reservations about the sentences given to offenders, which are often seen as 'paltry' and insufficiently punitive (see Chapter 7), or complain about a lack of prosecution – for example, in cases involving the death of workers. Victims may wish to see responsibility for deaths or injuries clearly established, which may spring from the experience of bereavement (Wells 1995), and 'justice' done. Such responses are more organized after 'disasters' that have caused mass victimization and these have, in the United Kingdom, triggered the development of more organized victim responses and support groups (Wells 1995; Pearce and Tombs 1998; Slapper and Tombs 1999). Indeed, these groups distinguish disasters from individual tragedies and perform both emotional and instrumental functions (Wells 1995). Emotionally, they provide a forum for sharing the experience of bereavement and seeking to explain what happened, which may include attributing legal responsibility. They also provide a channel for legal redress, either through compensation or, increasingly, through taking an active part in the legal processes after disasters. This may include being represented at inquests and subsequent inquiries and calling for the criminal prosecution of those seen to be responsible. Organized groups can better represent their case to the media and secure legal representation. There has, indeed, been the development of what Wells (1995) describes as a 'language of disaster' in which 'disaster lawyers' representing 'disaster groups' have become specialized and have campaigned for corporate manslaughter. There has also been the growth of well-established support groups. The Herald Families Association pressed for the criminal prosecution of P & O after the *Herald of Free Enterprise* disaster and the group formed after the *Marchioness* disaster undertook a private prosecution. The Hillsborough Families Support Group has also undertaken a private prosecution for corporate manslaughter of the two senior police officers whose decisions are said to have led to the fatal crush at the Hillsborough football ground (BBC news online 14 June 2000). In 1991, the group Disaster Action was formed with the stated priority of defining and establishing corporate responsibility and accountability. Similar groups have also formed around financial crimes such as the Maxwell pensions case. The growth of these groups is significant in that they contest the representation of many major corporate crimes as unavoidable accidents and attempts to blame the victims (Pearce and Tombs 1998). Most recently, the announcement that a new law on corporate killing would be introduced followed widespread complaints by the media and by the support group about an absence of prosecutions following the Paddington rail crash (*Guardian* 10 May 2000: 4). The way in which the law deals with corporate responsibility will be discussed in Chapters 6 and 7.

Concluding comments

This chapter has sought to explore aspects of victimization often neglected both in conventional victimology and in studies of white collar crime. White collar crime is often represented as 'victimless' and its effects on individual victims are seen as negligible. Yet, as seen above, individuals do suffer directly and indirectly from white collar crime and, like conventional crime, it affects the quality of life and has local and global consequences. It has also been seen that it is dangerous to make broad generalizations about victimization or to broadly compare this to conventional crime as different offences have different effects.

Moreover, although white collar crime is often associated with generalized groups of victims such as consumers, workers or the general public, it has a more patterned effect on specific groups and reflects wider inequalities of gender, age, socioeconomic status and expertise. In this way, argue Slapper and Tombs (1999: 84) in relation to corporate crimes, these crimes do 'more than rob from the poor to pay the rich: they exacerbate the structures of inequality and vulnerability which capitalism systematically generates'. This is evident only when the structural, as opposed to individual, aspects of victimization are considered, because conventional victimology has focused largely on the effects on individual victims of individual offences. The study of victimization from white collar crime therefore provides a good illustration of the utility of a more critical victimology which takes account of structural variables and 'looks behind our backs' at other aspects of victimization (Mawby and Walklate 1994; Walklate 1998). Moreover, there are signs that victims can and do feel sufficiently aggrieved to take action, which has implications for aspects of the regulation and control of white collar crime.

Further reading

There have been few works specifically devoted to the study of white collar crime and victimization. Walklate (1989) provides a useful overview and a brief section is also included in Croall (1999a). Levi and Pithouse (1992) report on a study of fraud victims and see also Levi and Pithouse (forthcoming). Szockyj and Fox (1996) contains a number of articles concerning women's victimization.

Explaining white collar crime

Popular and academic explanations of white collar crime play on broad themes. Offenders have been portrayed as 'rotten apples in the barrel' or are assumed to be motivated by 'greed' rather than the 'need' assumed to motivate conventional offenders. Some, particularly corporate offences, are often linked with a prioritization of profits over the interests of clients, consumers, workers or passengers. These conflicts are further represented as inevitable in free market, capitalist societies in which cultural values support the aggressive, individualist pursuit of monetary success. Although these kinds of explanations are oversimplified, they do indicate different levels of approach. Individual offenders may have a variety of motivations but at the same time white collar crime takes place in occupations and organizations, some of which are seen to encourage crime. Although offending is often associated with affluence rather than poverty, **anomie**, **subcultural** and other theories linking crime to inequality may also be relevant, as can those that explore how criminal activities are related to cultural values. Finally, although it may be over-simplistic to argue that capitalism produces white collar crime, it is important to look at its location in particular political and economic contexts.

This chapter will start by outlining some of the issues involved in analysing white collar crime before looking at how it has been incorporated into general theories of crime. It will then focus on individual perspectives and move on to considering how it can be related to organizational characteristics. The application of sociological, cultural and social structural approaches will be explored before discussing the extent to which white collar crime can be seen to be an inevitable feature of capitalist societies. As with other aspects of white collar crime, the absence of research impedes analysis. The restricted information about offenders means that less is known about their individual characteristics or personalities than is the case for conventional offenders. More importantly, the rich ethnographic accounts of offenders' motivations or subcultures, which have had such an important influence on theories of conventional crime, are not available for white collar crime, meaning that there is little primary research on the cultural norms and values that provide rationalizations for offending.

It was seen in Chapter 1 that white collar crime challenged criminological theories aiming to establish the 'causes' of crime and, despite the considerable theoretical advances made since Sutherland's early critique, it has remained largely excluded from criminological theory. Indeed, criminological theory could be characterized as 'blind' to the significance of white collar crime in much the same way as it has been criticized by feminists as 'gender blind'. As Slapper and Tombs (1999: 110) argue, 'most of what constitutes criminological theorizing has signally failed even to attempt to account for corporate offending'. This is related to the problematic criminal status of white collar crime, which produces initial difficulties of establishing what is to be explained and whether it can be approached in the same way as other crimes (Friedrichs 1996; Nelken 1997a). If, for example, white collar crime is 'crime', can and should it be incorporated into theories that seek to explain crime but that often exclude it? Alternatively, if it is counted as crime, do its particular characteristics necessitate different theoretical approaches? As will be seen below, many so-called 'general theories' of crime, which do incorporate white collar crime, are so broad that they can be criticized as overly simplistic.

It is also difficult to relate white collar crime to most well-recognized criminological perspectives. The traditional criminology of which Sutherland (1949) was so critical sought to relate criminal motivations to individual pathologies, yet white collar offenders less evidently showed any discernible physical or psychological abnormalities. Many of these abnormalities were also associated with the lower-class backgrounds from which conventional offenders were drawn. White collar crime also challenged the sociological and liberal association of crime with social inequality that was intrinsic to theories focusing on anomie, social disorganization and delinquent subcultures (Ruggiero 1996a), and it did not feature in the criminal 'areas' or delinquent subcultures that were the focus of attention. Later approaches, also critical of 'traditional' criminology, also tended to neglect white collar crime, focusing instead on the way in which labelling, law enforcement processes and the criminal law were used to criminalize the activities of lower-class groups, assuming, often tacitly, a contrast to the more favourable treatment of white collar and corporate offenders. These approaches also tended to focus on issues of control rather than on explanations, which was also the case with administrative criminology, which had itself turned to issues of crime prevention and crime management. Further criticisms came from those who argued that, in any event, as 'crime' is itself a contested category, encompassing diverse activities, there is little point in looking for any single perspective or set of perspectives to explain it.

Many of these issues are difficult to resolve. On the one hand, it could be argued that white collar crime is so different from conventional crime that it cannot be incorporated into criminological approaches and that different approaches, such as those which look at its organizational character, can and should be developed. Many criminological approaches look for explanations at the level of individual offenders, whereas white collar crime involves structural considerations. On the other hand, if the focus of some approaches on lower-class offenders is re-evaluated, these approaches can be relevant and useful. Moreover, as is the case with conventional crime, white collar crime can be analysed on several levels, with individual decisions to participate in crime being placed in the context of the organizational and structural location of offenders, cultural values and the wider social and economic system.

General theories of crime

Attempts to use general theories to explain all kinds of crime have had a continuing appeal, and Sutherland's initial work on white collar crime was linked to his desire to develop such a theory. Crime, he argued, is learnt behaviour resulting from a process of differential association in which an individual is exposed to more values favourable to the commission of crime than those which favour conformity to the law. Criminals learn the techniques and attitudes necessary to commit crimes in association with other criminals and whether or not they adopt these depends on the frequency, duration, priority and intensity of such associations (Sutherland 1947). Although some studies followed this approach, it has now been generally dismissed as superficial, over-generalized and 'banal' (Braithwaite 1985a; Nelken 1997a). As Slapper and Tombs (1999) argue, it does not tell us where the criminal values or crimes originate and may therefore explain the perpetuation of crime but not its origins. It does, however, direct attention to the importance of looking at how values supportive of crime are found in occupational settings (Nelken 1997a).

Another 'general' theory has been proposed by Gottfredson and Hirschi (1990). Using official crime data they found few differences in relation to age, social class and gender between white collar offenders, counted as all those in fraud categories, and conventional offenders. White collar crime also, they argue, involves the essential ingredients of crime, force and fraud. It is therefore little different from other crimes and needs no separate set of explanations. They go on to relate crime to human nature, seeing it as motivated by a self-interested pursuit of pleasure and the avoidance of pain. Short-term gratification is a feature of both conventional and white collar crime and they characterize criminals as more impulsive, aggressive and lacking concern for the opinion of others than non-criminals. Both their theory and methodology have, however, been subject to considerable criticism. Their use of uniform crime reports means that non-white collar frauds are included in the white collar category, and, in any event, as so few white collar criminals are convicted, their sample is biased towards lower-class offenders, with elite and corporate crime specifically excluded (Steffensmeier 1989; Friedrichs 1996). In addition, organizational crime involves actions related to organizational goals rather than individual desires for self-gratification (Friedrichs 1996). More fundamentally, the contention that crime, or any other form of behaviour, can be attributed to universal human nature, contradicts sociological and other arguments that human behaviour is strongly influenced by an individual's environment and social structural position and is subject to different cultural influences (Slapper and Tombs 1999).

Control theories also claim to have general application, although control theorists have largely been committed to a conservative, conventional view of crime which excludes white collar crime (Friedrichs 1996). To these approaches, crime results from a rational choice that will be made in the absence of sufficient controls. The question of why people commit crime is therefore replaced by the question of why they do not (Downes and Rock 1995). Controls include attachment and commitment to, and an investment in, legitimate and conventional lifestyles (Hirschi 1969). This could be taken to exclude white collar offenders, who, it could be assumed, have a stronger commitment to such lifestyles, although this could also lead to crime, should individuals perceive a threat to their employment or success (Nelken 1997a). In addition, controls could be neutralized by the justifications for offending learnt in an occupational setting (Nelken 1997a).

All of these theories, however, have a limited application to white collar crime or, indeed, to conventional crime. Seeing crime as a rational choice motivated by self-interest and uninhibited by controls says little about the complexities of motivations or about the way in which crime is socially patterned. As Friedrichs (1996) comments, only at a general level can some common motivation such as a desire for personal gain be shared by a mugger and a Wall Street insider trader. Whether or not crime can be seen as a rational choice, the kind of crime that individuals choose to commit is dependent on the range of opportunities provided by the different social and cultural settings in which they are located. In addition, what is or what is not a rational choice and how self-interest is perceived may also vary considerably in different settings (Slapper and Tombs 1999). Control theories also divert attention from the wider social structural and economic factors that have been associated with crime (Croall 1998c).

'Rotten apples in the barrel': individualizing white collar crime

These general theories focus on individual choices to commit crime. Other theories have located crime in individual pathologies and in characteristics assumed to differentiate offenders from non-offenders. As these 'pathological' or 'deficit' approaches were based largely on convicted offenders, they tended to exclude white collar offenders and were also seen as inappropriate. As Sutherland (1949: 257–8) famously commented, those suggesting that crime was located in individual pathologies:

> would suggest only in a jocular sense that the crimes of the Ford Motor Company are due to the Oedipus Complex, or those of the Aluminium Company of America to an Inferiority Complex, or those of the U.S. Steel Corporation to Frustration and Aggression, or those of Du Pont to Traumatic Experience, or those of Montgomery Ward to Regression to Infancy.

Nonetheless, there is still a tendency to attribute white collar crime to personality or other psychological traits or to 'rotten apples in the barrel' – a phrase often used in connection with police or political corruption (Doig 1984). This also serves an ideological function – blaming individual 'rotten apples' makes occasional offending seem unavoidable and diverts attention from the 'barrel', which would include the policies, practices and culture of the organization (Doig 1984).

There is also little evidence to support any association between white collar crime and individual pathologies. Few offenders are characterized as 'evil', 'crazed' or 'fiends' in the way that sexual or violent offenders are. Indeed, white collar offenders seem to be normal rather than abnormal and are portrayed as mentally disturbed only in exceptional cases. Although biographical accounts of notorious offenders have identified narcissism or an obsession with power and control as common traits, these are also attributed to many non-criminal people and overall there has been little or no evidence that these kinds of factors play any part in explaining white collar crime (Friedrichs 1996).

Indeed, some of the personality traits that have been linked with white collar crime are also associated with business success (Box 1983). Offending has been associated with characteristics such as a propensity to take risks, recklessness, ambitiousness, drive, egocentricity and a hunger for power (Friedrichs 1996), and Gross (1978: 71) characterized top executives as 'ambitious, shrewd and possessed of a non-demanding moral code'. Box (1983) suggests that one consequence of success may be a lessening of the moral bind of conventional values. Clinard (1983) found that managers more interested in financial prestige and quick profits were more likely to be 'unethical' than those with a more technical or professional outlook, and that mobile executives, recruited from outside the organization, were described as more aggressive and self-interested than those who had spent long periods in an organization. Many of these typifications, however, amount to little more than 'Dallas type sketches' (Box 1983), and the characteristics they identify are scarcely abnormal. On the other hand, it can be argued that personality and character are not totally irrelevant – 'some white collar crime does indeed seem to be difficult to explain without reference to personality and character' (Friedrichs 1996: 218).

These kinds of approaches also assume that most white collar offenders are successful executives, but, as seen in Chapter 3, many are not and some have also identified a 'fear of failure' (Wheeler 1992) as important. Some offending has also been linked to personal problems such as gambling or drug addiction. One study of embezzlers argued that offences originated in personal, non-shareable financial problems (Cressey 1986), and Weisburd *et al.* (1991) described the personal lives of many offenders as being in some disarray. Although these kinds of factors are more applicable to individual occupational offenders, financial pressures in a medium-sized or small business could also lead to offences such as neglecting safety or other regulations or setting fire to premises to obtain the insurance money.

Individual explanations are, however, limited. As for conventional crime, they do not apply to all cases, and identify problems or characteristics that are not always associated with crime (Croall 1998c). Nor do all self-seeking individuals or those with financial problems turn to white collar crime. Individual motivations must be located in the wider context of the organizations in which offending takes place and the cultural values that encourage or discourage offending. There is, additionally, little evidence to suggest that, particularly with organizational crime, offenders are especially 'bad people' (Punch 1996), and many offences are justified as being for the good of the organization. As Slapper and Tombs (1999) suggest, it is more fruitful to ask why, in the context of organizations, 'good people' indulge in crime? The relationship between individual, organizational and sociological factors is well summed up by Schraeger and Short (1977: 410), who point out that:

> preoccupation with individuals can lead us to underestimate the pressures within society and organizational structures which impel those individuals to commit illegal acts . . . recognizing that structural forces influence the commission of these offences does not negate the importance of interaction between individuals and these forces, nor does it deny that individuals are involved in the commission of illegal organizational acts. It serves to emphasize organizational as opposed to individual etiological factors, and calls for a macro sociological rather than an individual level of explanation.

'The buck stops here': criminogenic organizations?

To Punch (1996), the organization is the 'villain', and provides the means, the setting, the rationale, and the opportunity for corporate deviance. As with the pathological approach, research has investigated which, if any, features distinguish organizations or industries characterized by high amounts of offending – indeed, the Sheen Report following the *Herald of Free Enterprise* disaster portrayed the firm concerned as being 'infected with the disease of sloppiness' (cited in Wells 1989: 934). To others, organizations are seen as inherently criminogenic, because the diffusion of responsibility means that no one person assumes responsibility for questionable decisions and the structures and cultures of organizations reflect the prioritization of profit. Organizations also provide the 'illegitimate opportunity structures' for committing crimes, which are also related to the trust relationships inherent in occupational roles (Shapiro 1990).

Organizational pathology

A number of studies have explored the extent to which specific organizational features such as size, economic performance or rate of growth are related to offences, although no clear conclusions have emerged (Friedrichs 1996; Punch 1996; Nelken 1997a; Slapper and Tombs 1999). This may be because these factors have different effects in different circumstances. Offending has, for example, been related to the greater diffusion of responsibility in larger organizations as well as to the absence of clear operating procedures and lack of expertise in smaller ones. Poor economic performance could make offending seem a rational choice to maximize profits or to ensure the survival of a business, whereas it could also be argued that moral controls may be lessened in a prosperous organization. Indeed, Punch (1996) argues that managers may be capable of using any market to rationalize rule bending. The absence of reliable information about the extent of offending makes it difficult to test these assumptions. One major study, carried out by Clinard and Yeager (1980), which did suggest an association with economic performance, has been criticized for relying on official conviction records (Nelken 1997a). A further problem is the number of factors that have to be taken into account, including, for example, analyses of markets, the organizational structure, the relationship of different sub-units within it and the regulatory regime. As Slapper and Tombs (1999) argue, the mechanisms that lead to rule breaking are complex and difficult to link with any certainty.

Criminogenic occupations and organizations

Some occupations and organizational settings can be seen as more 'criminogenic', providing more opportunities for offending than others. Quite simply, if employees have no access to cash or goods, they cannot engage in theft and, even where they do, levels of supervision and the degree of trust placed in them will affect their opportunities. Mars (1982) contrasts 'hawk' jobs, such as those of sales personnel, that provide freedom and autonomy and thereby opportunities for fiddling, with 'donkey' jobs such as the supermarket checkout operator who is closely supervised and has few such opportunities. 'Wolfpack' jobs, which involve team work and access to cash tend to produce highly organized fiddles, as was the case in the docks industry. Some jobs are, he argues, particularly 'fiddle prone', including those that involve 'passing trade' – where employees have an economic relationship with people they will not see again, such as tourists – and jobs involving 'gatekeepers' who introduce purchasers and suppliers of goods or services, enabling the gatekeeper to extract a proportion of the payment. As seen in Chapter 2, this extends to 'brokers' who introduce clients to providers, which provides opportunities for bribery and corruption. Professional occupations also provide many illegitimate opportunities because employers, clients or customers are not in a position to challenge expert judgements about the nature or value of the service required. They also involve high levels of trust. Other occupations involving technical knowledge, such as car services, are also 'fiddle prone'.

Industries can also be particularly criminogenic. In respect of the car industry, for example, Leonard and Weber (1977) identify an oligopolistic market in which large motor manufacturers, who grant franchises to dealers, effectively force dealers to sell as cheaply as possible, gaining little profit. This leaves secondhand car sales and repairs as dealers' main source of profit, encouraging a variety of frauds. In the pharmaceutical industry the huge profits to be made by developing and marketing a successful product may encourage industrial espionage, the falsification of test results, the concealment of potential side effects and a variety of marketing offences including inducements to doctors to prescribe particular products (Braithwaite 1984). The food industry is also highly competitive but faces a relatively inelastic market. Food manufacturers may secure a competitive advantage by, for example, 'value adding' to basic foods to produce a greater range of food products – such as is the case with potato crisps, for example. Consumers end up paying more for basic foods and for products containing less 'real' food and more additives, which are often not fully declared on food labels (Cannon and Walker 1985; London Food Commission 1988; Croall 1992).

The search for profits

These examples indicate that the search for competitive advantage and profits may lead to law-breaking activity, and a simple explanation for organizational crime is that it arises out of the prioritization of profits over safety, health, quality or other considerations. This can, however, be criticized as over-simplistic. Although the cost of compliance with regulations may be high, law breaking, if revealed, can threaten the profitability and even the survival of an organization (Braithwaite 1984). If a company or business is found to have been responsible for incidents resulting in injury, death or serious financial loss, the ensuing publicity and loss of sales can be catastrophic. It is not, therefore, ultimately in a company's best interests to be seen to have committed offences – although the low risk of detection has itself been seen as a factor in producing crime. As will be seen below, the extent to which companies do prioritize profits, or can be seen as 'amoral calculators', has also been questioned and the relationship between profitability and offending is more complex.

Nonetheless, considerations of cost-effectiveness may affect the relative positions of different departments in organizations and affect crucial decisions. The priority accorded to profits can produce conflicts between production, sales and marketing departments and those concerned with quality control, safety or other aspects of compliance. In such situations, compliance may depend on which departments have more power to influence decisions – on who has more 'clout' (Braithwaite 1984; Pearce and Tombs 1998). Braithwaite (1984), for example, found in the pharmaceutical industry that pressure to cut corners on safety is more likely where quality control managers are directly responsible to sales departments rather than to senior executives.

One objection to the often made connection between white collar crime and profitability is that crime also takes place in public service organizations, where profitability is not the main goal, and that some forms of crime are not related to profits. As will be seen below, however, principles of cost-effectiveness have been introduced in many public service organizations and can be seen as criminogenic. Other offences may be produced by similar organizational 'strains'. Some forms of police deviance have been related to the conflict between 'crime control' – interpreted as the need to secure convictions – and due process – the need to stay within the law. Police officers may perceive securing a conviction for an offender they assume to be guilty as a 'higher goal' than conforming with the requirements of due process – which may provide the justification for a range of deviant and illegal activities, such as 'fitting up' suspects or using questionable means to secure confessions (Ruggiero 1996a; Croall 1998c). This may also account for some forms of police violence and, in other organizations, for the use of torture or other means of obtaining information – justified as being in the interests of the state.

Both private corporations and public service organizations have been affected by major changes, linked to 'post-Fordism', associated with flexible structures, decentralization, the creation of autonomous departments linked through internal market networks, and an increasing tendency to turn services into 'businesses' and contracting out different functions (Tombs 1995; Pearce and Tombs 1998). These can also be criminogenic. In a study of six multinational chemical corporations Tombs (1995) found that while senior management stressed the importance of safety, staff involved in safety lacked sufficient 'clout'. No company had a board member with specific safety expertise and efforts to develop monitoring systems and accountability for safety were piecemeal and ineffective. Workers, whose role in safety management had declined since the early 1980s, received little training in safety. Internal markets, he argued, 'commodified' safety as it became a service with a 'cost'. Contracting out maintenance could lead to a reduction of safety staff and has been seen by the Health and Safety Executive as contributing to 'accidents' and thereby to violations. Similar changes in public sector organizations have, as seen below, also been associated with offences.

Organizational cultures

Whether or not these criminogenic features lead to crime may depend on the cultures and subcultures in organizations. Looking at why violations are more common in some organizations than in others, Clinard (1983) and Clinard and Yeager (1980) point to the importance of the attitudes of senior managers. In some organizations, they suggest, law breaking may become a 'normative' pattern, with senior management setting a 'moral tone' that filters down to middle management. Where safety or quality have a low priority, top management may deliberately shield themselves from knowing about violations and exercise little control. In a study of mining companies, Braithwaite (1985b) found cultures where senior managers effectively say 'get it done but don't tell me how you do it'. He also points to the existence in some companies of a 'vice president responsible for going to jail' should violations be uncovered (Braithwaite 1984).

There may also be cultural conflicts in organizations between, for example, the professional values of lawyers or accountants and the commercial culture of sales or marketing personnel. The role of lawyers may become problematic in situations where their professional expertise and commitment to the law may give way to pressures to advise companies on how far they can 'get away with' sales or marketing practices (Braithwaite 1984). Scientists may face pressures to produce results quickly and to falsify findings and accountants to overlook illegal financial transactions. This can also be seen in public organizations, where the introduction of internal markets and commercial principles amounted to a 'cultural revolution' producing a state of 'marketisation anomie' (Hodgkinson 1997). This was illustrated in the Audit Commission reports into fraud in local government and the health service (Audit Commission 1993, 1994). Local government, it argues, has long been associated with public accountability and a reputation for honest and efficient administration, and the health service inherited a culture based on faith in standards of performance, public accountability and professional loyalty. Organizational changes, such as the delegation of financial and management responsibilities, the introduction of internal markets that gave officers access to bank accounts and the contracting out system, have increased workloads, altered priorities and created more opportunities for fraud and corruption. The Audit Commission also found a changed ethos in the health service that it linked with the introduction of business-oriented, risk-taking contemporary management, which was a deliberate move away from the image of the traditional, safe, risk-averse administrator concerned with correct procedures and protocols. In both reports, the commission identified a reluctance to acknowledge problems that, it argued, sent the wrong message to wrongdoers and created a culture conducive to fraud.

Individuals and organizations

Describing offences as organizational crime and seeing others as organizationally induced raises the problematic relationship between individuals and organizations. Can, for example, the organization be said to be 'responsible' when decisions are made by individuals? To some, organizations cannot be viewed as 'offenders' because they can form no intent, cannot learn and cannot be said to have motivations (Cressey 1988). On the other hand, as seen above, many organizational factors can be said to be criminogenic and a major feature of organizational crime is that it is related to decisions, or non-decisions, taken by senior executives or boards who, for example, sanction or do nothing to stop the marketing of dangerous products or the continuation of dangerous or fraudulent practices. In meetings, individuals' personal feelings may give way to a group consensus, particularly where they have no individual responsibility for what might otherwise be seen as unethical or immoral decisions. Slapper and Tombs (1999), for example, argue that the personality and moral code of individuals are less significant than the structural pressures that, in an 'unhealthy culture', can have devastating consequences, and institutional practices and collective decisions can be seen as more than simply the sum of individual actions (Fisse and Braithwaite 1993; Friedrichs 1996).

A good illustration of this is provided in Punch's (1996) analysis of why managers become criminals, in which he explores how an individual's morality may be suspended in the organizational setting. Managers, he argues, have to 'manage' the duality between clean and 'dirty' activities, between the image of the rational, ordered organization and the daily reality of work relationships. Managers become depersonalized as the diffusion of responsibility makes them feel far removed from the consequences of their actions. They develop a variety of rationalizations for unethical conduct similar to the techniques of neutralization used by delinquents – higher loyalties such as business values are invoked and they can readily claim that they were acting on orders, or that others have not carried out their orders.

Punch identifies a number of factors that explain how 'ordinary people' come to violate rules in organizational settings (Punch 1996: 239). Although profit is not a daily obsession, it underpins decision making at key moments, and managers become '*Homo economicus*'. Questionable decisions may become 'crimes of obedience' induced by feelings of loyalty. Punch also points to the processes of organizational selection and socialization that encourage an identification with, and commitment to, the corporation. This leads to the development of an organizational 'mind' that enables individuals to suspend their individual values and to prioritize the interests of the organization. Individuals lose internalized restraints and develop a tunnel vision. In a process of cognitive dissonance, evidence of the dangers of a product, for example, are rejected and managers persuade themselves to believe in it, filtering out damaging evidence. Managers become what he calls 'amoral chameleons', where they learn to live with the duality of their personal morality and corporate 'group think'. This does not happen universally; rather, managers may proceed through a variety of different 'moral careers'. In some cases, he argues, they approach deviance instrumentally and temporarily; in others, they blunder into misconduct; whereas in yet others, they engage in carefully crafted conspiracies over extended periods. In extreme cases, the organization itself becomes 'criminal' yet businessmen rarely see what they are doing as illegal, unethical or criminal.

Features of organizations are therefore a crucial element in explaining white collar crime and go some way towards answering the question posed earlier of why 'good' people make 'bad' decisions. As Pearce and Tombs (1998: 191) point out, 'criminogenic structures can exist in the absence of criminal individuals'. It is important, however, to place these organizational features in their wider cultural and economic context, which will be considered below, after exploring how white collar crime can be related to social structural factors.

Social structure: 'the needy and the greedy'

As seen above, white collar crime has presented a problem for perspectives relating crime to social inequality, although there have been attempts to re-examine how it can be incorporated into such approaches. It can be argued, for example, that anomie theory, the most enduring of approaches linking crime to structural inequalities, is particularly relevant to white collar crime. In Durkheim's original formulation of the concept, applied to suicide, he discusses the effects of the 'boundless aspirations' generated by economic change. These aspirations affect all individuals and, indeed, Durkheim argued that poverty operated against suicide, because those who have less are less tempted to indefinitely extend their needs. Wealth, on the other hand, may lead to feelings that unlimited success is possible and, he argued, 'wealth, exalting the individual, may always arouse the spirit of rebellion which is the very source of immorality' (Durkheim 1897, cited in Slapper and Tombs 1999: 133). This could be applied to the 'enterprise' culture of the 1980s with its emphasis on monetary success, individualism, risk taking and enterprise (Friedrichs 1996; Slapper and Tombs 1999), and some have referred to the 'anomie of affluence' (Stanley 1994).

Merton's (1938) modification of anomie theory assumed that the strain between materialistic success goals and legitimate opportunity structures would be experienced most acutely by those of lower status. The classic criminal response of innovation was a means of attaining goals of success while rejecting the legitimate means. Yet all face the same success goals and anomie can provide a persuasive account of many forms of white collar crime, which are also innovative. Indeed, 'entrepreneurship' has often been associated with 'innovative' economic activity (Ruggiero 1996a). It could also be argued that those who have achieved success will react strongly if that status is threatened, and, as seen above, success in itself may generate further ambitions. The conflict between profitability, cost-effectiveness and business survival and other considerations can be seen as a similar kind of strain (Box 1983), which may also lead to 'innovative' solutions. In corporations, argues Passas (1990), individuals come to realize that attainment of their own ends is related to the prosperity of the firm. Thus, white collar crime can readily be incorporated into the anomie paradigm.

Other approaches have sought to relate crime to aspects of social deprivation, unemployment or economic cycles, although even if white collar crime is excluded it is difficult to establish clear links (Box 1987). What has been suggested is that crime increases in situations of widening income differentials (Box 1987), suggesting to left realists that relative rather than absolute deprivation is associated with crime (Lea and Young 1993). This may occur where groups feel that they have a legitimate claim to be equal to another group, described as a reference group. Where these aspirations are blocked, they may experience **relative deprivation**, which can lead to crime if legitimate avenues of grievance are closed – as might be the case, for example, with the unemployed or minority groups. Such an approach, argue Lea and Young, can account for the property crimes of the disadvantaged and for white collar crime – although less attention was paid to this. As seen above, many offenders are not drawn from the top of the hierarchy and forms of financial crime could be related to feelings of relative deprivation where there is a perception that justifiable pay increases or promotion opportunities have been blocked. Although few studies have looked at higher-status employee crime, as seen earlier some lower-level occupational crime has been related to justifications that workers are attempting to secure a 'fair day's pay' (Ditton 1977). It is, however, easier to apply to individual offences than to organizational offences.

Often linked with left realism are critical approaches that relate conventional and white collar crimes to the nature of contemporary market society (Currie 1997; Taylor 1999). The market society has emerged out of the industrial upheavals that have led to the decline of stable manufacturing industries and the growth of flexible systems of organization often known as 'post-Fordism' in which notions of lifetime employment and welfare support have given way to high levels of unemployment and casual employment with minimal state support. This, together with the erosion of informal and communal networks of mutual support, a 'hard' materialistic culture, a tendency for many people to have to overwork and the weakening of social and political alternatives, can be related, it is argued, to the growth of violent and other forms of crime (Currie 1997).

Although these kinds of approaches tend to focus on lower-class crime, they, like others, can also be applied to white collar crime and to its links with organized crime. To Taylor (1999: 138), financial frauds and neighbourhood organized crime can be seen as explicable choices by individuals and social groups in particular market positions in market society. Post-Fordist organizations, he argues, are continually engaged in a struggle for 'market advantage' in 'niche markets' in which management must struggle to reduce labour costs and invest in technology to replace human labour. The liberalization of financial markets, with its consequent lessening of regulation and the privatization of publicly owned utilities, also vastly increased the risks and temptations associated with market competition. Different forms of financial crime are, he argues, common at all levels and it can readily seem that 'everyone is a capitalist, or that everyone is "on the take"' (Taylor 1999: 147). Financial crime is related to different levels of constraint or inducement – for those at higher levels, constraints or pressures focus on demands for continuing capital accumulation, whereas, at lower levels, pressures are related to survival where full-time employment is no longer a realistic option. Particularly significant for white collar crime, to both Currie and Taylor, is the predominant culture of market society. Currie (1997), for example, criticizes the emphasis, particularly in the USA, on links between crime and the culture of the underclass at the expense of the culture of the overclass and a common or dominant culture of exploitation, predation and indifference to human life – a 'culture of callousness'. Thus, he argues,

> Market society promotes violent crime in part by creating something akin to a perpetual state of internal warfare in which the advancement of some is contingent on the fall of others and in which a corresponding ethos of unconcern – of non-responsibility for others' well-being – often legitimized under the rubric of beneficent competition, pervades the common culture and the interactions of daily life.
>
> (Currie 1997: 163)

This suggests that social inequality can be related to both the crimes of the poor and the crimes of the affluent, and Braithwaite (1992), following Sutherland's concern with general theory, provides a powerful argument to this effect. To him, both 'need' and 'greed' are socially constructed. Needs can be interpreted as 'wants which can be satisfied', whereas greed is constructed as 'insatiable wants'. Wealthy individuals, whose needs are satisfied, may develop further goals and seek to accumulate goods for exchange, surplus to those required for use. They also have more opportunities for acquiring these than the poor. He contends, therefore, that inequality produces crimes of poverty motivated by need for goods for use and crimes of wealth motivated by greed for goods for exchange. In unequal societies, the poor, who are more likely to experience unmet needs, have little to lose from a criminal conviction. Whereas the wealthy may be deterred, they pursue further wealth to prove their success through, for example, conspicuous consumption or building an empire. In this way the blocked aspirations of the wealthy to, for example, become millionaires can encourage the use of illegitimate opportunities, and the 'fear of falling' referred to earlier can also be an important factor.

Conspicuous concentrations of wealth also increase the potential targets available to the poor and wealth itself can open up opportunities for crime – the wealthy can, for example, create illegitimate opportunities. Capital, Braithwaite argues, can be used to set up a company that can be used for fraud. Illustrating the different opportunities for the rich and the poor, he points out that although 'anyone can stage a bank robbery . . . it is not a particularly cost-effective form of illegitimate work' (Braithwaite 1992: 88). The rich have no need to rob a bank because, citing Pontell and Calavita (1992), he argues that 'the best way to rob a bank is to own one'. The wealthy can also use their resources to prevent detection and criminal sanctions and their power renders them unaccountable. Crime can also be motivated by a desire for more power, as seen in examples of the crimes of totalitarian rulers whose activities are justified on the grounds of gaining and maintaining power. Violent crimes can be similarly analysed, as, to Braithwaite, unequal societies are more humiliating. The rich humiliate the poor through conspicuous consumption and perceive exploiting the poor as legitimate, and the poor are exploited and regarded as failures. Ageist societies produce abuse of elders, and oppression also produces crime in racist and patriarchal societies. In patriarchal societies, although women may accept their humiliation, oppression may lead to crimes such as rape and the commercial exploitation of women described in Chapter 4. In totalitarian societies, atrocities by the state are also, he argues, enabled by disrespect for citizens. This can also be related to culture and political economy, which will be explored further below.

Cultural sources of white collar crime

The importance of cultural values in providing rationalizations for offending has already been seen, although, in relation to white collar crime, the 'culture of capitalism' or 'enterprise culture' rather than criminal *sub*cultures has been the source of attention. Subcultural theory has, however, been said to over-predict juvenile delinquency (Downes and Rock 1995), and linking white collar crime to culture can invoke similar criticisms. If, for example, so much is culturally tolerated, why is it not more widespread than it seems to be? Moreover, it is not universally tolerated. It is, albeit inadequately, regulated by law, and the unbridled pursuit of profit irrespective of ethical considerations does attract disapproval and, as seen above, culture conflicts have also been identified. White collar offenders, whether individual or organizational, provide rationalizations and accounts similar to Sykes and Matza's (1957) techniques of neutralization. The relationship between culture, subculture and white collar crime is therefore complex.

A close relationship between the values of capitalism and white collar crime has often been posited. Mills, for example, saw business as operating in a 'subculture of structural immoralities' (Mills 1956: 138), and one of the key features of white collar crime seen in earlier chapters is the blurred line between legality and illegality and between social acceptability and disapproval. Where, for example, is a line to be drawn between entrepreneurship, commercial innovation, sharp practice and fraud (Mars 1982; Ruggiero 1996a)? Some illegal activities are regarded as 'normal' business practice and others are readily justifiable as being for the 'good of' the organization. Cultural attitudes towards activities may also change over time. Often cited, for example, is the 'enterprise culture' of late capitalism which stressed values of individualism, symbolically expressed in the famous comment by the hero of the film *Wall Street,* that 'greed is good'. In both Britain and the USA these sentiments were also associated with a climate of deregulation supported by an ideology that too much regulation was a barrier to the pursuit of free enterprise (Punch 1996). This could be seen as 'criminogenic' not only by decreasing the risks of being detected but also by providing cultural support. Moreover, it may have led to the development of a subculture in 'the city' (Stanley 1992, 1994), in which, as Taylor (1999: 141) suggests, 'playing with other people's money built in an ethic of individual irresponsibility'.

Cultural values also feature in offenders' motivational accounts, which, although constituting *post hoc* justifications, are significant as they express an appeal to acceptable cultural sentiments, suggested in Sykes and Matza's (1957) analysis of techniques of neutralization. As seen in Chapter 4, white collar offenders often 'blame the victim', drawing on culturally acceptable notions in which consumers are expected to exercise caution and workers are blamed for neglecting safety instructions. Cohen (1996a) also points to the way in which state terror is justified by depersonalizing the 'enemy', implying that 'they had it coming'. Organizational offenders, assisted by the diffusion of responsibility and their indirect relationship to the victim, routinely deny any intent to harm (Croall 1988). Embezzlers deny the criminal nature of their actions by claiming that they were only 'borrowing' money (Cressey 1986). Denying blame by claiming that it was 'someone else's fault' (Croall 1988) or that offenders were 'only following orders' is a ubiquitous defence for organizational and state criminals alike (Cohen 1996a; Punch 1996). A major theme in such accounts is an appeal to higher, often business, loyalties. In court, one car dealer stated in mitigation simply that he 'was in the business of buying and selling cars' as if no further explanation was necessary (Croall 1988). Similarly, Benson (1985) found that anti-trust offenders frequently argued that their activities were part of the realities of the business world and excuses that 'business is business' are a recurrent theme (Cressey 1986). Much organizational deviance is justifiable as being in the interests of the 'company' or organization or, for state offenders, the 'nation' (Cohen 1996a). These kinds of arguments are often linked to an implicit or explicit criticism of the law which is seen to interfere with the legitimate pursuit of business interests. As Benson (1985: 588) argues:

> The widespread acceptance of such concepts as profit, growth, and free enterprise makes it plausible for an actor to argue that governmental regulations run counter to more basic societal values and goals . . . criminal behaviour can then be characterized as being in line with other higher laws of free enterprise.

The cultural conflicts in organizations outlined above reflect wider conflicts. Thus free market goals of aggressive individualism and the pursuit of wealth and profits have for long been seen to conflict with professional ethics or standards of public service (Doig 1984; Hodgkinson 1997). Cook (1989) also analyses the conflict between welfare and *laissez-faire* values. Under the latter over-taxation is strongly resisted as it is seen to stifle enterprise whereas welfare values stress collectivism and citizenship and the moral imperatives of taxation. Tax evasion can be justified by appealing to *laissez-faire* values by arguing, for example, that it is 'natural' to want to pay as little tax as possible or that the tax burden is excessive. At the same time, she argues, the unresolved conflict between the contradictory principles of citizenship and free market individualism set some boundaries – few would dispute that some taxation is necessary or support unlimited tax evasion.

Cultural and subcultural theories have also been criticized by feminists for failing to explore gender and the culture of masculinity. It was suggested in Chapter 3 that the preponderance of male white collar offenders could be linked to the 'macho' culture of business. To date, this has received little attention in comparison with violent crime and masculinity. Again the relationship is complex and some people warn of the dangers of associating crime with 'masculinity' as not all men display violent tendencies and there are different forms of masculinities (Levi 1994, 1997). It would nonetheless be interesting to explore the extent to which the aggressiveness, risk-taking and self-seeking pursuit of profit associated with white collar crime is linked to the masculinity of the business and commercial worlds (Messerschmidt 1993), or to what Taylor (1999) refers to as forceful managerial masculinity. Although, as Levi (1994) argues, financial frauds do not involve violence, they may be read as an expression of aggression which, in the business world, is associated with masculinity. Aggressive business executives are generally portrayed as male and he also points to the sentiments of merchant bankers that the 'City is a place for men, not for boys' (Levi 1994: 241). Punch (1996) also draws attention to the gendered language of business in which 'predator' companies are depicted as male and the language of war and competition routinely used. The phrase 'macho management' became commonplace to describe 'tough' aggressive management styles and, as Punch also points out, corporate 'heroes' and 'battles' are part of struggles for power and control. A 'macho' culture surrounding safety, which stresses dangerousness and downplays safety precautions, has also been associated by Charles Woolfson with a resistance to safety regulations in the oil industry (*Scotsman* 15 November 1997).

Although these observations are suggestive, and it might be interesting to explore the potential effect on such cultures of gender equality in the business world, as Heidensohn (1992) suggests in relation to the police, few conclusions can be drawn. There is as yet little evidence about the relative participation of female and male executives in organizational crime, and it remains an open question as to whether female executives who have succeeded are any less likely to engage in crime, or less likely to undergo the processes of 'cognitive dissonance' (Punch 1996) described above

(Friedrichs 1996). In addition, as Levi (1994) points out, linking corporate or white collar crime to masculinity over-predicts crime because many men do not turn to crime, and failure rather than the aggressive pursuit of success is also significant.

Is white collar crime endemic to capitalism?

All of the above approaches suggest a close relationship between white collar crime and capitalist social and economic organization. Corporations are structured around the profit motive, which is supported by cultural values, and capitalism also produces social inequality. To Marxist criminologists the origins of white collar crime lie in capitalism itself. Slapper and Tombs (1999: 141) identify the 'structural necessities of contemporary capitalism' as an issue of potential explanatory significance, as it underlies the prioritization of profit which leads to amoral calculations on the part of corporations, and affects the extent to which corporate crime is seen as more or less acceptable. Although not denying that individual business people care about ethics, they point out that doing business ethically may itself be a strategy to secure competitive advantage, such as the recent efforts by banks to encourage 'ethical investments'.

There are, however, many problems with seeing white collar crime as endemic to capitalism, some of which were discussed in the context of organizations. Serious violations of law, when detected, can threaten profitability, and taking account of safety or quality can be advantageous to long-term profitability (Nelken 1997a; Pearce and Tombs 1998). Like other approaches, such a view can also be said to over-predict white collar crime, because it becomes difficult to explain the relative stability of economic trade if crime is as prevalent as it would be were it an inevitable result of capitalism (Nelken 1997a). Moreover, there have been improvements in quality and safety and laws regulating business have been passed, questioning the view that laws inevitably reflect capitalist interests (Croall 1992; Nelken 1997a; Pearce and Tombs 1998). As Nelken comments:

> if it is somewhat over-simplified to argue that only a small proportion of businessmen are bad apples, it is not much more convincing to assume that all businesses act as amoral calculators and would choose to offend but for the availability of serious sanctions.
>
> (Nelken 1997a: 906)

A further problem is that such an approach can less easily incorporate law breaking in non-profit-making organizations, although, as seen above, these are increasingly affected by market considerations, and industries and state agencies in former non-capitalist or socialist societies were not 'crime free' (Friedrichs 1996; Nelken 1997a). The relationship between capitalist organization and ideology and white collar crime is therefore not straight-forward. Reviewing these points, Pearce and Tombs (1998: 134) nonetheless contest that there is an 'ultimate and inevitable truth' in the argument that they are related, and that it is 'accurate in the last instance'.

To support this contention, they critically explore explanations of accidents in the chemicals industry. It is often argued, particularly in industries using new technologies, that a certain number of accidents are 'inevitable' and that some risks cannot be foreseen. Similar arguments were advanced in the North Sea oil industry, where accidents were attributed to the 'frontiers of technology' (Carson 1981). Although, argue Pearce and Tombs (1998), there is an element of truth in these claims, they must be evaluated in the context of capitalist industrial development, in which risk assessment is premised on the need to make enterprises profitable. Advancement is there-fore seen as more important than safety – an order of priorities that is rarely questioned. Accidents and disasters also reveal the limits of scientific know-ledge, which is itself socially organized. Experts such as chemical engineers claim a monopoly of knowledge and competence to make plants 'safe', whereas workers, who experience the plants daily, are not viewed as credible. This provides an example, they argue, of Habermas' (1970, cited in Pearce and Tombs 1998: 142) notion of 'distorted communication', in which workers are not a 'source of serious statements'. Corporations thereby function by disempowering a range of stakeholders, including workers and trade unions. Far from being inevitable and unavoidable, accidents are routine occurrences, involve mismanagement, are rooted in the need to accumulate and are further related to the balance of power between capital and labour. Those who own and control chemicals corporations, they argue, structure operations in ways that produce accidents. An import-ant corollary of this is that operations could be organized in different ways (Pearce and Tombs 1998).

A further feature of capitalism is its tendency to 'commodify' social relationships (Friedrichs 1996; Slapper and Tombs 1999) by reducing 'risks' of death or injury to figures on a balance sheet in which they are balanced against profitability. In this way, argue Slapper and Tombs (1999: 144), 'capitalism relentlessly reduces all forms of social relationships into econ-omic ones'. The Ford Pinto case in which executives calculated the likely costs of lives being lost provides a stark illustration of this (Chapter 2). Slapper and Tombs (1999) argue that similar kinds of calculations are made in relation to safety at work and rail, sea and air travel, in all of which cost and expediency are balanced against known dangers, their chances of ma-terializing, the number of people who would be hurt and the gravity of injury that they might suffer. Decisions about the safety of roll on–roll off ferries, such as the *Herald of Free Enterprise*, involved considering how quickly ferries could turn around and were therefore related to the pressures of competition and the need for speed on highly competitive routes (Slapper and Tombs 1999). The decision in the United Kingdom not to install advanced equipment to prevent trains going through red lights, which might have prevented the Southall and Paddington rail crashes, provides a further illustration of the priority accorded to issues of cost-effectiveness.

To Slapper and Tombs (1999), these kinds of considerations illustrate the 'distorted gaze' that results from and reinforces the legitimacy of commercial considerations. This can be seen further in discussions of issues of quality and safety, many of which rely on economic rationalizations. In the United Kingdom, the Health and Safety at Work Act, for example, uses the notion of 'reasonable practicability', which ultimately implies cost-effectiveness. Some arguments for compliance stress that it is 'good' for profits. A recent campaign by the Health and Safety Executive centred around the theme that 'good health is good business' and stressed the costs of ill health. Slapper and Tombs argue therefore that all the evidence indicates that the preservation of human life and welfare is not the abiding principle of capitalism (Slapper and Tombs 1999).

One criticism of these kinds of approaches is that it is not easy to identify exactly what capitalist interests are, far less to equate these with the state which does pass regulatory legislation, although the relative ineffectiveness of that regulation could be taken as a further example of the state operating in capitalist interests. Some Marxist approaches have, however, moved beyond more mechanistic models and recognize that capitalist interests may not be unitary (Pearce and Tombs 1998). Specific forms of white collar crime should therefore be located in their specific political and economic context. Pearce and Tombs (1998) argue that the Bhopal disaster can be fully understood only in the context of relationships between multinational corporations and host governments and the local context of the pesticides market. The capitalist class cannot be assumed to use the state as its instrument. Some conflicts, such as those against the working class, unify the capitalist class, whereas others, such as competition between corporations for markets and capital, divide it. Thus the 'unity of the capitalist class can be real enough but is often fragile' (Pearce and Tombs 1998: 209). Nor should the state and its agencies inevitably be seen as operating in capitalist interests, although on occasion their respective interests may coincide. In his work on regulation in the North Sea, Carson (1981) argues that coincidence of corporate interests in developing the oil fields and the UK government's interests in speedy development to capitalize on revenue produced a 'political economy of speed' in which safety, despite campaigns for tougher regulation, took second place to development (Carson 1981).

Whether or not white collar crime is seen as endemic to capitalism, these arguments do point to several of its criminogenic features and suggest that some could be changed (Pearce and Tombs 1998). It should also, however, be pointed out that other systems of social and economic organization also have criminogenic features. In non-capitalist economies, for example, pressures of production, quotas and targets are also prioritized over safety or environmental considerations, as was the case in former state socialist systems of production (Nelken 1997a). In addition, Nelken (1997a) points out that while not underestimating the fruitfulness of hypotheses based on the capacity of capitalism to generate business crime, it is also prudent to point out that all organizations, capitalist or otherwise, can be criminogenic insofar as they tend to reward achievement at the expense of external considerations. As seen above, public organizations such as the police, army or government also generate crime and corruption. Moreover, not all white collar crimes are in the interests of capitalism because some threaten it economically and others endanger the legitimacy of finance, commerce or government (Nelken 1997a).

Concluding comments

It is clear, therefore, that many different kinds of approaches can be used to reach a fuller understanding of white collar crime and that although it is generally excluded from criminological theory, similar approaches can be applied. Its occupational location makes an analysis of organizations essential which is also the case for organized crime. Indeed it is the relevance of organizational characteristics and organizational theory that leads Ruggiero (1996a) to conclude that corporate and organized crime should be jointly analysed. It may also be useful, as Pearce and Tombs (1998) suggest, to distinguish between 'first order' and 'second order' causes of crime. The immediate cause of many white collar crimes lies in the individual decisions to engage in activities that can be defined as crime, whereas second order causes relate to the structural and economic background within which these choices are made. Individuals' choices must be located in their specific occupational or organizational settings which, in turn, have to be placed in the context of their environment, in their particular market and in a social and economic system that prioritizes goals of profitability. Although this may be seen as of more relevance to organizational than to occupational crime, this too is located in a work environment and in an organizational and cultural context. Offences also take place in the context of the unequal societies that produce anomie or relative deprivation and the 'insatiable wants' that have been associated with the crimes of the poor and the wealthy (Braithwaite 1995b). As Ruggiero (1996a) points out, wealth as well as poverty can lead to crime. Some of these approaches are also relevant to the study of the control of white collar crime; indeed, many have focused more on control than on explaining activities. It has been seen, for example, that within *laissez-faire* values regulation and laws are seen as undesirable. This will be further explored in the next two chapters.

Further reading

A good summary of many explanatory approaches along with an exposition of the Marxist approach can be found in Slapper and Tombs (1999), and a more detailed development of this approach can also be found in Pearce and Tombs (1998). Punch's (1996) analysis of 'why managers break the law' is also interesting and further points about organizational analysis are provided by Ruggiero (1996a). Braithwaite's (1992) article gives a clear exposition of his argument that unequal societies produce crimes of the poor and of the wealthy. Nelken (1997a) and Friedrichs (1996) also contain comprehensive summaries and critiques of the major approaches to explanation.

chapter six

Regulating white collar crime: law and policing

The most marked distinctions between white collar and other crimes are found in the way in which they are criminalized, policed and punished and the ambiguous criminal status of offences and distinctive features of law enforcement have been outlined in previous chapters. In general terms, white collar crimes are associated with lower rates of prosecution and, for many offences, the use of private and administrative measures outside the formal processes of criminal justice. The involvement of agencies other than the police underlines these distinctions, as Levi (1995: 181) comments, 'at a crude level, if the police deal with it, it is crime; if other agencies deal with it, it is not crime'. The term regulation, generally used to describe the structure of law, enforcement and sanctions surrounding most offences, is accompanied by a different language from that used in relation to conventional crimes (Cook 1989). 'Crimes' and 'offences' such as theft or fraud are represented as being subject to 'control', 'criminal justice', 'policing' and 'punishment' whereas the activities encompassed by white collar crime, often described as 'wrongdoing', 'malpractices', 'violations' or 'rule breaking', are seen as subject to 'regulation', 'negotiated agreements', 'settlements' and 'sanctions'.

As is the case with other aspects of white collar crime these contrasts should not be overdrawn because not all detected conventional offenders are prosecuted. The distinction between individual offences, occupational offences and organizational crime is also particularly marked and discussions of regulation most often relate to corporate crimes in areas such as health and safety, consumer protection or environmental crime (Slapper and Tombs 1999). Fraud and financial offences are, as seen in earlier chapters, more readily regarded as 'criminal', subject to criminal law and sanctions and more likely to be subject to police investigation. Organizational crime, on the other hand, involves activities subject to criminal law not because they are seen as morally wrong but on the grounds of public protection. Laws are enforced by a variety of enforcement agencies and inspectorates, whose main role is the maintenance of standards and public protection. What is often called **social regulation** is therefore associated with a distinctive set of law and procedures and 'regulatory' and 'criminal justice' approaches are often contrasted. This can be further related to Pearce's (1976) distinction between activities that threaten the interests of capital, as fraud and theft ultimately do, which are likely to be subject to stronger criminalization than those that do not threaten the pursuit of profitability. As will be seen below, this does draw attention to significant differences, although the regulation of both groups of offences shows similar features.

Many issues have been involved in the study of regulation. As seen in previous chapters, its different and purportedly less severe nature has been widely assumed to reflect the influence of high-status and powerful offenders although, as seen in Chapter 3, direct class bias on the part of enforcers is less easy to establish. Others also dispute that regulation is less stringent, arguing instead that the differences between white collar and other crimes necessitate different laws and enforcement. In turn, however, these arguments have been strongly criticized for accepting the ideological distinction between white collar crimes and other crimes (Hawkins 1990; Pearce and Tombs 1990; Snider 1990). Regulation has been subject to considerable research, theorizing and academic and political discussion. Studies in the sociology of law have examined the nature and development of regulatory law along with the activities of enforcers and the role of class and power. Discussions have also focused on the most appropriate and effective means of preventing white collar crime. This chapter will start by placing regulation in its historical context before exploring further its major characteristics. It will then outline the major debates surrounding its efficiency and the extent to which it can be seen as reflecting the power of business over its own regulation. Finally, some alternative approaches to regulation will be introduced. This chapter will focus largely on law and its enforcement, leaving related discussions on sanctions and punishment to Chapter 7.

The development of regulation

The characteristics of **regulatory enforcement** can be appreciated more clearly by briefly exploring its historical context, which involves the tension, outlined in Chapter 5, between free market, *laissez-faire* principles under which legal intervention is resisted and liberal, welfare values under which legal intervention is justified as necessary for public protection. To advocates of free market principles, intervention is seen as unnecessary because market forces can themselves ensure high standards of production and protect the public. Workers, it is argued, will refuse to work in unsafe workplaces and consumers will avoid buying substandard or unsafe goods. On the other hand, industrial development has continually presented dangers that have not been prevented by market forces. In Britain in the nineteenth century, concerns centred around the long hours, poor conditions and low wages of factory workers (Carson 1974), and the health of the public was affected by pollution and widespread food adulteration – in one incident in Bradford adulterated lozenges poisoned 200 people, of whom 15 died (Paulus 1974). Mass production of consumer goods made it more difficult to sustain the principle of *caveat emptor* as manufacture became separated from selling and buyers could no longer judge the origins, quality or contents of goods (Borrie and Diamond 1981). Technological development in the twentieth century continued to pose risks to individual and public health, which was particularly marked in the chemicals, food and pharmaceutical industries and in transportation. Protective legislation was therefore justifiable, but its development has generally been premised on an assumed need to strike a balance between the interests of public protection and industrial or commercial development and profitability.

The struggle between conflicting ideologies and interest groups is well illustrated in studies of the development of regulatory laws, notably the nineteenth-century Factory Acts (Carson 1971, 1974, 1979, 1980) and food and drugs legislation (Paulus 1974). The eventual form of law resulted from a lengthy process of conflict, negotiation and accommodation between *moral entrepreneurs*, who campaigned for criminalization, governments and industrial groups. Specific campaigns led to the development of legal principles in one area, which were then applied to other areas, including pollution, factories, food and drugs and, later, consumer protection (Paulus 1974). These campaigns, often triggered by specific incidents, led to the criminalization of what were seen at the time as 'normal' trading or manufacturing practices. In the first instance, laws included requirements of *mens rea* (criminal intent), but were often symbolic rather than instrumental as they did not provide for sufficient enforcement and it was difficult to obtain convictions. Emergent enforcement bodies such as the Factory Inspectorate and Public Analysts, responsible for testing food, then became part of the process leading to subsequent reforms.

The now familiar pattern of enforcement and strict liability emerged out of these negotiations. Initially, business groups were hostile to regulation and factory inspectors recognized that they could better gain acceptance by persuading businesses to comply and engaging in only selective prosecutions. Gradually, argues Carson (1979), they distinguished between 'acceptable' and other violations and industrialists came to see the law as less of a threat. Enforcers argued that strict liability was necessary to obtain convictions, but accepted that prosecutions would be selective. Some industrialists also accepted that some form of regulation was in their own interests – it could, for example, price smaller competitors out of the market, and food manufacturers found that it prevented the use of cheaper substitutes by competitors. Strict liability also led to smaller penalties and to the distinction between 'real' and 'technical' crimes, which are often described as 'quasi criminal'. Often quoted in legal texts is the case of *Sherras* v *De Rutzen* ((1895) 1 QB 918), in which strict liability offences were described as 'not criminal in any real sense'. As Carson (1979; 1980) argues, offences were thereby 'conventionalised' and seen as substantially different from other crimes. Similar justifications and arrangements were subsequently applied to consumer protection laws during the twentieth century. In the development of the Trade Descriptions Act, some business groups supported the law because it would control unscrupulous sales practices, whereas others feared that it would bring retailing to a 'grinding halt' (Croall 1987). It was stated, however, by the Minister of State of the Board of Trade that the bill was 'not expected to lead to a great number of prosecutions' (Croall 1987).

Formal statements of the aims of laws and agencies therefore tend to stress the need to secure a fair balance between the interests of business, industry or commerce and those of consumers, workers or the general public. Moreover, their main aim is said to be to protect the public by encouraging high standards of trading or commerce, with the detection and prosecution of offences being one among other strategies. Regulatory agencies are not seen as, nor do they see themselves as, 'industrial police officers' but as expert advisers or consultants whose aim is to secure compliance to laws and regulations.

Particular legal problems have also surrounded the criminal liability of companies. Some of the problems of 'blaming' organizations for offences were seen in Chapter 5, and, even if companies can be seen as morally responsible, establishing legal liability is extremely difficult. It is often argued that the criminal law, which relies on notions of individual blame and responsibility, is not well adapted to dealing with companies (Wells

1993; Ross 1999). Considerable difficulties surround establishing intent, or *mens rea*, along with recklessness or gross negligence, where companies rather than individuals are involved because corporations are legal abstractions and have no 'soul' or 'mind' capable of forming criminal intent. To establish corporate liability, the law has relied on attributing a 'personality' to the corporation by identifying its 'controlling mind', a test that requires that directors who can be prosecuted are identified, who can be shown to have been in a position to act as the controlling mind as opposed to being servants or agents of the company (Ross 1999; Slapper and Tombs 1999). This has proved extremely difficult in practice, and there have been few successful prosecutions of companies for corporate manslaughter, particularly in cases involving mass deaths. In the case against P & O after the *Herald of Free Enterprise* disaster, the court also rejected the principle of aggregation in which fault on the part of several directors could be aggregated to incriminate the company. Intent must legally be attributed to individual directors, meaning that 'the rules work in a way which is more accommodating to corporations than to individuals' (Slapper and Tombs 1999: 32).

This has several consequences. It may result in individual employees being 'scapegoated' by being prosecuted in situations where the company is perceived to be morally responsible. As seen in Chapter 5, individuals and companies can also attempt to 'pass the buck' by claiming either that they were only following orders or that orders issued had not been followed, and convictions may be easier where the company is small, with a more identifiable person to be held responsible – as was the case with OLL Ltd, which was convicted following the deaths of teenagers in Lyme Bay. The prosecution of larger companies may involve lengthy, costly trials with a high risk of failure (Slapper and Tombs 1999). Many companies are therefore prosecuted for breaches of 'regulatory' statutes such as those under the Health and Safety at Work Act rather than for manslaughter.

A good illustration of some of these problems is the case following the outbreak of *E. coli* in central Scotland, which involved the firm John Barr and Sons (Croall and Ross 1999). In one prosecution, in October 1997, John Barr himself was prosecuted for the common law offence of culpable and reckless conduct relating to supplying contaminated meat – because no death had occurred from this specific meat he could not be charged with culpable homicide. There was, however, insufficient evidence to prove that he had supplied the meat either knowing that it might be infected with the bacterium or indifferent as to whether it was or not. A second prosecution was brought in January 1998 against Mr Barr, two other partners and the firm for offences under the Food Safety Act 1990 and food hygiene regulations. Charges against the individuals were dropped, however, in exchange for the firm pleading guilty to charges of selling meat unfit for human consumption and a breach of hygiene regulations – regulatory offences not requiring *mens rea*. This arguably enabled the individuals involved to avoid responsibility and led to relatively small fines for violations of regulations that did not seem to reflect the harm done – in this case 21 deaths. This raises issues of whether individuals or companies should be prosecuted, and also illustrates the problems of prosecuting on the basis of the regulation that has been broken rather than the outcome.

Although these considerations apply more specifically to social regulation, similar tensions emerge in relation to financial regulation. Under free market principles, intervention, even where directed against fraud, can be resisted and the fine line between fraud or theft and 'normal' business practices has been seen to be subject to different constructions. Many financial institutions such as the stock exchange used to be subject to self-regulation and outside intervention was resisted. During the 1980s, however, there were strong imperatives to strengthen regulation that protected investors and to enhance the legitimacy of the financial market, because the government wished to privatize industries that had been publicly owned and regulated and to encourage investment by new groups of small investors (Punch 1996; Levi 1999a). Privatization in itself created the need for new regulatory arrangements (Slapper and Tombs 1999). This led to the formation of the Serious Fraud Office (SFO) and a new structure of financial regulation.

Laws against fraud and corruption also seek to secure a balance between protection, the need to maintain standards of commerce and the interests of industry. Levi (1987a: 85) points out that laws against fraud are formulated not just to deal with fraud but 'to provide a regulatory framework within which commerce can function', and the maintenance of standards in finance or commerce is a feature of much financial legislation (Clarke 1986). Laws in relation to bribery and corruption are directed not only at offences but aim to maintain the 'highest standards of integrity and propriety in public life' (Doig 1984: 344). It was seen in Chapter 5 that the conflict between *laissez-faire* and liberal values also affects taxation, which is seen as a threat to free enterprise and initiative (Cook 1989). In the United Kingdom, many agencies are also less concerned with prosecution than with prevention or achieving compliance. Whereas police agencies such as the SFO and the Crown Prosecution Service (CPS) focus on criminal prosecution, the main role of the Bank of England and Self-Regulatory Organizations (SROs) is 'prudential or preventive' and the Inland Revenue and Customs and Excise perceive their task as being the 'maximization of revenue' (Levi 1995: 186).

These kinds of considerations do broadly distinguish the nature of white collar crime regulation, although this varies between different kinds of offences and difficulties are particularly acute where companies rather than individuals are involved. The rationale for the use of law forms the context in which the specific characteristics of law enforcement, discussed below, must be placed.

White collar law enforcement

One of the most immediate features of white collar law enforcement is the large number of different agencies involved. Providing a full list of these would be a prohibitive task, and this section will focus on their general characteristics. Some indication of the range of institutions involved can nonetheless be indicated. The regulation of fraud, for example, involves government departments responsible for taxation, such as Customs and Excise and the Inland Revenue, along with the Department of Trade and Industry (DTI), which is responsible for many other financial offences and for overseeing the work of the SROs involved in different areas of City fraud. The Bank of England and the stock exchange also perform regulatory functions, together with the Securities and Investments Board (SIB) (Levi 1995, 1999a). The SFO was set up in 1988 to provide a unified body for the investigation and prosecution of serious fraud, and is responsible for frauds where amounts at risk exceed a minimum level that has ranged from £1m to £5m. It has a limited caseload of about 100 cases a year and other frauds are dealt with by the Fraud Investigation Group (FIG) of the Crown Prosecution Service (CPS) and by regional fraud squads (Levi 1995). Regulatory crimes are the responsibility of a variety of inspectorates. Consumer protection laws are largely the responsibility of local authority consumer protection or trading standards departments (Scott 1995); food hygiene and some pollution matters are the responsibility of environmental health officers (EHOs); safety in the workplace falls under the remit of the Health and Safety Executive (HSE) and some EHOs; and water and other pollution matters are dealt with by the Environment Agency. Trade associations and professional bodies also have regulatory functions and, in large companies, lawyers, accountants, compliance officers, quality control and safety managers and security departments are all responsible for aspects of compliance. Despite the wide range of bodies involved and the different nature of offences, some common characteristics of regulation can be discerned, with, as indicated above, some differences between financial and social regulation.

Prosecution as a 'last resort'

Principal among these common characteristics is the tendency of most agencies to see prosecution as a 'last resort', reserved for a relatively small proportion of detected offences. This is particularly pronounced in areas of social regulation where, as seen in Chapter 2, only a small number of complaints and incidents eventually lead to prosecution. Non-prosecution is also a feature of the regulation of fraud (Levi 1995). For example, in its first four years the SIB prosecuted only one case involving an unauthorized investment business, although it claimed to have detected 50 cases of fraud, which were passed on to the police or the SFO resulting in 22 convictions. Levi further identifies the Inland Revenue as being the most selective agency in respect of prosecutions.

Compliance strategies

The lack of prosecutions is attributed to the use of what are described as **compliance strategies**, which are most often associated with social regulation but also apply to financial regulatory bodies. These derive from the nature of regulatory law which, as seen above, produces a situation in which agencies' main role is seen to be the maintenance of high standards and compliance with regulations. Many pursue advisory and educative roles in which visits or inspections are used to offer expert advice as well as to detect violations. Enforcement officers and businesses are involved in a continuing relationship (Hawkins 1984) in which persuasion is seen to be a better means of encouraging cooperation and compliance. It is often argued that a strict prosecutorial approach could damage this relationship and alienate businesses. When offences are detected, a typical approach is to persuade businesses to remedy the situation before resorting to informal and formal measures (Cranston 1979). These measures range from verbal advice, warnings and cautions to more formal written notices requiring improvements and formal cautions, in what has been characterized as a 'graded letter system' (Richardson *et al.* 1982). Prosecution is considered only if these options fail and offences persist.

Out of court settlements

Compliance strategies are also related to the range of powers possessed by agencies, many of which are seen as more effective, and on occasion more Draconian, than prosecution. Some agencies have powers to grant or withdraw licences necessary for a business to operate, and others can close a business, particularly where it poses a direct danger to public health or where previous warnings have been ignored. In some cases, these powers underlie negotiations, and a business may agree to a temporary closure while improvements are carried out. These powers are considerable because they directly threaten the profitability or survival of a business, although they are often used sparingly (Croall 1992). Other regulatory bodies have powers to disqualify company directors, and professional bodies can also 'strike off' or otherwise disqualify members. Some agencies can additionally negotiate out of court financial settlements and impose financial penalties. The Inland Revenue, for example, can negotiate repayment along with fining tax evaders. In companies, individual offenders may be dismissed rather than prosecuted because companies may fear that publicity could damage their public reputation. Many offenders are therefore dealt with and sanctioned without resort to criminal proceedings.

Cost-effectiveness

Many of these strategies are based on considerations of cost-effectiveness. In addition to being seen as less appropriate, prosecution may be avoided on the grounds that it is costly and often risky. It has already been seen, for example, that the complex nature of offences makes them difficult and costly to investigate, detect and prosecute. Many offences are detectable only through inspections and investigations that involve time and resources. Some investigations require expensive tests – for example, on the contents of foods and other consumer goods or the nature of emissions. Serious frauds are particularly costly to investigate because they often involve many participants and have taken place over long periods of time. They may also require the collection and examination of a long 'paper chain' of thousands of documents or interviews with many witnesses, many of whom may be located abroad.

These problems are exacerbated where prosecution is contemplated because evidence must be carefully prepared to satisfy legal requirements that are often complex. Many fraud trials are lengthy, and establishing that offences have been committed, and which defendants are responsible for which actions, may involve technical legal arguments. Defendants may also have sufficient resources to obtain expert legal and financial advice and to provide sophisticated defences (Mann 1985). Trials have gained the reputation of being 'risky' after some high-profile acquittals, such as the failure to convict in the Maxwell pensions case. In the celebrated Blue Arrow case, defence costs were estimated at £30m, with the prosecution amounting to £2m, and the Maxwell prosecutions cost £25m (Levi 1995). The complexities of fraud trials have been widely acknowledged and have led to suggestions for creating special procedures and dispensing with the use of juries. It was also seen above that the prosecution of companies for criminal offences such as manslaughter also involves lengthy and risky trials. In other, less serious regulatory cases, agencies may balance the time and costs of prosecution with the lower costs of persuasive strategies, especially where only a low fine may result from a prosecution (Cranston 1979; Hutter 1988; Croall 1992).

Who is prosecuted?

The low rates of prosecution inevitably raise questions about which offences and offenders are most likely to be prosecuted, particularly in relation to class bias. Regulatory enforcement was subject to considerable research in the 1970s and 1980s, in which the attitudes and day-to-day practices of enforcement agents were studied to explore the relationship between the 'law in action' and the 'law in books' – particularly in areas of social regulation such as pollution (Richardson *et al.* 1982; Hawkins 1984), health and safety (Carson 1971), consumer protection (Cranston 1979; Croall 1987) and environmental health (Croall 1987; Hutter 1988). Far less qualitative material is available in respect of areas of financial regulation. These studies also revealed how the tension between prosecution and persuasion are played out in practice and variations between and within agencies.

These studies largely confirmed that, in general terms, prosecution was reserved for what were seen as deserving cases – characterized as the 'big and the bad' (Hawkins 1984). For example, it was more likely in cases with a high public profile, such as major pollution incidents or 'accidents' involving members of the public (Hawkins 1984; Hutter and Lloyd Bostock 1990). Although these are serious offences, seriousness in itself is not necessarily a major factor because cases resulting in individual deaths have been found to be no more likely to be prosecuted (Carson 1971). Rather, judgements were made about the character of offenders – for example, whether they were likely to comply or had ignored previous warnings. In this way enforcement agents' decisions reflected judgements of 'blameworthiness' with a disregard for warnings being interpreted as blameworthy and 'recalcitrant' offenders more readily typified as 'criminal' (Carson 1971; Cranston 1979; Richardson *et al.* 1982; Hawkins 1984; Hutter 1988).

Within this, there was considerable variation both between and within agencies, with some pursuing more aggressive or punishment-oriented strategies and others more persuasive ones. Cranston (1979) found that some consumer protection departments used prosecution sparingly, others were 'prosecution minded' and still others neither encouraged nor discouraged prosecution. Hutter (1988) and Croall (1987) found both persuasive and insistent attitudes among environmental health departments. These differences were commented on by officers. In one study two neighbouring departments openly discussed their different styles, with those in an 'action' department criticizing the adjacent department for its 'writing one letter, then another' approach (Croall 1987). In other departments, purges or blitzes on particular offences may be carried out (Braithwaite and Vale 1985; Croall 1987). Some departments consciously use publicity as a deterrent, such as the Environment Agency's 'Hall of Shame' referred to in Chapter 2. Although prosecution and persuasion are often portrayed as alternative policies, in practice they are often combined and persuasion is backed up by the ultimate threat of prosecution. Braithwaite (1984) characterized enforcers as 'walking softly while carrying a big stick' and Hawkins (1983), described day-to-day enforcement as a process of 'bargaining' and 'bluffing'.

As seen in Chapter 3, enforcers also have stereotypes about types of businesses where offences are most likely to occur, and 'rogues' and 'cowboys' are found across a wide range of enforcement areas – indeed, they are the equivalent of the 'usual suspects' of the police. This may lead to some businesses being visited more often and being seen as deserving of prosecution. It was also seen in Chapter 3 that there has been little evidence, in Britain at any rate, of the kind of class bias often alleged, although these kinds of offenders are often of a lower status than others. Compliance strategies are also based on the assumption that most businesses are likely to comply and more 'respectable' businesses conform more readily to this assumption. Moreover, in some areas of enforcement, particularly those involving self-regulatory bodies, the attitudes of regulators and offenders about which activities are 'criminal' may be very close (Bosworth-Davies 1993). Assessing the extent to which non-prosecutions are related to class bias must also take account of the difficulties and costs of prosecution, particularly where proof of intent is required (Levi 1995). The issue of class bias must also be placed in the wider political and economic context of business regulation, which will be discussed below.

Issues in regulatory enforcement

The nature and practice of regulatory enforcement have been subject to extensive public and academic debate. The effectiveness of regulatory enforcement has been questioned and the low rate of prosecutions said to be insufficiently deterrent, although to advocates of free market principles the same rates of prosecution can be seen as excessive. It is seen to constitute favourable treatment for one class of offenders, which raises questions about the fairness and impartiality of criminal law and justice. At the same time, however, the extent to which it does constitute lenient or unfair treatment can be questioned and it can also be argued that the regulatory approach is necessitated because offences are more difficult to detect and prosecute than other crimes and some argue that it is also the most appropriate approach. The arguments of what is often called the 'compliance school' have in turn been subject to criticisms that they accept the fundamentally ideological nature of the distinction between white collar and other crimes along with the rationales for regulatory enforcement (Hawkins 1990; Pearce and Tombs 1990). These different views are linked to alternative approaches to the reform of regulation, which will be the subject of the final section.

Criticisms of ineffectiveness have been levelled at both financial and social regulation, although Slapper and Tombs (1999) argue that financial regulation attracts stronger public reaction. The DTI was severely criticized for the length of time it took to take action in cases including that of the fraudster Peter Clowes, and the SFO has been caricatured as the 'Serious Farce Office' following high-profile acquittals – although at the same time it has also been criticized for being too aggressive (Levi 1999a). It is difficult to assess these criticisms. Levi (1999a) points out that there are evidential difficulties and that the SFO has taken on cases that would not previously have been tackled. Highly publicized failures have also, he argues, to be placed against a conviction record of about 75 per cent. At the same time, however, other agencies do use prosecution sparingly and a low priority is given to fraud within the police, illustrated by the low level of resources given to fraud squads and an absence of pressure to do more about fraud (Levi 1999a).

Some high-profile cases have also attracted critical attention to social regulation. The failure to prosecute companies for corporate manslaughter following mass deaths and injuries has led to considerable public and academic criticism (Slapper 1999), and also draws attention to the policies of enforcement agencies. In the fatal accident inquiry (Cox 1998) following the outbreak of *E. coli* referred to earlier, the enforcement department was severely criticized for not making sufficiently rigorous or frequent inspections and it called for more resources for food safety enforcement. Moreover, the low rates of prosecution in both financial and social regulation, coupled with what are seen as lenient sanctions, can be interpreted as amounting to a licence to carry on offending. If the threat of prosecution is to be seen as a deterrent, it is argued, it should be a real one, and the widespread use of out of court settlements, which means that many offenders are not publicly prosecuted, compounds these problems.

It can also be argued that treating one group of offenders differently undermines the claim of the law to be 'fair' and impartial, especially as these offenders tend to be drawn from higher-status groups. It was seen in Chapter 3 that although allegations of direct class bias are difficult to substantiate, it can nonetheless be argued that higher-status offenders are structurally advantaged. In general terms, the outcome of compliance strategies is that white collar offenders, who are more often of middle-class status, are less likely to be prosecuted than conventional offenders and it is also the case that some, often more 'respectable' or large businesses, are less likely to be targeted for surveillance or prosecution. The use of negotiated settlements can also be seen as advantageous, because, irrespective of their effectiveness, they result in fewer prosecutions and may lead to a situation in which wealthy offenders can 'buy' themselves out of public prosecution, which carries a greater stigma. Some offenders may also be able to exert political pressure in relation to investigation and prosecution, as has been the case where the investigation of serious frauds has been subject to political intervention (Levi 1999a).

In addition, although the law, particularly in relation to social regulation, is seen primarily as a deterrent, the criminal law also carries implications of moral disapproval and its legitimacy rests on assumptions of equal treatment. Irrespective therefore of whether prosecution is 'cost-effective', it is justifiable on moral grounds. As Levi (1995: 194) argues:

> granted that *some* forms of securities and insurance misconduct can be
> dealt with more expeditiously . . . by the appropriate regulatory bodies,

is this . . . form of diversion for adult offenders really fair on people prosecuted for minor offences in the 'blue collar' field? And, more sociologically, what would be the effect of such an explicit policy on the ideology of equality before the law (assuming that the public got to hear about it)?

Moreover, arguments about the cost-effectiveness of prosecution are applied less to conventional offenders. It could be argued, for example, that it is not particularly cost-effective to prosecute a burglar in that it may not compensate victims, stop the individual burgling or deter other burglars, yet few would dispute that burglars *should* be prosecuted (Croall 1992).

The rationale for compliance strategies therefore rests on assumptions that differentiate white collar offences and offenders from other offenders. In addition to pointing to the complexity, organizational location and invisibility of offences, which hamper law enforcement, advocates of compliance strategies make a number of assumptions about offenders. It has been argued, for example, that white collar and particularly organizational offenders differ from conventional offenders because their activities are socially productive and should not be curtailed, and that they are not 'recalcitrant' criminals but otherwise law-abiding citizens who are amenable to persuasion (Kagan and Scholz 1984). Offences are seen to be a result of incompetence or lack of expertise rather than criminal or deliberate intent and as incidental rather than central to the operations of the business. Businesses can be persuaded to comply because, ultimately, offending is not in their long-term interests, despite being motivated by short-term desires to avoid the costs of regulation. Corporations are seen as being capable of being 'socially responsible' and are not therefore necessarily or only 'amoral calculators'.

These assumptions have been contested by those adopting a Marxist approach, who, as seen in Chapter 5, relate white collar crime to capitalism and the profit motive. To such critics, regulation must be located in the political and economic structure of capitalism (Snider 1990; Slapper and Tombs 1999), and in a number of publications Pearce and Tombs (1990, 1997, 1998) have provided a detailed and extensive critique of the compliance school. In particular they challenge the contention that businesses are not 'amoral calculators'. Although individual managers and corporations claim to be socially responsible, they nonetheless have a legal responsibility to act in the interests of shareholders and are continually under pressure from shareholders and market and competitive considerations to maximize profits at all costs. These pressures 'necessarily push managers to develop an amoral, calculative attitude to economic activity, in other words, to try to act as rational economic actors' (Pearce and Tombs 1997: 82). Moreover, they argue, the assumption that businesses are persuadable is related to a view that illegalities are marginal to business operations, which accepts business rationalizations and is contradicted by the widespread and 'normal' nature of law violations. This view also accepts the ideological distinction between white collar and other crimes.

To Marxist approaches, the nature of regulatory enforcement and its accompanying rationale are, as seen in earlier chapters, indicative of the power of business over the criminal law and its enforcement. In instrumentalist or 'ruling class' models, business interests were seen as predominant and identifiable with the interests of the state and its agencies. Although the existence of laws against business seems to contradict this argument, it was contended that the limitations of these laws rendered them merely symbolic, thereby serving capitalist interests. As McBarnet (1984: 231) explains:

> Law was made by the state: the state was run by the ruling class; and law was obviously in the interests of the class which made it. Law which at first sight did not quite fit with the model, such as health and safety regulation or pollution control could be readily dismissed as merely ideology, ineffective in practice, or in the 'real' interests of capitalist class – if not in the short term, in the long term, if not in their financial interests, in their ideological interests, if not in the interests of individuals nonetheless in the overriding interests of the survival of the class.

Some of the problems of instrumental approaches are illustrated in the analyses of the development of regulatory law outlined above. Although laws were resisted, some capitalist groups accepted that regulation was in their interests, particularly when it was seen to present less of a threat. In addition, there were conflicts between different groups and it may not be possible to identify the interests of capital as a whole, as opposed to the interests of specific groups of capitalists (Levi 1987b). The negotiations leading to legislation often involve conflicts between different groups about how laws will impinge on their activities and specific groups lobby on their own behalf. Such 'special interest' lobbying occurred in the United Kingdom in the build-up to the Financial Services Act during the 1980s, where conflicts emerged between the interests of finance and industrial capital (Levi 1987b). The long history of negotiation involved in nineteenth-century legislation also revealed considerable differences between larger and smaller manufacturers, and in the development of the Trade Descriptions Act, diverse groups such as coal merchants, bakers and biscuit manufacturers sought to exempt their operations from controls, with, for example, biscuit manufacturers being particularly influential in preventing controls over deceptive packaging (Croall 1992).

Although the state is often identified with capitalist interests, the role of government may be to mediate between these sectional interests and government may also have a wider interest in promoting the public health through controls over food or the environment. In respect of financial regulation, which may be subject to more stringent controls, government may also need to protect the legitimacy of financial institutions. As seen above, apparently tougher controls were imposed in relation to financial services during a period associated with free market values which was also associated with the government's priorities of opening up financial markets to a wider range of investors. Regulation was therefore seen as necessary to encourage new investment.

Nonetheless, industrial influence on the law is strong and extends beyond law making to the setting of standards and regulations. Regulatory laws typically involve broad prohibitions or standards which are accompanied by detailed regulations (Scott 1995). Standards are set by committees on which business groups are represented, representation that often exceeds that of other interest groups such as workers, consumers or environmentalists (Croall 1992). The use by business of scientific and technical expertise is also crucial. As business groups often have more resources to fund research than governments or interest groups, they are in a better position to influence the determination of appropriate standards. In this way, business definitions of reasonable regulations tend to predominate (Yeager 1995; Pearce and Tombs 1998). Although business influence may not therefore be a 'conspiracy' nor can 'business interests' always be clearly identified, their effect on law and regulation is considerable and pervasive. As Nelken (1983) argues, this effect amounts to a coherence without a conspiracy in that:

> if it is proper to resist the assumption that legislation inevitably serves to reinforce the existing distribution of power in society it is also wise to note that most legislative intervention does have this effect – even if the route which it follows to this end is uneven and not necessarily consciously designed.

Some Marxists move beyond instrumentalist perspectives by using the Gramscian notion of hegemony in which class rule or hegemony is not seen to be absolute but is seen as emerging out of recurrent struggles between competing groups. Regulation is thereby represented as the outcome of conflict, negotiation and class compromise, processes within which agency struggle and resistance are intrinsic (Pearce and Tombs 1998). There is no one pattern of regulation, different forms emerge in different states and for different industries, and its effects are not predetermined. Moreover, they argue, there have been real improvements – workplaces have been made safer and safety is not inimical to capitalism although, in some circumstances, particularly in Britain, it is often resisted. As Slapper and Tombs (1999: 193) comment, corporate power is not a resource 'which in a simple and once and for all fashion constrains, but . . . [is] . . . a phenomenon which takes many forms, and which is always ubiquitously and unevenly available'. Hegemony is never complete as the struggle for dominance is never finally achieved, and it is subject to continual challenge and legitimation crises. To Slapper and Tombs this lays open the possibility of regulatory reform.

Criminalization, regulation and self-regulation

These debates are related to analyses of how regulation can and should be reformed. At extreme ends of the spectrum lie free market and economist arguments advocating decriminalization and deregulation and Marxist and critical arguments advocating greater criminalization and stronger enforcement. Most arguments take less extreme positions and, despite considerable differences, some of the approaches outlined above are not incompatible. Many accept, for example, that white collar crimes do present particular difficulties for law and enforcement and that some regulatory options can be as effective as, if not more effective than, criminal prosecutions and few would advocate prosecuting all detected offences. There is also some agreement that, ultimately, organizational offences are best prevented in organizations – by, for example, creating 'cultures of compliance' in which compliance is seen as a major goal and rewarded. However, there remain important differences as to what constitutes the most effective mixture of strategies. To the compliance school, cooperative methods of regulation are seen as more effective, whereas Marxist scholars such as Pearce and Tombs advocate punitive policing strategies. Yet other approaches attempt to combine the strengths of self-regulation and tougher criminal measures.

Particularly influential has been the approach taken by Braithwaite, who, along with collaborators, has advocated a combination of persuasive and self-regulatory approaches along with stronger sanctions that he characterizes as an enforcement pyramid (Braithwaite and Fisse 1987; Fisse and Braithwaite 1993). At the base of the pyramid, to be used for a large proportion of offences, lie advice, informal warnings and cautions. At the next level lie civil and monetary penalties, followed by voluntary disciplinary measures and/or remedial investigations to be undertaken within companies. These latter are described as accountability *agreements*, distinguished from the next stage, accountability *orders*, in which similar investigations are imposed by courts (Fisse and Braithwaite 1993). Further up lie criminal prosecutions, which should involve both individuals and corporations, and at the top of the pyramid lie severe sentences. The strength of such an approach, based on models of successful regulation, lies in its recognition that persuasive strategies and self-regulation can be effective only if backed up by the threat of tough and credible sanctions. Thus,

> compliance is . . . understood within a dynamic enforcement game where enforcers try to get commitment from corporations to comply with the law and can back up their negotiations with credible threats about the dangers faced by defendants if they choose to go down the path of non compliance.
>
> (Fisse and Braithwaite 1993: 143)

In support of this model, it is argued that full law enforcement is not realistic

for either conventional or white collar crime and that it is also not a particularly effective strategy. Self-regulation has several advantages, not least
of which is placing the costs of enforcement on corporations themselves. In
addition, company investigators or 'private police' have more expertise and
more knowledge about internal procedures and can make more frequent
inspections than external inspectorates. Those best placed to identify and
take action about violations are those who are closest to them in the organization – thus 'whistle blowing' should be encouraged. Companies can be
encouraged to comply because they do have some commitment to compliance, are concerned with their reputations and may choose to expend effort
and resources in self-regulation when faced with the threat of greater external regulation (Fisse and Braithwaite 1993).

Although many people accept the basis of these arguments, particularly
that self-regulation is ultimately more effective and is strengthened by
tougher sanctions, differences emerge in how much reliance should be
placed on self-regulation as opposed to external regulation. Placing so much
responsibility on companies themselves could perpetuate what is seen as a
weakness of current approaches, as companies may not respond or only pay
lip service to persuasion or voluntary agreements. Pearce and Tombs (1997,
1998), although not disagreeing with aspects of the enforcement pyramid,
argue for a speedier escalation to tougher sanctions, and take issue with the
strong reliance on self-regulatory arrangements. External regulators, they
argue, are necessary precisely because self-regulation is ineffective in practice and compliance can too easily become cynical and symbolic. In addition,
they contend that arguments advocating self-regulation can readily be incorporated into arguments for deregulation and decreasing the resources of
enforcement agencies (Snider 1990). Thus,

> arguments for self-regulation in a hostile economic and political climate
> are likely to be expropriated by dominant economic and political
> forces, and used in ways that differ markedly from the intentions of
> those who had originally espoused them. Thus such arguments are
> often represented as arguments for deregulation, as has been the experi-
> ence in both the USA and the UK in recent years.
>
> (Pearce and Tombs 1997: 97)

Although Marxist analyses are often criticized for presenting few alternatives, Pearce and Tombs do suggest that some changes are possible and desirable, and can be brought about by concerted campaigns on the part of
workers, consumers and other social movements. As outlined above, to
Pearce and Tombs, hegemony is never closed and constructions of crime can
be challenged and changed. They further argue that as corporations are
amoral calculators, they can be deterred, provided that there is a realistic
threat of action. As is the case for conventional crime, however, deterrence
may lie in the chances of being detected rather than in the eventual

punishment. Detection is often hampered by enforcement agencies, lack of resources, and it could well be argued that increasing these resources and thereby the chances of detecting offences could have a real effect (Levi 1987a; Croall 1992; Pearce and Tombs 1998). In addition, although conventional offenders may not be deterred, because they underestimate their chances of being caught and are not fully informed of the likely sanctions they will face, white collar offenders are well informed and can make rational calculations. More realistic chances of detection and prosecution would also, Pearce and Tombs argue, empower enforcement agencies and those in corporations who do prioritize compliance. Moreover, although out of court sanctions can be seen as less of a deterrent than public prosecution, more use of the strongest of these, such as withdrawing licences or disqualifying directors, can be a considerable deterrent.

Pearce and Tombs, along with other academics, also argue that some of the limitations of criminal law in relation to corporations can be ameliorated. In the United Kingdom, there have, for example, been recurrent calls from academics and victim and other interest groups for reforms to the law relating to corporate liability, which restricts the possibility of convicting companies on manslaughter charges. The Law Commission has recommended a new offence of 'corporate killing', which would make a company liable for prosecution where 'management failure' results in death, provided that the failure constitutes conduct far below what could reasonably be expected – thus judging the corporation by its collective efforts (Law Commission 1996). This would considerably strengthen the law, although it could also lead to a downgrading of corporate manslaughter, as it would be seen as a lesser offence (Ross 1999). It was announced in May 2000, after the start of the inquiry into the Paddington rail crash, that the government intends to introduce this legislation in the near future. Pearce and Tombs (1990, 1997) have also suggested the application to companies of strategies developed for motoring offences, in which offences such as careless and reckless driving indicate degrees of liability – why not, they argue, careless or reckless employing (Pearce and Tombs 1990, 1997)? The recently announced proposals do include reckless killing and killing by gross carelessness (BBC news online 23 May 2000).

Concluding comments

The regulation of white collar crime therefore involves complex issues. This chapter has focused on the debates and analyses surrounding regulation and cooperative or compliance models, which have dominated the study of white collar law enforcement, and which tend to focus on the contrast between policing crime and regulating business. As with other areas, however, these contrasts should not be overstated. Increasingly, the policing of conventional crime involves a wide range of agencies and what some see as a 'mixed economy' of social control, involving private policing, the increasing use of surveillance and more sophisticated methods for detecting fraud and corruption. As seen in earlier chapters, as white collar crime becomes more transnational and global in nature, so too has its regulation, as is also the case with conventional crime. As Nelken (1997b) points out, globalization, although often exaggerated, may also affect definitions of crimes, offenders and victims, with growing attention being given to international war crimes tribunals or 'sex tourists' who victimize children abroad. The close links, seen in earlier chapters, between some forms of white collar crime and organized crime are also significant for law enforcement, with the growing 'war' on organized crime such as the drugs industry, the illegal arms market, illegal trades in cigarettes and alcohol and the trafficking of illegal immigrants involving aspects of both. All of these tendencies raise further issues about the accountability of law enforcement and the way in which different groups of offences are regulated. Surveillance and the use of closed-circuit television (CCTV) in the workplace, for example, is primarily targeted at the offences of lower-level employees (McCahill and Norris 1999). Although much discussion of these developments has focused on the policing of conventional crime, they also raise issues about how law enforcement strategies are differentially directed against different groups of offenders.

Rather than being seen as part of the 'war' on different kinds of crime, discussions of the regulation of white collar crime move beyond those usually included in discussions of policing and criminal justice to wider political and economic considerations of business regulation. The laws and distinctive pattern of regulation applied to many forms of white collar crime, both financial and regulatory, have emerged out of recurrent negotiations between government, business and different groups. They are located in the tension between free market principles under which interventionist legislation is resisted and seen as an example of the 'nanny state', and liberal values under which protectionist laws are justified. For many offences, particularly those involving social regulation, criminal law is justified on the grounds of efficiency rather than being a moral condemnation of the activities it seeks to control, although here a distinction emerges between fraud and dishonesty, which are more readily regarded as criminal, and organizational offences. This justifies the compliance strategies adopted by enforcers, which are seen as more cost-effective than criminal prosecution and which are additionally accounted for by the difficulties of detection and prosecution posed by the nature of many offences. At the same time, however, current practices can be criticized both on the grounds of deterrence and on the moral grounds that they treat one group of offences and offenders differently from another, and the rationales supporting current regulatory practices can be seen to rest on the ideological distinction between white collar crimes and other crimes.

These different approaches have produced major disagreements over how to account for current regulatory practices and how they can, or should, be reformed. Despite this, however, it has been seen that it is possible to accept that the nature of white collar crime does pose considerable problems for its control and also to recognize that the rationales supporting current regulatory practices are fundamentally ideological. Levi (1995), for example, considers contrasts as part ideological and part pragmatic, and Pearce and Tombs (1998) also describe the distinction between traditional and regulatory offenders as containing both real and ideological aspects. It is also important to recognize that, as Nelken (1994b) points out, the compliance system described above is not found in all jurisdictions. In Italy, for example, white collar crimes are policed in a more similar way to conventional ones. Compliance strategies are therefore related to cultural values about the significance of different forms of crime.

It is also possible to discuss a mixture of approaches to regulation. It was seen, for example, that most writers accept that, ultimately, self-regulation is likely to be more effective than external regulation. But, for this to work, it must also be backed up by realistic deterrents in the form of prosecution and sanctions. Laws can be strengthened and the criminal law could be better adapted to suit the corporate form. If the ideological nature of the distinction between white collar crimes and other crimes is recognized, then moral as well as deterrent arguments for tougher regulation can be made and, as seen, there are public criticisms of the weaknesses of some aspects of regulation. It could, however, be argued that calls for tougher regulation or for greater use of self-regulation are less than realistic (Nelken 1997a) and that the criminal law is inevitably limited – as it is also limited in the control of conventional crime. This will be further discussed after looking in more depth at issues of punishing white collar crime in Chapter 7.

Further reading

As outlined in this chapter, there has been a considerable volume of work on the issues surrounding regulation and many texts such as that by Slapper and Tombs (1999) devote considerable attention to it. Debates over the compliance approach are found in Pearce and Tombs (1990) and Hawkins' (1990) response. Pearce and Tombs (1997, 1998) develop these arguments and their critique of the compliance approach. Braithwaite's work on the enforcement pyramid and his argument for self-regulation can be found in Fisse and Braithwaite (1993). The regulation of fraud is discussed at length in Levi (1987a) and an updated account is provided in Levi (1999a).

Regulating white collar crime: punishment

The sentencing of white collar offenders is an important part of regulation because the prospect of meaningful sanctions is crucial for deterrence and punishment and also reflects moral condemnation of activities. Although sentences for white collar offenders attract less public attention than those for conventional criminals, they do attract criticism where, for example, serious fraudsters receive short prison sentences or companies blamed for deaths or injuries are given a relatively small fine. They are often described as 'paltry' and criticisms reflect concerns that they undermine the deterrent power of the law and are 'unfair', considering the harm that has been done. Sentencing raises similar issues to those encountered in relation to law and its enforcement. Its assumed lack of severity is often cited as one of the major features of white collar crime and is popularly and academically thought to result from the high class of offenders. As is the case with prosecution, it is not easy to validate such claims and sentencing is also related to the characteristics of offences. It has been seen throughout the book, for example, that the diffusion of responsibility and ambiguous criminal status characteristic of so many offences reduces the apparent blameworthiness of offenders and this inevitably affects sentencing. Moreover, as with other aspects of white collar crime, there are differences between offences – those whose criminal status is less ambiguous do, on the whole, warrant a wider range of sentences than others. The sentencing of organizations presents particular problems because many forms of punishment, devised for individual offenders, are inappropriate – organizations cannot, for example, be sent to prison. A major issue therefore is the extent to which white collar offenders can or should be sentenced in the same way as others.

This chapter will start by outlining the kinds of sentences used and some of the criticisms they attract. It will then explore how sentencing outcomes can be accounted for by looking at the many factors that affect sentencers, including the extent to which class bias plays a role. Attention will then turn to discussions of how the theories of punishment that are applied to conventional offenders can be related to white collar offenders, before exploring the potential application of a wider range of sentencing options.

White collar sentences: slaps on the wrist?

There are clear differences between the sentences given to companies, for which the fine is the only option, and those given to individual offenders, who can be and are imprisoned. In 1998, in England and Wales, 4100 out of a total of 19,600 individuals sentenced for fraud and forgery were given immediate custodial sentences and about 3000 received absolute or conditional discharges, fines, probation orders and community service orders (Sisson *et al.* 1999). For men aged 21 and over sentenced in crown courts, 57 per cent sentenced for fraud and forgery received immediate imprisonment, compared with 64 per cent for all indictable offences, 79 per cent for burglary, 92 per cent for robbery, and 57 per cent for theft. Average lengths of sentence for fraud and forgery were 16 months, compared with 23.6 months for all indictable offences, 21 months for burglary, 47 months for robbery and 12.4 months for theft. Fraud sentences were therefore below the average, substantially lower than those for burglary or robbery and closer to those for theft.

The number and length of custodial sentences has increased in the United Kingdom since 1993, as is the case for all offences, although Levi (1999a) points out that, in 1989, only five people received sentences of over five years' imprisonment and 59 received sentences of over three years for fraud; in 1995, the numbers were five and 48 respectively, despite increasingly heavy sentences for violent offenders. Few details are available for specific patterns of fraud and any consideration of sentences must also take into account the large number of cases that are settled without prosecution. The Inland Revenue, for example, imposes financial penalties out of court and prosecutes only a small number of the most serious cases, most of which do receive prison sentences – nearly all prosecutions listed in 1999 on the Revenue's website received prison sentences ranging from nine months to three years, nine months for a fraud involving an estimated £1m.

Most prosecutions under regulatory law lead to a fine, although amounts vary considerably, ranging from hundreds to, in rare cases, millions of pounds. There has been some evidence of increasing levels (Slapper and Tombs 1999), with a succession of 'record' fines being announced. Total fines of £1.7m, described as the biggest single fine under the Health and Safety at Work Act, were given in February 1999 to Balfour Beatty Civil Engineering Limited and Geoconsult ZT GmbH after the collapse of tunnels at London's Heathrow Airport in October 1994 (hse.gov.UK), and the £1.5m fine imposed on Great Western Trains following the Southall rail crash, which led to seven deaths, was also hailed as a record (*Guardian* 28 July 1999). Fines vary considerably and differ between regions. David Bergman has, for example, calculated that the average fine for health and safety cases in London is £10,250, compared with £37,000 in Wales and the West Country and £5000 in the Midlands (*Guardian* 3 November 1999). Leading the Environment Agency's 1999 'Hall of Shame' was a £300,000 fine imposed on ICI for polluting groundwater in Runcorn, although other fines were substantially lower – in May 1998, the agency estimated an average fine of £4300 (BBC news online 29 May 1998). Fewer large fines are reported for consumer offences.

On occasion, individual directors and employees are given other sentences, and car dealers have received prison sentences (Croall 1991). Two company directors were recently given community service orders following a conviction for employing teenage boys to remove asbestos. In this case, the judge commented that they were not sent to prison only because the law's maximum sentence did not permit it and that 'only time will tell whether the development of diseases caused by asbestos will cause Parliament to look at the maximum sentences for these offences' (*Guardian Unlimited* 13 April 1999).

Criticisms that these sentences are too small reflect different arguments. Morally, they can be represented as unfair in comparison with the higher sentences given for conventional crimes and in relation to the harm that has been caused. Even six-figure fines for companies can be seen as trivial when the considerable resources of companies are taken into account, reducing their deterrent value. It is difficult to evaluate these criticisms in the absence of any benchmark of what would represent a tough or soft sentence and it is also difficult to compare sentences for different crimes. The circumstances of offenders, which are also taken into account, also vary considerably. Nonetheless, the volume of criticism, from diverse commentators such as academics, enforcement agencies, the media, victims, interest groups, politicians and on occasion the comments of sentencers themselves, indicate several concerns.

The lower use and shorter lengths of imprisonment imposed on fraudsters whose offences involve large sums of money can, for example, be interpreted as lenient. Although a sentence of three years in prison is considerable, it can be seen as low where, as in cases of tax fraud, the total sums involve £1m. As an illustration, Levi (1999a) describes the 'modest' sentences received by the four principal Guinness defendants. After reductions by the court of appeal one defendant was imprisoned for two and a half years, one for 21 months, one for a year along with a £5m fine, and another received a £3m fine and was stripped of his knighthood. Those sent to prison went to open prisons and received parole. There was also considerable press reaction after the release, after serving less than the 10-year sentence originally imposed, of Peter Clowes, who defrauded £16m from elderly investors. One former investor was reported as commenting that 'I want him to come out penniless and facing a struggle, but I'm sure that won't be the case' (*Herald* 23 February 1996: 4).

Fines given to companies are often derided as 'slaps on the wrist' and said to amount to a licence to break the law because they bear little relation to the gains of offending (Box 1983; Braithwaite 1984; Cranston 1984). In May 1998, British Gas was fined £10,000 after admitting faulty servicing of, and failing to monitor work on, a central heating system in Dunfermline that led to the death of a 36-year-old man and injuries to his parents. The parents are reported to have commented ' . . . what's £10,000 to this billion pound company . . . just peanuts to the likes of them' (*Herald* 6 May 1998: 9). In another case, after the death of an oil rig worker, Shell was fined £2000 and Expro, a contractor, £1000. The relatives' solicitor is quoted as commenting that 'it (is) almost impossible to relate the impact which these fines will have on two major companies to the devastating impact which . . . [the] family have suffered at the loss of their son' (*Herald* 19 August 1998: 9). Even cases with 'record' fines attract similar criticisms. After the £1.5m fine on Great Western Trains, Louise Christian, a solicitor representing the victims, commented that although the fine seemed a lot 'it will not hurt Great Western Trains in any way. The company has a turnover of £300 million, and £5 million would have been more appropriate'. The widow of one victim commented, 'there is no justice. What is £1.5 million today?' (*Guardian* 28 July 1999). The fine of £2500 imposed on the butcher involved in the *E. coli* case was also widely criticized by the media, victims and their representatives and members of Parliament, one of whom expressed an intention to ask the then secretary of state for Scotland to consider tougher penalties (*Herald* 21 January 1998: 1). The sentencing sheriff had indicated that he had taken into account the loss of business suffered by the company, to which one victim responded: 'how can anyone talk about a business's financial loss when 20 lives were lost and hundreds of people were made ill?' (*Guardian* 21 January 1998: 7).

Enforcers have also been critical of fines. In 1998 the Environment Agency called for higher fines, pointing out that the average fine of £4300 was equivalent to a person earning £30,000 a year paying a fine of £5 (BBC news online 29 May 1998). It was also seen in Chapter 6 that small fines may deter prosecution and are seen by enforcers as undermining their activities (Cranston 1979; Richardson *et al.* 1982; Croall 1987; Hutter 1988). Higher fines are, accordingly, publicly welcomed – after the £300,000 fine for ICI in relation to pollution offences, the chief executive of the Environment Agency was reported as commenting that it would 'send a signal to boardrooms that pollution does not pay' and hoped that the scale of the fine was an indication of courts' appreciation of the impact of industrial pollution (*Guardian* 13 March 1998: 6). Courts have also considered that fines, particularly in respect of health and safety, may be too low to be effective. After the Health and Safety Commission in 1991 criticized the then average fine of £732, the maximum fine following summary prosecution was raised to £20,000 and by 1997–8 it had increased to £6223 in magistrates' courts in England and Wales and to £17,768 in crown courts, where fines are unlimited (Croall and Ross 1999). These figures are taken from a case in the English Court of Appeal (*R v F Howe & Son (Engineers Ltd)* [1999] 1 All ER 249) in which these totals were seen as too low.

Understanding sentencing

Any exploration of what factors affect sentencing must take into account the complexities of sentencing decisions. Sentencers are informed by a combination of deterrent, retributive or other rationales for sentences that are applied in different circumstances (Ashworth 1997; Davies *et al.* 1998). They also take into account the activities involved, the harm that has been done and the individual circumstances of offenders, all of which may serve to aggravate or mitigate individual sentences, and they are also highly dependent on the quality and quantity of information made available to them. Comparing any group of sentences is therefore difficult, given the large number of factors to be considered. This is exacerbated for white collar crime because so few cases ever reach the sentencing stage and so few details are available about offences or offenders. Even more problems are encountered when considering the potential effect of class and status. This is not routinely recorded and it was seen in Chapter 3 that white collar offenders are not all from high-status groups. As Levi (1999a: 159) points out, there are too few members of the 'socioeconomic elite convicted to draw any conclusions about the leniency or severity of their treatment compared with others'.

Irrespective of class and status, the now familiar characteristics of white collar offences could be expected to lead to lower sentences. Many are not seen as 'really criminal', others harm individual victims only slightly and in yet others blame is not easy to attribute to individuals. Difficulties of detection and the occupational location of offences also mean that many offenders have not been in court before, and therefore have few previous convictions. On the other hand, some offences, as seen in Chapter 2, do involve extremely large sums of money and evident breaches of occupational trust can attract a strong reaction. Offences may therefore show what have been described as aggravating or mitigating features producing a 'paradox of leniency and severity' rather than a uniformly lenient pattern (Wheeler *et al.* 1988). In a major study in the USA, in which judges dealing with individual offenders were interviewed, three 'core legal norms' of harm, seriousness and blame emerged as crucial factors influencing decisions. Judges also took into account previous convictions and the effects of prosecution on defendants (Wheeler *et al.* 1988). Although there is no similar research for Britain, analyses of sentencing guidelines and individual cases indicate a broadly similar approach (Levi 1989a; Croall 1992). Sentencing guidelines for fraud, for example, indicate that defendants' character, the length of time over which frauds have been perpetrated and the amount of money involved are all significant and similar factors may affect companies.

Before exploring these aspects in more detail, it is important to look at how cases are presented in court, as this affects the information available to sentencers. In any criminal trial both 'sides' engage in an information game (Carlen 1976) in which they seek to restrict damaging information. For white collar offenders, the distinctive characteristics of the law provide a number of opportunities for information control (Mann 1985; Croall 1988). The difficulties of establishing *mens rea*, and, in offences of strict liability, the absence of a need to prove intent, enable defendants to deny that they intended any harm and the prosecution need not contradict this. Guilty pleas can also be used strategically to limit the information provided by the prosecution because, particularly in regulatory cases, defendants can claim that a plea of guilty indicates their acceptance of their legal responsibility while arguing that, in this particular case, offences were unavoidable (Croall 1988). Defendants may also claim that they have taken all reasonable steps to prevent offences, offering what could be used as statutory defences to mitigate the sentence (Croall 1988). What would, in a full trial, be complex legal arguments become part of what has been described as an 'adversarial sentencing process' in which, while pleading guilty, defendants deny blame in mitigation (Mann 1985; Wheeler *et al.* 1988).

Also absent in court is the long history that often precedes prosecution and, in some cases, the full amount of offending. Many offences take place over a long period but evidence is produced only for a selected number of charges. For example, although individuals may have been evading taxes for many years, they may be charged for only one year. With regulatory offences, charges may relate to only some regulations although others may also have been violated. The full history is not relevant to the court and many white collar offenders can be presented as first offenders with an apparently 'blame-free' record.

This gives offenders the opportunity, in court, to strategically offer accounts, similar to the techniques of neutralization described in Chapter 5, that can be described as strategies of defence and mitigation (Croall 1988). A classic example of this is to claim that offences were someone else's fault. Individual defendants may claim that they were only following company procedures, and companies claim that their systems have not been followed or that workers have been careless or consumers insufficiently vigilant. Another common strategy is to claim that, given the technology used, occasional 'freak' accidents are inevitable. Systems for checking that regulations are complied with are described in great detail, often with the assistance of expert witnesses, building up to an argument that violations have to be seen in the context of an otherwise problem-free history.

Business values and practice provide the basis of further arguments that implicitly criticize the law by implying that to comply fully with legal requirements would substantially endanger profitability. Defendants may also claim that their actions are 'common practice'. In commercial fraud cases, for example, 'custom and practice' defences have been accepted by judges and have led to acquittals (Levi 1987a), and tax evaders claim quite simply that 'everybody does it' (Benson 1985; Cook 1989). The ambiguous criminal status of offences is used by defendants who claim that cases are trivial and not 'really' criminal. Intent to do any harm or any imputations of dishonesty are denied and defendants portray themselves as honest, responsible and reliable – in contrast to the unscrupulous 'rogues' against whom the law is really directed. Offences are thus presented as (merely) 'technical' rather than criminal and, on occasion, defendants point out the considerable harm they could cause if they were 'really' dishonest (Benson 1985; Mann 1985; Croall 1988, 1992). A final and, many people argue, particularly influential argument is to claim that heavy sentences are not deserved because defendants are respectable, law-abiding citizens who have otherwise blame-free records. Businesses advance, where possible, their long history and reputation and their absence of previous convictions.

The credibility of these strategies is enhanced by the inability of the prosecution to counter them, because the long history preceding prosecution is not, as seen above, relevant. In court, for example, officers expressed frustration when such arguments were offered. They operate, therefore, as important strategies of information control that may affect sentencers' perceptions of the seriousness of offences and the degree of blame to be attached to offenders. In addition, they may benefit defendants who can present themselves as 'respectable' or responsible. All of these factors are important in affecting sentencing, as will be seen below.

The seriousness of offences

The seriousness of offences is indicated by the level of harm done and the costs involved, and, as indicated above, white collar offences may be perceived as less serious where there is less direct victimization or physical injury. One judge in the US study commented, for example, that 'the most distinctive thing about white collar crime is the lack of violence' (Wheeler *et al.* 1988: 63). In financial offences, this may be offset by the large amounts of money involved in serious frauds. In England and Wales, for example, guidelines suggest a sliding scale of sentences according to the sums of money involved (Levi 1989a). The nature of victimization is also important, with organizational victims being considered as 'less victimized' (Wheeler *et al.* 1988) and relatively defenceless victims being perceived with more seriousness (Levi 1989a).

Actual or potential physical harm is involved in regulatory offences and does have some effect on sentencing – in consumer cases, for example, food hygiene cases that involve a risk of food poisoning have attracted higher average sentences than other food offences (Croall 1991), and it has also been suggested that fines for workplace safety cases are higher when accidents are involved (Hutter and Lloyd Bostock 1990). On the other hand, as seen in Chapter 6, one problem with regulatory prosecutions is that the regulation broken rather than the outcome is the subject of prosecution, which in turn reduces the sentence (Wells 1993; Slapper and Tombs 1999). Deaths and serious injuries may, however, be taken into account. In *R v F Howe*, referred to earlier, the court took the view that sentences could be increased where deaths were involved. Although it was acknowledged that whether or not death or serious injury resulted was a 'matter of chance', it was nonetheless felt that penalties should reflect 'public disquiet at the unnecessary loss of life, indicating a move away from the situation in which consequences are not relevant' (Croall and Ross 1999). The large fine for Great Western Trains was also justified on the grounds that it had to take account of the extent of the disaster and the number of people killed or injured (*Guardian* 28 July 1999). In practice, however, these considerations may be offset by others – in the *E. coli* case, for example, the fine did not take account of the loss of life and the sentence was reduced by taking account of the loss of revenue that the business had already suffered.

Characteristics of offenders

The apparent blameworthiness of offenders is related to evidence of intent, deliberateness and the degree of trust that has been violated. In offences involving *mens rea*, degrees of deliberateness and dishonesty are crucial – Wheeler *et al.* (1988: 94) found, for example, that judges' perceptions of culpability were affected by evidence of 'scheming', planning and calculation, and Levi (1989a) comments that sentencers distinguish between deliberate 'pre-planned' frauds and those indicative of a 'slippery slope' where honest business people have resorted to reckless trading. With regulatory offences, the absence of intent also accounts for lower sentences and higher sentences are given for those that more clearly involve dishonesty. Car dealers who have turned back odometers, more readily seen as deceptive, can, for example, be imprisoned. In one leading case in trade descriptions law, *R* v *Gupta* [(1985) *Criminal Law Review* 81], it was argued 'that this kind of fraud called for an immediate custodial sentence'. In addition to degrees of planning, the extent to which offenders have profited from offences and the length of time over which they have taken place also increase sentences (Wheeler *et al.* 1988; Levi 1989a).

Although these factors are more specifically relevant to individual offenders, they may also be important for companies – in *R* v *F Howe* the court argued that the gravity of offences was affected by whether or not the company fell far below a 'reasonably practicable' standard in committing the offence. A deliberate breach with a view to profit was described as 'seriously' aggravating the offence and also important were the degree of risk and extent of danger created by the offence and the extent of the breach, in particular whether it was an isolated incident or continued over a period.

The extent to which offences involve a breach of occupational trust also affects sentences. Occupational offences receive a fuller range of sentences and a study of Court of Appeal judgements found that breaches of trust were taken seriously over and above other mitigating factors such as 'blame-free records' or loss of employment (Thomas 1979). This is particularly the case with public servants, professionals or politicians – one US judge expressed the opinion that whereas tax evaders were 'simply stealing public money', in cases of political corruption offenders were 'endangering the very foundation of government itself' (Wheeler *et al.* 1988: 79). Although this is often seen as particularly relevant to financial and individual offences, it can also feature in organizational ones, particularly those involving deaths and injuries to passengers. Sentencing a train driver following a rail crash in which five people died and 87 were injured, the judge stated that 'those who provide services to the public should do so carefully . . . passengers put themselves in a very special sense in the hands of the driver . . . they trust him entirely . . .' (*Financial Times* 4 September 1990: 10).

The seriousness of offences can therefore increase sentences although this may be offset by other considerations and by the ability of defendants to restrict damaging information. As seen above, many white collar offenders are apparent first offenders and many also claim that they have been particularly damaged by prosecution and in any event will not be in a position to commit offences again – thus, they claim, the 'process is punishment' (Levi 1989b). They may argue that they have lost their jobs, businesses or reputation, and that their innocent families will be harmed by further sentences. Small businesses may claim that they cannot survive and that the loss of their reputation has adversely affected trading, and larger companies may claim that they have already taken steps to remedy the situation (Croall 1991).

These kinds of arguments do affect sentencers who quite legitimately take individual circumstances into account (Wheeler *et al.* 1988). It is difficult, however, to evaluate the extent to which white collar offenders are more adversely affected by prosecution. Weisburd *et al.* (1991) attempted to explore this and found that bank embezzlers, who tended to be of a lower status than other offenders, more often lost their jobs in comparison with taxation and anti-trust offenders who were more likely to remain owners and officers of companies. This could be linked, they suggest, to the lower stigma surrounding these offences, whereas embezzlement is directed against employers. Although they could neither support nor reject the hypothesis that detection and prosecution constituted major forms of punishment, they suggest that defendants' images of suffering overstate their real experiences.

These kinds of arguments may also provide judges with a dilemma. Many judges reject any implication that the status of defendants is an advantage, but do consider how much they have already lost. In refusing the Guinness defendants' leave to appeal, Mr Justice Henry commented that while imprisonment and a fine were required to meet the 'gravity' of offences, 'punishments are after all intended to be punitive and the court must ensure that a man's wealth and power does not put him beyond punishment' (*Guardian* 3 October 1990). Nonetheless, it could reasonably be argued that to take such factors into account for offenders who have a lot to lose is unfair in comparison with offenders who are unemployed at the time of offending and therefore have no jobs or a respectable lifestyle to be endangered (Croall 1992). This raises the issue of class and status.

Class, status and sentencing

As is the case with prosecution, it is difficult to estimate the independent effect of class and status, for so long held to be a major factor in sentencing. In some situations superior status can indeed be a disadvantage and high-status offenders have been found to attract higher sentences, possibly because judges perceive an abuse of the trust accorded to persons in high positions as particularly blameworthy. Indeed, sentencers may see the activities of high-status offenders as 'letting the side down' (Levi 1989b; Croall 1991), and some have also, as in the Guinness case, expressed strong feelings that it should not count. Studies of sentencing have not in general found any consistent bias or sympathy for offenders of similar social status. Although some sympathy may be expressed, this can reflect sentencers'

agreement with appeals to business values or an acceptance of the predominant view that white collar offences are less serious than other crimes (Croall
1992).

It is also assumed that the ability of higher-status offenders and large corporations to employ expert legal advice assists them in relation to prosecution and sentencing decisions. Evaluating this assertion is, however, difficult
because of the variation between white collar offenders and the problems of
estimating the effect of such representation. Lower-status white collar
offenders are less well represented, as are small businesses (Croall 1988).
This affects how successfully defendants can use the strategies of defence
outlined above. In one study, unrepresented defendants were more likely to
reveal damaging information such as, for example, their ignorance of regulations or of their own legal responsibilities, and they could incriminate
themselves by claiming that they were not responsible for offences and failing to appreciate the complexities of strict liability (Croall 1988). Weisburd
et al. (1991) also found that many white collar offenders, particularly those
of lower status, were not legally represented, and for those who were, a
major advantage was the ability to choose which judge would hear the case.

As was seen in relation to law enforcement, higher-status offenders may be
advantaged in less direct ways. To the extent that arguments that the 'process
is punishment' do reduce sentences, some are advantaged over those who
cannot produce similar arguments (Croall 1992). Defendants who can reasonably claim that they have much to lose by the notoriety of conviction tend to
be of higher-status whereas lower-status defendants have less to lose. In
addition, some white collar offenders, particularly those of higher status, are
better able to conceal incriminating information and use strategic arguments.
They may also be able to 'buy themselves' out of prison by being able to afford
heavy fines and negotiate out of court settlements. Larger companies are similarly advantaged – sentences can be mitigated by, for example, evidence that
defects have been remedied or that they have made substantial contributions
to local communities, tactics less available for smaller companies. In comparison with conventional offenders, many white collar offenders are also
advantaged by the credibility of arguments that their offences are less 'criminal' and carry less stigma. Although sentencers may not be affected directly by
the class or status of individual offenders, they may be culturally predisposed
to accept these arguments. Some offences are more likely to be seen as 'criminal', however, and sentences reflect the distinction between 'pro-capitalist' and
anti-capitalist activities, with fraudsters receiving a wider range of sentences.

White collar crime and punishment

Sentencing outcomes are therefore strongly related to the perceptions of white
collar offences and offenders, which also affect the law and prosecution. They

also reflect an assumption that only a restricted range of theories of punishment and sentencing options are appropriate for white collar offenders. For regulatory offences, as seen in Chapter 6, the law is justified largely on deterrent grounds and even for offences more readily regarded as criminal, such as fraud, some sentencing options, such as community sentences, are less often considered. The legal problems of attributing responsibility to a company extend to sentencing, where, as seen above, the fine is virtually the only option. For offences subject to a regulatory as opposed to a 'criminal justice' route, the emphasis is on the effectiveness of sanctions, and punishments justified on the basis that offenders have done wrong and 'deserve' it are seen as less relevant. It can, nonetheless, be argued that punishment rationales applicable to individual conventional offenders can be applied to white collar offenders, including organizations, and could lead to a wider range of sentencing options. This section will briefly explore how the main principles of sentencing can be applied to white collar offenders before exploring this range of options.

Deterring white collar crime

The importance of a deterrent rationale was seen in Chapter 6 and indeed it could be argued that deterrence is more effective for white collar offenders than for conventional offenders because their offences are so often assumed to be rationally motivated. Individual offenders, who can be assumed to be in employment, face powerful threats of losing their jobs, status and being imprisoned (Punch 1996). Companies, often seen as 'quintessentially rational' and future-oriented (Braithwaite and Geis 1982), are also deterrable as they risk losing reputation and custom. Sentences are, as seen above, often criticized on the basis that they undermine deterrent objectives, suggesting that they should be strengthened along with the chances of detection. As will be seen below, fines could be increased, and the use of other options that directly threaten the ability of offenders to stay in business, such as licensing powers or disqualifications, could be increased.

There are, however, limits to deterrence, and a major problem with severe penalties, such as extremely high fines or closing businesses, is often described as the 'deterrence trap' in which the effects of heavy sentences 'spill over' on to innocent parties. Shareholders may lose income, consumers may face higher prices and workers' employment is threatened. Moreover, while companies may be amoral calculators, they do not always recognize the benefits of compliance and, as seen in Chapter 5, attitudes supporting non-compliance may be prevalent in corporate cultures (Pearce and Tombs 1998). Deterrent policies also do little to ameliorate the conditions in which offences proliferate or the criminogenic features of organizations (Moore 1987) and they may leave the perpetrators in the same positions. For individual offenders, the potential of the law to deter can also be overstated and, as Levi (1987a) argues, the 'fall from grace' may be exaggerated. Many offenders are not dismissed and continue their careers or start new ones. Some may indeed make money from selling their memoirs. Deterrent approaches alone therefore may not be sufficient and they do not in any event fully address the moral dimensions of the law.

'Just deserts' for white collar offenders?

The moral dimensions of the law are expressed in retributive principles under which offenders are punished on the basis that they have done wrong and deserve punishment, and such principles are also related to proportionality – sentences should reflect the harm that has been done. As seen above, many criticisms of sentences reflect these sentiments and lenient sentences can also be seen as unfair. Although retributive principles do not necessarily argue for heavier punishment (indeed, some advocates of just deserts principles argue that punishment for all offences should be kept to a minimum (Ashworth 1997)), tougher sentences can be justified on the grounds that they should better reflect the harm done and should be in proportion to the offender's circumstances. As seen above, even large fines for companies can be perceived as disproportionate to their resources, and the amounts of money and breaches of trust involved in serious frauds are not reflected in the length of prison sentences when compared with other offenders. Just deserts policies have several limitations, however, in relation to both conventional and white collar offenders (Braithwaite 1982; Braithwaite and Pettit 1990). As such policies rely on notions of guilt, blame and seriousness, which are so often denied by white collar offenders, they do not necessarily lead to heavier sentences. In addition, prosecuting greater numbers of white collar offenders would be prohibitively costly (Braithwaite and Pettit 1990). Just deserts models also raise the problem of who defines the seriousness of offences and the pervasive ideological view that white collar offences are less serious would, in any event, lead to lower sentences (Hudson 1987).

Rehabilitating white collar offenders

Rehabilitation has been a major goal of sentencing for conventional offenders, although its effectiveness has been questioned. It has, however, not been generally regarded as appropriate for white collar offenders, who have, as seen in Chapter 5, not been considered to suffer from the kinds of individual or social problems at which rehabilitative policies have been addressed. White collar offenders are therefore less likely to be seen as being in need of help and advice or as amenable to strategies aiming to change their motivations. Rehabilitation is also aimed at individual offenders and not at organizations, which, as seen in previous chapters, have no 'mind' or 'soul'. The assumed inapplicability of rehabilitative principles can nonetheless be related to the individualist bias of the criminal law (Wells 1993; Croall and Ross 1999) and there have been persuasive arguments that organizations may be more rather than less responsive to rehabilitative approaches. Braithwaite (1984), for example, argues that standard operating procedures and organization charts are easier to change than individual psyches and that the criminogenic features of organizations can be changed. Although deterrent policies do little to intervene in organizations, rehabilitative strategies could be aimed at poor monitoring of standards, a lack of accountability and corporate cultures (Braithwaite 1984; Punch 1996; Slapper and Tombs 1999). Interventionist policies could also strengthen the persuasive strategies of enforcers (Pearce and Tombs 1998), and there is less risk of the spillover effects associated with deterrence. Rehabilitative policies could also be particularly useful for small businesses, where offending is often seen to be associated with ignorance rather than deliberate intent (Croall 1992). As will be seen below, therefore, rehabilitative policies such as probation or community service orders could be adapted for white collar offenders.

Incapacitating white collar offenders

A popular principle underlying sentencing is incapacitation, in which sentences aim to render offenders unable to commit further crimes. Capital punishment is the most extreme way of doing this, and other incapacitative sanctions include disqualifying dangerous drivers or using lengthy prison sentences. These kinds of policies have not been widely applied to white collar offenders, who are not included among the dangerous or persistent offenders at which these policies are generally directed. Some sanctions against white collar offenders are nonetheless primarily incapacitative, such as disqualifications, withdrawing licences or ordering a business to cease trading. Many people argue that these could be used more extensively as part of sentences.

'Shaming' white collar offenders

These approaches have nonetheless been found to be relatively ineffective in preventing large amounts of conventional crime, and Braithwaite (1989) has argued for the adoption of policies that enhance offenders' experience of shame. This is linked to his views that many people choose not to commit crime because of the shame that would follow detection, as happens, for example, in families and in communitarian societies. To him, white collar offenders, including companies, who have a high stake in their public reputation, are capable of feeling shame and examples of policies include wider publicity for offences and settlements involving victims that underline the harm done and enhance feelings of shame. Shaming, however, should not involve degrading offenders, which could lead to the development of organized cultures of resistance, and should seek to be rein-tegrative. They should aim to underline the moral aspects of law – for most kinds of white collar crime, he argues, 'the moral educative functions of the law are sorely neglected by insufficient levels of formal punishment coupled with state shaming' (Braithwaite 1989: 132). Shaming strategies lie mid-way up the enforcement pyramid – if they fail, incapacitative policies are necessary.

Alternative approaches to sentencing white collar offenders

These arguments suggest that a wider and stronger range of penalties could be developed to meet criticisms of sentencing patterns. Wells (1993: 35), for example, argues that 'it is essential that any discussion of corporate sanctions addresses the question of how to introduce more variety in the calendar of penalties', and Braithwaite (1995a) points to the dynamic relationship between different strategies – if persuasion fails, he suggests, deterrent strategies can be used and if these fail, incapacitative strategies can be used. As was seen in relation to other regulatory policies, a mixture of strategies are therefore most appropriate and Pearce and Tombs (1998) argue that strengthening deterrence and using more rehabilitative measures can be positive rather than negative and limiting. Such a mixture could include some of the following options.

Monetary penalties

As seen above, heavy reliance has been placed on financial penalties, particularly for corporate offenders. These reflect primarily deterrent principles but can also be retributive and incapacitative where the survival of a business is threatened. It has been seen, however, that monetary penalties are often considered to be too low, leading to suggestions that they should be substantially increased. They could, for example, be better related to the resources of a company and, in some jurisdictions, equity fines are directly related to a company's turnover and profits. In one Scottish appeal case, *Topek (Bur) Ltd* v *H.M.A.* (1998 SCCR 352), the High Court of Justiciary upheld a £20,000 fine against a company following the death of a worker, the amount representing half their net annual profit. The sentencing sheriff had argued that a substantial fine was necessary 'to express society's disapproval' of such failures, especially where they led to a fatality, and, as the company were substantially to blame, considered the correct level of fine to be half the company's annual net profits.

Directly linking fines to an offender's resources can be limited by the difficulties of ascertaining these resources. Although a full statement of offenders' means, along with a social inquiry report, is routinely given for conventional and some individual white collar offenders, this is not the case in regulatory offences, where information about company finances can be haphazard – indeed, companies are more likely to claim a poor financial position to mitigate sentencing (Croall and Ross 1999). This could be remedied by the introduction, suggested by Bergman (1992), of a form of 'corporate inquiry report', which would provide accurate financial information, such as the company's turnover and annual profits, along with information about the history of its relationship with the regulatory agency or its general health and safety record (Bergman 1992; Slapper and Tombs 1999). This could partially overcome the problem of defendants attempting to control the information available to the court (Croall and Ross 1999).

The limitations imposed by the potential spillover effect of heavy penalties and the risk of putting companies out of business can also be contested. In the case of R v F Howe, discussed above, the court rejected the notion that a fine should take into account whether or not the company should stay in business, with Lord Justice Rose commenting 'there may be cases where the offences are so serious that the defendant ought not to be in business' (Croall and Ross 1999). Effects on 'innocent' shareholders could also make shareholders question management (Geis 1978), and it can also be argued that they take a risk by investing (Braithwaite 1984) and indirectly profit from offences (Pearce and Tombs 1998). Some of this has been recognized by courts. Imposing one of the biggest fines in a Scottish court, £250,000, on Royal Ordnance after an explosion that seriously injured a worker and after revelations of a 'sad history' of compliance, the sentencing judge acknowledged that the fine would fall on innocent shareholders but trusted that they would take action to prevent similar accidents (Herald 27 February 1998, cited in Croall and Ross 1999).

There are, nonetheless, problems with relying on financial penalties. To make them sufficiently deterrent, for example, astronomically high fines would be necessary because, assuming that companies are rational calculators, the size of fines would have to take into account the low chance of detection and prosecution (Etzioni 1993; Slapper and Tombs 1999). This could be politically unacceptable. In the USA, fines based on such calculations were suggested by the Sentencing Commission but had to be withdrawn following strong objections by business groups (Etzioni 1993). Extremely high fines could also exacerbate differences between larger and smaller companies because large corporations can more easily afford to pay (Croall 1992; Pearce and Tombs 1998). Moreover, fines for companies cannot be backed up with the threat of prison, as they are for individual offenders (Wells 1993). They may also not be as deterrent as is often assumed – Slapper and Tombs (1999) claim that the increasing size of fines for occupational safety cases has not led to a decrease in prosecutions and, like deterrent approaches, they do little to remedy the situation that has led to offending nor do they fully underline moral disapproval (Wells 1993).

Community sentences for white collar offenders?

Arguments that more use could be made of rehabilitative and other sentences have led to the introduction, in some jurisdictions, of probation and community service orders that have been adapted for corporate offenders. Probation orders can target company policies and operating procedures, and objections that employing a new body of 'company probation officers' would be prohibitively costly can be met by requirements that costs are borne by companies (Box 1983; Braithwaite 1984). Courts could also require companies to employ staff who are specifically responsible for monitoring compliance (Slapper and Tombs 1999). In the UK, the Law Commission, after consultations and representations by groups such as Disaster Action, included a provision in its draft bill on corporate killing enabling courts to make a 'remedial order, which would require a corporation to take steps to remedy the "management failure" leading to a death, failure to comply with which would lead to a fine' (Law Commission 1996: 7.15–7.16). Probation orders could also be particularly suitable for small businesses, many of which could not afford larger fines.

In the USA, corporate probation is accompanied by other sentences and, in some cases, companies have been required to send executives to work on community programmes (Wells 1993; Punch 1996). Although community service has not been widely used for either individual white collar or corporate offenders, it has also been argued that, specially adapted, it would be particularly appropriate for offenders whose talents and resources could be better used by serving the community than sending them to prison. The undoubted financial or managerial skills of individual offenders could be useful to community groups (Levi 1989a), and Braithwaite (1995a) points out that Michael Milkin, of the notorious junk bonds, could have been better employed by following his own suggestion of working with banks to find creative solutions to third world debt. For corporate offenders, innovative ideas have included requiring polluting companies to fund leisure amenities, requiring executives in car companies who have produced unsafe cars to do voluntary work in emergency rooms, or requiring companies found guilty of food adulteration or manufacturing unsafe toys to provide free food or toys to children's homes (Box 1983; Croall 1992; Etzioni 1993; Slapper and Tombs 1999). These kinds of options reflect a variety of punishment rationales, as do community service orders for conventional offenders. They can be seen as potentially rehabilitative, they express symbolically the idea that corporate crime harms communities, they can maximize publicity, they are retributive, they can be part of reintegrative shaming strategies, and they also avoid the deterrence trap. Nonetheless the practicality of implementing such orders could be questioned and they may have high administrative costs. It might also be objected that, as is the case with conventional offenders, they could be seen as 'soft options'.

Shaming strategies

As seen above, it has also been argued that white collar offenders are amenable to shaming because they have a strong investment in respectability and there is some evidence that companies and individuals do worry about the effect of publicity (Benson 1985; Hutter 1988) and that companies do feel that their reputation has been damaged (Fisse and Braithwaite 1983). Many offences, particularly regulatory ones, are not widely reported, and the use of 'publicity orders' or corporate atonement policies where companies are required to pay for advertisements correcting misleading ones have been suggested (Fisse and Braithwaite 1993). The effectiveness of this can be limited by the tendency of companies to place corrective advertisements in specialist journals. It has also been suggested that publicity orders be used as a formal sanction along with calling press conferences immediately after corporate convictions (Fisse and Braithwaite 1993). More recently, there have been attempts to 'name and shame' offenders in areas such as pensions misselling and, as seen in earlier chapters, environmental and safety offences.

Other shaming strategies include adaptations of those used for young offenders, such as conferences and meetings with victims. Braithwaite (1995a) provides examples of small 'shaming ceremonies' in which senior executives of an insurance company that had deceptively sold insurance policies to people living in remote Aboriginal communities were sent into these communities to negotiate settlements. This involved coming into immediate contact with victims and living in the same conditions as they did, and Aboriginal community councils played a strong role in negotiations. This, he argues, is an example of the middle level of the enforcement pyramid and, along with education and shaming, it also involved more deterrence, compensation, internal discipline and correction of standard operative procedures than any court case could have provided. Executives were treated as people expected to act responsibly.

Incapacitation

Many ways of strengthening the role of incapacitation have also been suggested. Wells (1993) looks at corporate dissolution, disqualifying companies from government contracts and banning products – like heavy fines, however, these can have consequences for workers, consumers and shareholders. Nonetheless, many people argue that incapacitative strategies are necessary and justifiable for public protection if all other strategies fail. Although companies cannot be sent to prison, more prosecutions of individual directors could lead to greater use of imprisonment and Fisse and Braithwaite (1993) have suggested corporate capital punishment, where senior executives are removed and companies nationalized for a period of time as an ultimate sanction. Other incapacitative strategies include increasing the powers of both enforcers and courts in respect of licensing and disqualification, which could also enhance the power of regulators (Pearce and Tombs 1990, 1998). These options are limited to situations where licences and other qualifications are necessary, but the number of businesses requiring licences could be increased. The introduction of stricter registration and licensing requirements have, for example, been suggested for food businesses after the *E. coli* outbreak, and for landlords after deaths in unregistered properties (Croall 1999c). In the financial area Levi points out that prevention mechanisms against company directors are more limited than they are for people selling financial services, who have to be deemed 'fit and proper' before being granted a licence. He comments that there is no bar, however, 'upon anyone setting up in business, however ill qualified they may be by competence and/or morality' (Levi 1999a: 162). Individuals have set up new businesses after being released from prison following fraud convictions and, although between 1986 and 1997 a total of 4800 directors were disqualified, the effects of such disqualifications are unknown. Former directors may set up a business under a new name, although this is a criminal offence. In short, 'even where bans are in force and activities are known to the authorities, commercial incapacitation can be incomplete' (Levi 1999a: 163).

Despite the limitations of many of these strategies, they can be used in combination and Braithwaite's notion of a pyramid suggests that they can be arranged in increasing severity. The introduction of new alternatives and the strengthening of others could also add considerably to the available options for the courts. Whether or not such suggestions are seen as realistic, however, may depend on the extent to which offences are seen as serious enough to merit their adoption, which returns, yet again, to the problematic criminal status of offences.

Concluding comments

The issues raised by sentencing and punishment are therefore similar to those raised by regulation as a whole. Although it is often assumed that the lenient sentencing of white collar offenders is attributable to their high status, the sentences are also strongly related to the nature of offences themselves and, in particular, to the perception that they are less serious than other crimes. This is particularly the case with regulatory and organizational offences whose problematic status as crimes, and the difficulties of viewing companies as 'offenders', have severely limited sentencing options. Activities and offenders more readily seen as criminal do receive heavier sentences, although these can also be viewed as lenient in comparison with others and as related, albeit indirectly, to their status. As is also the case with other aspects of regulation, however, stronger options can be considered and sentences, like prosecution policies, can be justified as being more effective and as necessary to back up other regulatory strategies. Furthermore, concepts such as 'corporate killing' or sentences such as corporate probation or corporate community service orders underline the moral disapproval of activities and in themselves challenge the construction of white collar crime as not 'really' criminal (Pearce and Tombs 1998).

Discussions about regulating white collar crime also raise wider issues concerning the role of the criminal law as a means of regulating harmful activities. Although it is often argued that white collar crime raises particular problems that justify a different range of measures, it is now recognized that the criminal law and criminal justice processes are severely limited in their ability to reduce substantially the volume of conventional crime. The 'criminological project' associated with traditional criminology, which aimed to develop measures to reduce crime and stressed reductionist sentencing principles such as rehabilitation or deterrence, has now largely been abandoned. It has been argued that a 'new penology' has developed that is less concerned with the moral justifications for punishment and uses the language and techniques associated with risk management and actuarialism with a view to managing and preventing crime rather than reducing it (Feeley and Simon 1996). More attention has accordingly turned to crime prevention strategies and to managing offenders assessed on the basis of their risk of re-offending. Although much of this has been focused on conventional crime, it indicates that the limited role of the criminal law in reducing crime is not restricted to white collar crime. It has also been accompanied by the development of a 'populist punitiveness' (Bottoms 1995) in relation to those conventional offenders seen as most dangerous, which has not included white collar offenders. A process of bifurcation has also been identified in which diversionary programmes for some less serious offenders are also seen as appropriate. There is therefore considerable variation in approaches to dealing with conventional offenders, which strengthens the arguments of those such as Braithwaite (1995b) and Braithwaite and Pettit (1990) that similar approaches could be adopted for all kinds of crime.

Nonetheless, the use of regulatory rather than criminal procedures for white collar crime remains premised on the ideological assumption that white collar crimes are different from, and less serious than, others. Subjecting offenders to a wider range of sentences and to more 'punitive policing' (Pearce and Tombs 1990, 1998) becomes less problematic if this assumption is challenged. This returns to the moral and symbolic role of the criminal law, and campaigns that include calls for criminalization on the part of consumer, trade union or environmental groups are an important feature of such a challenge (Braithwaite 1995b; Snider 1990, 1996; Pearce and Tombs 1998). The criminal law, it can be argued, remains the most powerful expression of moral disapproval of harmful activities. Considerations of regulation therefore involve some of the major themes involved in the study of white collar crime, which will be returned to in the concluding chapter.

Further reading

There is a considerable literature, particularly in the USA, on sentencing the white collar offender, summed up in Friedrichs (1996) and Braithwaite (1982) and Braithwaite and Geis (1982). Issues of class bias are discussed in Wheeler *et al.* (1988) and, for the UK, Levi (1989a, 1989b) provides a good summary of financial offences and Slapper and Tombs (1999) consider corporate offenders. Braithwaite's approach to the sentencing of both conventional and white collar offenders is discussed in several publications, particularly Braithwaite (1989, 1995a) and Braithwaite and Pettit (1990). The fullest exposition of Pearce and Tombs' approach can be found in the concluding chapters of Pearce and Tombs (1998).

chapter eight

White collar crime
and criminology

The concept of white collar crime
One law for the rich? Class, power and the role of criminal law
Criminology and white collar crime

Many of the themes and issues that have recurred throughout the study of white collar crime remain unresolved. It might indeed be suggested that there has been little change since Sutherland (1947) first identified the concept. He drew attention to a hitherto neglected area of crime, associated with high-status individuals and companies, and to the different way in which they were dealt with by law and the criminal justice process. In so doing, he challenged what is now described as the 'criminological project', which located the causes of crime in the pathologies of individual offenders, social disorganization, social structural strain, social inequality and poverty. He was criticized for including harmful activities that were not, legally, crime and the subject became associated with a critical challenge to criminological theory and to the definition of crime. His work, however, foreshadowed and informed later critical approaches that explored the social construction of crime and the role of powerful groups and the state in criminalizing lower-class activities and individuals. The study of white collar crime has, however, remained marginal to criminology, although it retains its fascination and its critical role. Its existence continues to question representations and measurements of the crime problem, which exclude it, theories of crime which fail to explain it, and the criminal justice system, which is widely perceived as treating it more leniently than its seriousness justifies.

This book has nonetheless illustrated the considerable volume of work that has been carried out on white collar crime. Its widespread nature and considerable impact has been shown, and analyses of regulation have considerably increased an understanding of the role of class and power in the development and implementation of criminal law. These analyses also raise important questions about the strengths and limitations and wider role of the criminal law. Theoretical work has explored how it can be explained, looking at the application of theories of crime and also seeking to account for it in the cultures and structures of occupations and organizations and of capitalism itself. Many issues continue to be problematic, however. The definition of white collar crime is contested and its relationship with other crimes remains unclear – indeed its ambiguous status as 'crime' permeates discussions of virtually every aspect of it. It can be questioned whether it remains a useful or meaningful category, particularly in view of the major distinctions between, for example, occupational and corporate crimes. Its identification with class status and power can be questioned and the problems it poses for regulation move beyond those traditionally associated with criminal justice. Taken together with the continuing tendency of 'establishment' or 'administrative' criminology to focus on largely conventional crimes, it could be asked whether it can, or should, be included in criminology.

This chapter will draw together these themes and address some key issues. It will briefly explore the utility of the concept, its identification with class and status, its relationship to other crimes and variations between forms of white collar crime. It will then summarize discussions of the relationship between class, power and the role of the criminal law and criminalization. The significance of the concept in criminology will then be addressed and it will be argued that it remains an important subject. Finally, the chapter will briefly outline some priorities for the future study of white collar crime.

The concept of white collar crime

The problems of conceptualizing white collar crime have been encountered throughout previous chapters, and defining the category involves, as Slapper and Tombs (1999: 9) point out, 'disagreements about values, politics, theory, epistemology and methodology'. Particularly disputed have been whether it is 'crime', and what it should include. Is it, for example, to be restricted to activities encompassed by criminal legislation? Should it restrict itself only to activities of high-status or powerful offenders? Including activities not legally defined as crimes readily attracts accusations of political bias and subjectivity, as does its identification with high-status offenders and corporations. Restrictive definitions, on the other hand, preclude explorations of how and why some harmful activities are defined as crime. They also limit research agendas and preclude potentially illuminating comparisons of differences between and within categories of white collar crime. Nonetheless, broad, inclusive definitions do make the category so large that it could be argued that it is less meaningful. Can it, for example, be distinguished from other crimes? Are the differences between white collar crimes so great as to make the category too diverse? The phrase 'white collar crime' can itself be seen as anachronistic and definitional difficulties and the confusing terminology surrounding it can lead to arguments that it has outlived its usefulness. All these questions affect how its extent and impact can be measured, how it can be explained and analysed and how its regulation and control can be evaluated and reformed.

One of the most intractable problems with the concept is the contested criminal status of offences which, as illustrated in earlier chapters, underlies their exclusion from so many discussions of crime, criminal justice policy and criminology. This enables offenders to claim that they and their activities are not 'really criminal' and prevents victims from being seen, and seeing themselves, as victims of crime. The assumed distinction between white collar and 'real' crimes underpins the rationale for compliance strategies and contributes to lower rates of prosecution and less severe forms of punishment.

It has nonetheless been shown that this distinction is ideological and that crime itself is socially constructed. Indeed, as Nelken (1997a) points out, it is 'somewhat odd' that criminologists should spend so much time debating this issue when it is recognized that 'crime' is a highly debatable concept. Many criminological and sociological texts on crime begin with an extended discussion and deconstruction of the concept, arguing that it has no intrinsic or 'essential' features (Muncie 1996; Croall 1998c). As seen in Chapter 2, a fine line divides what are seen as 'normal' practices and tolerated 'fiddles' and 'scams' from 'malpractice', deception and fraud. Moreover, white collar crimes are not, as seen above, the only crimes with an ambiguous criminal status that can be related to issues of class and power. Feminist critiques exposed the extent and impact of domestic violence, which was also excluded from criminological discussions of crime, and related this to the patriarchal nature of criminal law. The slow recognition and criminalization of racial violence can also be related to racial inequalities. Challenging these constructions was also criticized as subjective and politically motivated. Some criminologists have further suggested that the concept of crime should give way to an analysis of harms (see, for example, Muncie 1998), which would enable a fuller exploration of the different ways in which harms are socially constructed, defined and made subject to the criminal law. Definitions and categorizations of any form of crime are therefore subject to construction and deconstruction.

How, therefore, should white collar crime be defined? It was argued in Chapter 1 that an inclusive approach should be adopted, incorporating all violations of law taking place in a legitimate occupation, irrespective of the class and status of offenders or whether violations were against the criminal law. This has proved useful in that it enables comparisons to be made between different groups of offences and offenders. It further allows analyses of the range of illegitimate opportunities available to different occupational groups and of how the social status of perpetrators can affect how their activities are perceived and subjected to criminalization. This can lead to a fuller understanding of the role of class and status by investigating and establishing, rather than assuming, their importance. It was suggested in Chapter 3, for example, that those occupying higher-status positions may have greater opportunities to commit more serious crimes (Weisburd *et al.* 1991) and, as seen in Chapter 5, wealth and power may be criminogenic (Braithwaite 1992). Similarly, including activities that are not legally criminal or dealt with by non-criminal sanctions enables an exploration of the different way in which the harmful activities associated with occupations and organizations are constructed as criminal or as 'malpractice' and raises important issues in relation to regulation. Thus, for example, low-status car mechanics who overcharge for unnecessary repairs are more readily regarded as 'cowboys' or 'villains' than doctors or dentists who claim for treatment that has not been undertaken. Including the 'crimes of the middle classes' also draws attention to crime across the employment spectrum, correcting the restricted criminological focus on the contrasting crimes of the underclass and the upperclass (Weisburd *et al.* 1991).

An inclusive definition does, however, attract criticisms that it creates a large category that lacks any distinguishing features. Nonetheless, the significance of the occupational location of offences has been seen throughout. It makes them relatively invisible and the trust and knowledge involved in occupational roles are crucial aspects of the activities. This in turn means that many are complex and highly organized. All of these features make it difficult to establish the extent and impact of offences. White collar crimes are particularly difficult to detect and, in many cases, it is difficult to provide evidence of offenders' culpability. Attempts to explain offending must take into account how different occupational settings provide space for offending along with supporting cultural justifications. The threat of losing employment can also be used to mitigate sentence. All of this does distinguish occupational crime from other crimes and exposing the vast range of crimes in employment questions general associations between crime and unemployment, and draws attention to the complexities of crime and work connections (Davies and Jupp 1999).

On the other hand, it could be asked whether the differences between occupational and other crimes are such as to constitute a separate category. It was argued above, however, that any categorizations of crime are subject to a variety of constructions and the difficulties of drawing clear lines between white collar and other crimes have been illustrated. It was also argued in Chapter 1 that many of the features that are taken to distinguish white collar crime from other crimes can better be represented as continua and this has been subsequently illustrated. More visible crimes are easier to detect and those that involve more measurable, direct harms are more likely to be regarded as criminal than those that involve indirect harms and a diffusion of responsibility. This is also the case with conventional crimes. The relative invisibility of many sexual offences and assaults within the family also present problems for exposure, detection and control, and the absence of direct victimization in, for example, drug offences can also be related to an ambiguous criminal status and problems of control. Exploring how these features affect the criminalization of particular activities may therefore be as important as attempting to draw artificial lines between groups of offences. Drawing attention to the specific features of crimes committed during the course of occupations can also be useful for the analysis of abuses of occupational roles that are less often defined as white collar crime. Organizational analyses such as those outlined in Chapter 5 can assist understanding of sexual and other forms of physical abuse in institutions and violence in state organizations.

A further problem with attempting to compartmentalize different forms of crime is the blurred boundary, seen in previous chapters, between forms of white collar crime and conventional crimes, particularly organized crime (Ruggiero 1996a). Many so-called white collar crimes involve both legitimate and illegitimate businesses along with businesses whose activities encompass both legal and illegal activities. Indeed, in post-industrial economies, an 'enterprise' culture may attract individuals to a combination of legitimate and illegitimate work (Hobbs 1995; Taylor 1999). At a global level, activities such as cross-border taxation frauds, subsidies frauds, illegal arms trading, people trafficking and counterfeiting involve legitimate and illegitimate industries, and money laundering well illustrates the fine line between 'dirty' and 'clean' money, and between illegitimate and legitimate industries. At a local level, enterprises that deal in stolen and counterfeit goods along with legitimately acquired 'bargains' are related to these global enterprises (Hobbs 1995), and to the illegitimate labour market (Ruggiero 1996a). Analyses of 'crime as work' can therefore be enhanced by looking at its multi-faceted relationships with 'crime at work' and it is also useful to explore how some business or occupational activities come to be defined as legitimate and illegitimate (Ruggiero 1996a). Segregating different kinds of crime into tightly constructed categories can therefore hamper analysis.

It could nonetheless be argued that this leaves an enormously large category of crime about which few generalizations can be made, and it could also be objected that class and status are intrinsic to the conceptualization of white collar crime. Differences between crimes committed by individuals for their own benefit and crimes committed largely on behalf of organizations, for example, have been illustrated throughout. Individual, occupational crimes such as theft or fraud are more readily definable as crime and do on the whole attract stronger condemnation and more severe 'criminal' sanctions. Organizational crimes more often involve a diffusion of responsibility, an apparent lack of intent to do any harm and more indirect victimization. They can more easily be justified as 'normal' business or commercial practices and distinguished from 'real' crime, all of which serves to justify a regulatory rather than a criminal justice approach that is associated with less severe sanctions. This can be further related to the interests that they threaten – fraud and theft more clearly endanger capitalist interests, whereas regulatory offences, particularly corporate crime, can be seen to be more clearly related to goals of profitability (Pearce 1976; Pearce and Tombs 1998). It has also been argued, however, that these distinctions can be overstated. As argued above, their occupational location does distinguish them from other offences and many are not prosecuted. Forms of theft and fraud can be organizational as well as individual and some corporate forms of fraud, such as the savings and loan frauds in the USA, can attract a strong reaction as they can be presented as striking at the basis of capitalism (Calavita and Pontell 1995). On the other hand, frauds can also be subject to regulatory rather than criminal procedures and the sentences that they attract can often be criticized as too lenient. Furthermore, their regulation also rests on the assumed need to balance the interests of the development and pursuit of commercial, industrial and financial enterprises against collective, welfare and protectionist values.

Nonetheless, the differences between types of crime make it likely that the current tendency to focus on individual, often financial forms of white collar crime or on areas of corporate crime will continue – as will other subdivisions such as those of safety, environmental or state crime. This is also related to practical research considerations because research is necessarily restricted to a limited number of activities or industrial areas. Investigating specific areas necessitates an understanding of the nature of the activities and organizations involved, along with the complexities of laws, regulations and enforcement. This also, as seen in Chapter 6, extends beyond considerations of crime and criminal justice to areas such as business regulation, the environment, consumer protection, occupational health and safety, civil liberties and human rights. Each of these has a distinctive set of laws, enforcement practices and discourse that form an important part of analysis.

It is also likely that the identification of the category with class, status and power will continue. This is not only because of the polemical or ideological function that exposing the extent and different control of white collar crime undoubtedly plays (Ruggiero 1996a; Nelken 1997a). It is also justified by the significance of class and status for so many aspects of white collar crime, irrespective of whether they are part of its definition. As argued above, the 'respectability' or social class of offenders may affect how their activities are constructed and how they are dealt with by law enforcers. The thefts and frauds of lower-level employees may be more vulnerable to surveillance, prosecution and heavier sentences whereas senior employees are accorded more trust. The activities of small businesses are also more likely to be regarded as 'criminal' than similar activities of larger ones and they are also more likely to be targeted by law enforcers. Wealthy individuals and large corporations can use their positions and greater 'illegitimate opportunities' to commit more serious offences and can use their resources to affect their chances of detection, prosecution and punishment. They may be able to influence the law and the regulatory structure. Distinctions between offences and offenders incorporating both the kinds of activities involved and the social characteristics of perpetrators, such as those illustrated in Chapter 3, can therefore usefully be developed.

Despite these variations, it can be argued that the concept of white collar crime is useful. It draws attention to some of the key features, which, taken in combination, do distinguish this group of offences. These provide a useful basis for exploring differences between white collar offences and for contrasting white collar crime with other forms of crime. Whether the phrase white collar crime is still appropriate, given the many problems associated with its use, is more debatable. As argued in Chapter 1, however, it retains a popular and academic resonance and is widely recognized. Developing an alternative could add to the linguistic confusion surrounding the subject.

One law for the rich? Class, power and the role of criminal law

Another major theme dominating popular representations and academic analyses of white collar crime is the assumption that its treatment is determined by the social class of offenders and amounts to 'one law for the rich and another for the poor'. Class and power are assumed to influence the designation of activities as crime, the laws that are used to control them, the enforcement of these laws and the severity of sanctions received by offenders. At an individual level, offenders are assumed to be dealt with more sympathetically by prosecutors and sentencers. At a structural level, the ideological distinction between white collar and other crimes and that between regulation, policing and punishment is assumed to result from the ability of the powerful to influence law and enforcement.

Closer analysis suggests, however, that a more nuanced approach to issues of class and power is appropriate and one of the strengths of including offences and offenders taken from a wide variety of employment positions is that the effect of social status can more clearly be illustrated. A large number of offenders are not in any event of high social status and some offences and offenders do attract heavier policing and punishment strategies. Irrespective of status, the nature of many offences does pose particular problems for detection and prosecution. Their complexity makes it difficult to unravel offences and to attribute responsibility. The absence of direct and measurable victimization also affects sentencers although sentencing may also be severe for high-status offenders who can be seen as especially blameworthy for abusing trust or 'letting the side down'. It has also been seen that, although the prosecution of companies for criminal offences poses particular problems, there is an increasing tendency to call for more prosecution and severe sentences where they are clearly to 'blame' for serious offences.

On the other hand, the significance of class and power has been shown and it has also been seen that offenders enjoy a number of structural advantages that produce variations in treatment between different groups of white collar offenders as well as between white collar and conventional offenders. Their resources can be used to negotiate favourable settlements and in some cases to deter prosecution, and these resources may also affect the extent to which they can mount successful defences that limit the information available to sentencers. The ability of individual offenders to claim that the 'process is punishment' gives them an advantage over offenders who cannot credibly make such claims and they can more readily claim that prosecution and punishment are unnecessary as they will take steps to comply with the law. Underlying the credibility of such claims is the widespread perception that many offences are less serious and less 'criminal' than others.

This can readily be attributed to the assumed ability of high-status and business groups to affect the nature of law. It has also been seen, however, that this is not as straightforward as is often assumed and the deficiencies of instrumental approaches to law have been illustrated. Laws protecting consumers, investors, workers, the public health and the environment do exist, and the maintenance of high standards and legitimacy in business, commerce and government can be seen as a priority overriding the objections of different industrial or other interests. On the other hand, these laws can be represented as reflecting the prioritization of capitalist interests in development and profitability – not only in terms of weaknesses in enforcement but also in terms of what are seen to be reasonable assessments of safety and risk. Decisions that balance the costs of safety procedures against the risk of harm, for example, can be seen to prioritize cost-effectiveness. The nature of regulations and enforcement can therefore be related to the 'hegemony of corporate capital' which can nonetheless, argue Pearce and Tombs (1990, 1998), be challenged and changed.

This raises the question of the extent to which the criminal law can be used to control and prevent white collar crime, which, as seen in Chapters 6 and 7, has been subject to considerable dispute. On the one hand, it can be argued that, given the complexities of many white collar crimes and their location in occupational and organizational settings, the criminal law is ineffective and inappropriate. Ultimately, self-regulation and persuasive and cooperative strategies are likely to be more effective means of protecting the public, particularly from the harms of corporations and organizations. The criminal law is seen as costly and cumbersome and ill adapted to deal with the problems of organizational offences. Sentences which appear to be insufficiently stringent can also be seen as an inadequate deterrent. Some of these arguments are persuasive, as white collar crimes do pose particular problems and, as seen in Chapter 6, few people dispute that self-regulation is ultimately more effective. Nonetheless, this does not necessarily distinguish white collar crime, as it has also been argued that the criminal law is of limited use in controlling or preventing any form of crime. For conventional crime, as seen in Chapter 7, this has led to more attention to strategies for 'managing' and preventing crime. It also strengthens arguments by those such as Braithwaite (1995b) for a mixture of diversionary, mediatory and criminal sanctions which can be applied to all forms of crime.

A major thrust of the study of white collar crime has, however, been to argue for a greater use of the criminal law and tougher sanctions against white collar offenders. Indeed, Cohen (1996b) points to the irony that critical criminologists who used to identify the 'old criminalization' with the interests of the state have become linked to progressive forces such as the environmental and consumer movements seeking 'new' criminalization. Thus, 'the very social forces which in the 1960s were so critical of Leviathan – which argued for decriminalization – now take as their success the creation of new laws' (Cohen 1996b: 14). Given the recognition that laws regulating business are limited, why argue for its retention and extension? Pearce and Tombs (1998), for example, as seen in Chapters 6 and 7, argue for a combination of criminalization, punitive policing, deterrent and rehabilitative strategies.

In part, strengthening law and enforcement can be justified on the grounds of reducing the apparent unfairness of treating one group of criminals different from another. It can also be justified on the grounds of effectiveness because current strategies have not to date been effective in preventing white collar crime. In addition, many authors argue that the use of criminal law is still important because it underlines the moral nature of offending and remains the most powerful moral condemnation of harmful activities (Braithwaite 1995b; Snider 1996; Nelken 1997a; Pearce and Tombs 1997). Its use is therefore partly symbolic – as Snider argues,

> criminal law is universalistic and absolute, and those who offend against it are *criminals*, a term fraught with connotations of evil. Transforming corporate criminals into regulatory evaders who have failed to 'cooperate' makes their transgressions seem pale by comparison.
>
> (Snider 1990: 385)

The symbolic role of the criminal law is also seen in the use of state as opposed to private punishment, and as seen in earlier chapters, in terms such as corporate killing, corporate homicide or corporate probation (Pearce and Tombs 1998). Campaigning for criminalization is also a means of exposing harmful activities and changing perceptions of their seriousness.

To many people, challenging the constructions of which crimes are considered as more serious than others is a crucial task (South 1998a), given the pervasiveness of the ideological distinction between white collar crime and 'real' or serious crime. Such a challenge links the theoretical concerns of criminologists with wider social movements such as environmental and consumer groups, trade unions, and victim and women's groups (Braithwaite 1995b; Snider 1996; Pearce and Tombs 1997, 1998; South 1998a), for whom criminalization may be one part of wider campaigns. In support of this, Braithwaite (1995b) points out that conceptions of the seriousness and criminal nature of activities have been affected by social movements. This happened, he argues, with what, to him, are those crimes inflicting greatest harm – domestic violence, white collar crime (particularly in the pharmaceutical industry), occupational health and safety and drunken driving. In addition, there is what some people see as a growing tendency to 'blame' corporations and to wish to see them made accountable for their actions (Wells 1995), and the victim support groups formed after disasters have played a major role in calling for greater corporate accountability (Pearce and Tombs 1998). In the UK this was evident most recently in connection with railway safety and the proposed introduction of the new offence of corporate killing. Increasing attempts to subject those responsible for 'war crimes' and human rights abuses to the criminal law, such as has been the case with General Pinochet and those involved in 'ethnic cleansing' in former Yugoslavia, is a further illustration of the symbolic role of criminal law, as is the 'movement' against political corruption (Cohen 1996b; Levi and Nelken 1996).

Criminology and white collar crime

A further theme running through this book has been the marginal status of white collar crime in criminology. It is not 'counted' as crime and it has been seen that it is generally excluded from theories attempting to explain crime, which remain centred on the crimes of lower-class young men. These theories – including those that purport to be able to incorporate white collar crime, such as left realism – have focused largely on individual offenders making it difficult to incorporate the structural aspects of offending and victimization involved in white collar and particularly corporate crime (Ruggiero 1992; Pearce and Tombs 1998). Research initiatives tend to focus on established 'law and order' or 'crime' problems such as violence – there has, for example, been no major research programme in Britain for white collar crime. Texts and discussions of policing tend to talk about 'the' police in relation to conventional crime and, although there is now a growing concern with private policing and surveillance, this often excludes the private or state policing of white collar crime. The growing significance of victimology has not, as seen in Chapter 4, included the victims of white collar crime, although some forms could be included in victim surveys and white collar and corporate victims have great significance for critical victimology. The many threats posed by fraud, safety, environmental, food, transport and consumer offences to individuals' economic and physical security and to the quality of life in neighbourhoods and communities is also largely absent from discussions of crime and community safety or the 'fear of crime' and from local crime audits and multi-agency crime prevention initiatives (Croall 1998a).

Despite its critical role therefore, the study of white collar crime has had little impact on 'mainstream' criminology. In this respect it compares unfavourably with other critical approaches – although criminology remains far from gendered, feminist criticisms and campaigns have placed women's victimization and issues of crime and masculinity on the criminological agenda, and family and racial violence now feature in the British Crime Survey. Much work on white collar crime, on the other hand, takes place on the margins of criminology. It could therefore be suggested that the study of white collar crime cannot be incorporated in a criminology that continues to accept state agendas in respect of researching, defining and developing policies for crime. Many criminologists who exclude the study of white collar crime from their work accept the ideological distinction between white collar and other crimes. In addition, a full understanding of white collar crime has been seen to necessitate analyses encompassing broader areas of business regulation, economics and issues of safety, the environment or consumerism. It could therefore be argued, similar to feminists who argued that 'malestream' criminology could not fully analyse the gendered nature of crime (Cain 1990; Smart 1990), that criminology has little to offer the study of white collar crime, which could be pursued more fruitfully outside the confines of criminology.

Although this argument might seem persuasive, there are also strong arguments to the contrary. It has been seen, for example, that relatively few scholars are engaged in research in white collar crime and setting up some alternative forum could mean more, rather than less, fragmentation of its study, with increasing divisions between specific areas such as safety, the environment or business regulation, which do, as seen above, share similar features. Criminology, for all its faults, draws together these disparate areas with its focus on criminal law and criminalization and issues of prevention and control. It has also been argued that no categorizations of crime constitute watertight compartments and many links with conventional, organized and white collar crime have been illustrated. Furthermore, perceptions of which activities constitute serious crimes do change – some white collar crimes are considered to be crime – and it has also been seen that criminological agendas can be changed. Here again there are parallels with feminist or critical 'race' perspectives. Gelsthorpe (1997) argues that the criminological project is in transition and that feminists can work 'within and against criminology' (Daly 1994, cited in Gelsthorpe 1997: 528). Slapper and Tombs (1999: 13) argue that one of the legitimate tasks of white collar criminologists is to reshape the nature and boundaries of criminology while accepting the poverty of its dominant discourses, which to them are a site of struggle. In this way, the study of white collar crime can be situated within but also explore the limits of criminology. In any event, criminology itself has been characterized as 'fragmented' (Ericson and Carriere 1996) with many different perspectives and its boundaries are not tightly delineated. Sparks (1997: 411) argues that criminology 'cannot "police" its ever-porous boundaries with other disciplines: neither can it renew itself intellectually entirely from within'. It is, he argues, an empirically complex, policy relevant and politically contentious field of study.

It is possible, therefore, to use criminological theories and perspectives in the analysis of white collar crime while at the same time pointing to the challenge that it poses for conceptions of crime and criminological agendas. Although white collar crime does involve looking at issues outside those traditionally associated with crime, this is also the case with the analysis and control of other forms of crime, which involve looking at, for example, social inequality, social structure, the family, the economy and social and economic change. Theoretically, it has been informed by sociological theories such as symbolic interactionism, Foucauldian perspectives, historical sociology and feminism, and it is relevant to explore the significance of social theory (Sparks 1997). It can further be argued that criminology can be enriched by fully recognizing the significance of white collar crime. Again drawing an analogy with feminism, although at present discussions of white collar crime, as was the case with gender and crime, tend to be 'tacked on' to criminology (Heidensohn 1996), they could be incorporated. As feminists criticized criminology for its exclusion of half of the population, white collar criminologists can point to its exclusion of the crimes of the employed rather than the unemployed, the powerful rather than the powerless and of organizations rather than individuals. And, as feminists argued that theories should be capable of incorporating gender, it can also be argued that theoretical explanations and analyses of crime and criminal justice should be capable of incorporating, not excluding, white collar crime.

It was seen in Chapter 5, for example, that whereas white collar crime seems to contradict theories locating crime in poverty and social exclusion, some approaches linking crime to structural inequalities can incorporate white collar crime by viewing inequality and the pursuit of wealth as criminogenic (Braithwaite 1992; Ruggiero 1996a). Analyses of market societies also suggest that the individualistic culture of market societies is linked to both white collar and conventional crime (Currie 1997; Taylor 1999) – thus, the economic, social and cultural changes that have been related to conventional crime are also important for white collar crime. Moreover, it has been seen that the post-industrial economy may also blur the relationship between legitimate and illegitimate work and business enterprises at a global and local level. The gender and racial inequalities that contribute to individual acts of sexual or racial violence also provide the basis for economic exploitation, which was seen in Chapter 4 to be a factor in victimization. Moreover, as argued above, organizational analyses developed in respect of white collar and corporate deviance can be of use for understanding other crimes that take place in organizations and organized crime. Considerations of policing, crime prevention and criminal justice policy can also be enhanced by taking white collar crime into account. Although white collar crime, and particularly corporate crime, are often seen as being under-criminalized and subject to too little intervention, it can also be argued that some forms of conventional crime are over-criminalized and that intervention should be minimal. As Braithwaite and Pettit (1990) argue, it is not necessary to argue for greater prosecution and punishment for white collar offenders to remedy inequalities of treatment but to argue that similar policies can be adopted for both forms of crime. It has already been argued, for example, that conventional criminals might benefit by the adoption of more 'regulatory' strategies because it is not necessarily cost-effective to prosecute such high numbers, just as theories of punishment primarily applied to conventional offenders could be usefully applied to white collar and corporate offenders who could be subject to community sentences, rehabilitation and incapacitation. In addition, as seen in Chapter 6, legal concepts such as 'reckless driving' could also be applied to corporations.

Further ways in which the study of white collar crime could 'revitalize' criminology are suggested by South (1998a) in relation to his proposal for the adoption of a 'green perspective' in criminology. He argues that because considerations of environmental damage are closely linked to the study of white collar crime and the crimes of the powerful, such a perspective could provide a unifying theme and rallying point for hitherto disparate work and add power to its accumulation as an identifiable field in criminology. He further argues that a criminology relevant to the next century should have the 'intellectual breadth' and 'constitutional space' to be able to embrace environmental, human and animal rights issues as related projects (South 1998a: 220). Among the advantages of a 'green' criminology would be the involvement of criminologists in regulatory issues and in interdisciplinary work. The symbiotic relationships between legitimate businesses, organized crime and states in relation to illegal waste transfer provide a further focus – he argues, for example, that late modern society is a consumption society, which is also a 'throwaway' society. Environmental issues are not only crucial to the study of risk but also to the criminological study of other 'new' topics such as war crimes and violations of human rights. Moreover, he argues, criminologists should engage in 'futurology' by exploring the potential damage of crimes and injuries generated by the 'manipulation of environmental resources and human and animal populations by corporate interests and governments in pursuit of "expedient solutions", greed and profits' (South 1998a: 226). Among these he includes the unknown consequences of genetically modified food.

It could be asked what such a perspective might include. It would clearly incorporate environmental, food and some safety issues, but how far would a green perspective be able to address other areas encompassed by white collar crime? If some issues were to be excluded, the adoption of such a perspective could lead to more rather than less fragmentation. The consumption society, for example, generates not only waste but also the many fraudulent and harmful practices directed against consumers outlined in Chapter 2. Would these be seen as part of a 'green' perspective where they do not involve primarily environmental issues? Nonetheless South's argument does point to the importance of developing a rallying point and to the possibilities of developing a distinct perspective – there is, for example, no widely recognized 'white collar perspective' equivalent to those associated with feminism or critical race approaches. A green perspective also provides a strong argument that criminology should address contemporary analyses of society based on the changing nature and organization of risk.

Although it lies beyond the scope of this book to explore the significance of analyses of the risk society or contemporary criminological concerns with risk assessment, these have affected criminology (Sparks 1997; Walklate 1998). Thus far, however, criminology has tended to explore risk in terms of crime prevention and criminal justice policies. Victim surveys, for example, have focused on the risks faced by different groups with a view to reducing risk. Risk has, argues Walklate (1998), been largely absent from discussions of corporate crime or fraud, and been related to issues of cost-effectiveness and use of resources. Criminological work on risk has largely not looked at what she describes as the 'risks we do not see', and has not explored the extent to which scientific enterprise has contributed to rising levels of risk as well as seeking ways to control it. Criminology has therefore accepted the scientific agenda and has not worked more critically with the concept of risk. On the other hand, broader analyses of the 'risk' society (Beck 1992), which see risk as a central feature of contemporary life and discuss the role of scientific knowledge and pressures for holding 'experts' accountable, have focused on broad issues such as the environment and said less specifically about crime (Sparks 1997).

White collar crime raises many issues of relevance to discussions of risk. It deals with the many risks faced in everyday life, from those associated with transport, workplace safety, food and the environment to the risks of investment and other areas of consumption. As seen in earlier chapters, it also involves crucial questions of the social organization of expert knowledge and the risks associated with scientific and capitalist development. Analyses of the systems and cultures in organizations in which regulatory violations are sanctioned also reveal that many of these risks, far from being inevitable, are avoidable and preventable, thus challenging 'expert' assessments of safety (Pearce and Tombs 1998). Furthermore, as seen in Chapter 4, analyses of victimization, which cannot follow the standard pattern of 'risk assessment' of conventional victim surveys, reveal the often hidden victimization that follows traditional patterns of gender, class and age, rather than, as some analyses of the risk society suggest, being distributed irrespective of these divisions. Analyses of white collar crime can therefore address the social distribution of risks along with, as Walklate suggests, the crucial role of scientific knowledge. In addition, it has been seen that white collar crime also involves analysing the social organization of trust (Shapiro 1990), which, like risk, is seen to be changing in contemporary societies, with the breakdown of communities and face-to-face interaction (Walklate 1998). Critical issues are also raised about the degrees of trust accorded to corporations and professional groups and how different groups are trusted in different cultures (Nelken 1994b).

What might be the agenda of a potential 'white collar crime' perspective, linked to a green perspective? Much is suggested in the above analysis. It would clearly be linked to other critical approaches by seeking to place white collar crime more centrally in the criminological agenda, thus challenging constructions of crime and victimization and raising key questions about the process of criminalization. There is also, as Nelken (1997a) suggests, always a need to expose the many crimes of elites and powerful groups and to point to the crimes of those in employment. It could also address the many areas of white collar crime that have been seen to be under-researched. Whereas the difficulties of researching the area have been illustrated, new and innovative methodologies could be developed (Davies and Jupp 1999). Previous chapters have illustrated many examples of research and of how social scientific methods (Tombs 1999) can be used.

Understanding of many aspects of white collar crime could be enhanced by such a research agenda and a forum for developing theory and research methodologies. Chapter 2 illustrated the absence of knowledge about the extent and impact of many serious offences – such as tax fraud, corruption and other serious frauds – which have a diffuse effect on the public as individual taxpayers, residents or patients. It is indeed relatively surprising, in view of the losses to the public purse, that not more is known about many of these offences, particularly in the public sector. The full nature and extent of organizational crime affecting consumers, workers and the environment is also ill understood and developing methods for 'counting' and exposing these, such as those used by Tombs (1999) in relation to safety crime, could further reveal their extent and increase awareness of the harms that they cause. Although the invisibility and indirect impact of offences on victims renders victim surveys inappropriate for some areas, other offences, particularly consumer frauds, employment and safety offences, could be incorporated into crime surveys such as the British Crime Survey, as shown by Pearce (1992). Other aspects, particularly where they affect individuals in the home and in local neighbourhoods, could be incorporated into crime and community safety audits, which often include the non-criminal 'incivilities' largely attributable to young persons and noisy neighbours. The equally distressing 'incivilities' of large and small companies, utility providers, factories that cause pollution, unsafe construction sites and noisy businesses could readily be incorporated into such estimates. Although it is often argued that information is difficult to access, it is not impossible, and, as seen in earlier chapters, a considerable amount of information is now available by careful searching on the Internet.

Information about offending and offenders is also sparse and could be the focus of more in-depth research and analysis, particularly in relation to class and gender, which was seen to be far less well researched in white collar crime than in other areas of crime. An understanding of the sources of white collar crime could also be enhanced by more work focusing on the 'fiddles' and 'perks' routinely engaged in not by the blue collar workers that have been the subject of previous studies, but by more senior employees and executives. This work could also explore the cultural values supporting such activities, and their gendered nature. Research in organizations could also examine the distribution of opportunities for the abuse of occupational roles and the social distribution of trust (Shapiro 1990) along with its relationship to social status and gender. The crimes of professional groups such as doctors, lawyers or accountants also raise crucial issues in relation to trust and expertise, particularly how these may protect such groups from investigation, as the recent case in the UK of Dr Harold Shipman dramatically revealed. Research in organizations could also vastly enhance an understanding of internal systems of compliance (Tombs 1999) and other criminogenic organizational features. Funding could also be sought for more detailed studies of white collar offenders and criminal justice – there have been few detailed studies, particularly in Britain, of the kind carried out in the USA (Wheeler *et al*. 1988; Weisburd *et al*. 1991), which, although limited to individual convicted offenders have nonetheless enhanced understanding of patterns of offending, the characteristics of offenders and the way in which they are processed and sentenced. The activities of law enforcement agencies, particularly those dealing with fraud, have also been relatively under-researched.

A major feature of such an agenda should also be the development of comparative research. Discussing the need for such research, Nelken (1994b) points to the significance of transnational and cross-border crimes involving fraud, money laundering, tax evasion and crimes against the environment – the control of which involves many jurisdictions with different cultures. In addition, comparative work is crucial if other countries seek to 'borrow' laws from other states (Nelken 1994b: 221), which must also take account of these differing legal and social cultures. Ethnocentrism should therefore be avoided. Nelken (1994b) also points out that the contrast between 'compliance' and 'policing' so prominent in work on regulation is less marked in Italy. This he relates to patterns of trust in different countries – in Italy, he argues, such a discretionary style of enforcement would be seen as an excuse for corruption, whereas more groups are trusted in the British system which also functions more directly in the interests of business. This affects what is seen as criminal, which groups are more likely to be targeted for surveillance and how they are sanctioned. As seen in Chapter 7, a number of alternative sanctions for corporate and white collar offenders are used in different jurisdictions, which could also provide a focus for comparative research.

White collar crime is still an area that raises many unanswered questions. It is, however, a subject that continues to be important for many aspects of criminology, however much the concept itself has been contested and the problems that it raises have been neglected. It involves issues of significance not only for criminology but for wider sociological analyses of risk and trust. The harms that it involves also relate to key aspects of contemporary life involving, as they do, issues of economic security, the legitimacy of financial institutions and state organizations along with the economic and physical dangers posed by industrial and technological development. Exposing these harms, many of which are shrouded by their invisibility, continues to be an important task in itself and one that also raises fundamental questions about the policies and practices used in their policing and control. Exposure is also necessary to bring about changes in these policies, which have been seen to be rooted in the conception that they are not 'really' crime. Challenging these perceptions is therefore a major task facing those who wish to see those harms reduced.

Glossary

Terms that are cross-referenced in the glossary are indicated in italics.

Administrative criminology   A term used to describe criminological research and policy developed to assist the administration of criminal justice and the prevention of crime. Also referred to as 'establishment' criminology, reflecting its organization around administrative and government priorities.

Anomie   A term first associated with the work of Durkheim (1897), who drew attention to the absence of norms that could occur in periods of rapid social change, which he associated with anomic suicide. He also pointed to the problems that could occur in periods of 'infinite aspirations' which could not be satisfied. Later reformulated by Merton (1938), who pointed to the strain or disjunction between societal goals of material success and the restricted legitimate opportunities for achieving these goals – crime was seen as an 'innovative' response to such a strain.

Compliance strategies   A term often used to describe the policies and practices of *regulatory enforcement* agencies, in which prosecution (often contrasted with compliance) is seen as a last resort. A compliance approach involves a mixture of persuasion, education and advice, aiming to secure the cooperation of business in complying with regulations.

Consumer crime   A term often used in relation to crimes whose main victims are consumers and which is related to laws protecting consumers, such as food, trade descriptions, labelling and weights and measures legislation.

Control theories   Theories that relate crime to an absence of formal or informal controls.

Conventional victimology   A term used to describe perspectives in *victimology* that explore how different groups are more at risk of being victims and that adopt largely conventional definitions of crime. These have largely excluded violence in the home and *white collar crime*, thus adopting conventional constructions of crime.

Corporate crime   Crimes committed by and on behalf of corporations as opposed to those crimes carried out for individual gain. Examples include violations of safety, health, environmental, financial or consumer regulations.

Corporate killing   A term used in proposed new legislation in the UK to reform the law on *corporate manslaughter* to enable companies to be convicted.

Corporate manslaughter   A term used in the UK in relation to offences in which a fatality is found to be the legal responsibility not of an individual but of the 'company' – for example, through a failure to ensure the safety of workers or clients. In practice, because of the difficulties of establishing corporate as opposed to individual liability, convictions have been rare and the new offence of *corporate killing* has been proposed.

Corruption   The abuse by an employee or politician of their position to gain material advantage in return for some kind of favour.

Crimes of professional occupations   Crimes committed by those in professional occupations such as medicine, law or accountancy, which usually involve an abuse of professional ethics or expertise. They are distinct from '*professional crime*'.

Crimes of the powerful   A phrase widely used to describe the crimes of those in powerful positions, such as senior executives, corporations and those occupying senior positions in government and state agencies. It is often used to distinguish these offences from the 'crimes of the powerless' and to reflect the exercise of power over the criminalization process.

Criminalization   The application of criminal law to activities. Widely used also to refer to the association of a 'criminal' label with specific groups of the population. As a process, it involves the development of criminal law and the application of law enforcement and criminal sanctions.

Criminological project   A phrase associated with traditional, positivist criminological concerns to establish the 'causes' of crime and develop policies to 'cure' and reduce crime.

Critical criminology   A range of criminological perspectives that question the focus of much criminological research and analysis around conventionally defined crime problems and government priorities. It encompasses approaches also known as 'radical' criminology, based on conflict and Marxist theory, 'left idealist' (as opposed to *left realist*) approaches and 'critical race' perspectives.

Critical victimology   An approach to *victimology* that is critical of the conventional construction of crime adopted in *conventional victimology*.

Elite crime   A term sometimes used in place of *white collar crime, corporate crime* or *state crime* that restricts its focus to the crimes of larger corporations, senior executives, politicians and state agencies.

Embezzlement   Dishonestly appropriating money or property of an employer.

Environmental crime   A term used to describe offences that violate regulations seeking to protect the environment, such as pollution, waste disposal and emissions of chemicals.

Feminist perspectives   A range of perspectives that aim to prioritize the study of women and gender and that are critical of, and seek to expose, the male-centred nature of many academic disciplines. Often distinguished are liberal, radical, socialist, standpoint and postmodern feminist approaches.

Fraud   A vast range of offences that involve obtaining material advantage by making a false representation.

Insider dealing   Using information gained (often in confidence) by virtue of 'inside' knowledge to undertake advantageous financial transactions.

Institutional violence   A term used to describe harmful practices of organizations that cause injury, illness or death but that are not included in the social construction of violent crime. Although there may be no individual intent to cause such harm, these practices can be seen to arise from acts or omissions taking place in organizations, which are often sanctioned by or not prevented by organizational practices and policies.

Labelling perspective A theoretical approach to crime and deviance based on the premise that no individuals or actions are intrinsically criminal or deviant until labelled as such by control agents.

Left realist/realism A term used to describe the perspective developed by Young and his colleagues from Middlesex University (see, for example Lea and Young 1993; Young 1997), in which the 'reality' of crime is recognized. It is associated with a 'square of crime' in which any form of crime can only be analysed fully by recognizing the interconnections between the victim, the public, the offender and the state.

Occupational crime Refers to the broad range of crimes committed in the course of a (normally legitimate) occupation. Incorporates both white collar and blue collar crime. Also sometimes referred to as crime at work (as opposed to crime as work).

Organizational crime Crime committed by, or on behalf of, organizations. The term may be used in preference to *corporate crime*, as it incorporates public sector and voluntary organizations as well as private corporations. It should not be confused with *organized crime*.

Organized crime Crime committed by illegitimate, 'criminal' organizations such as the drugs industry, which involve organization around primarily criminal goals.

Political crime A phrase used in two main contexts. One refers to crimes committed for a largely political motive such as terrorism. It is also used to refer to crimes committed by politicians that involve an abuse of their position either for personal gain or in pursuance of, or to maintain, political power.

Professional crime Crime committed by perpetrators who make a living from crime and who use some expertise, such as 'professional burglars' or pickpockets. It is often linked with *organized crime*.

Regulatory enforcement The policies and practices associated with *regulatory law* and *regulatory offences*. It generally involves a distinctive pattern of negotiation, advice and warnings that leads to relatively low rates of prosecution, often described as *compliance strategies*.

Regulatory law When used in relation to *corporate* and other *white collar crimes*, this refers to a body of regulations, violations of which are often distinguished from 'crimes' and criminal law. It further incorporates distinctive patterns of law, regulation and sanctions, which can be contrasted with criminal law and policing. See also *social regulation*.

Regulatory offences A term used to describe offences that involve a breach of regulations, such as those covering health, safety or the environment, by businesses and organizations. In general terms, these are often distinguished from other offences by the use of strict liability and are counted as non-indictable rather than indictable. See also *regulatory enforcement* and *regulatory law*.

Relative deprivation Often contrasted with absolute deprivation, this term refers to perceptions of deprivation in comparison with a reference group whose status or condition can legitimately be compared to one's own. It has been linked to crime by the *left realist* approach, which argues that groups who cannot pursue grievances through legitimate means might turn to crime.

Self-regulation A term used to describe the situation in which industrial, commercial or financial institutions are responsible for regulating themselves without external regulation.

Social regulation   A term sometimes used to describe the *regulatory law* and *regulatory enforcement* associated with offences where the criminal law is primarily justified on the grounds of public protection, such as consumer, safety or environmental law, giving it a broader social function than that often associated with the criminal law.

State crime   Crime committed by or on behalf of governments and state agencies such as the police or military. Where individuals break rules on behalf of the state or for its perceived benefit this is often referred to as 'state organized' crime.

State organized crime   A term used to describe crimes which are committed by official agents of the state (such as the police) in the pursuance of their duties where such crimes are condoned or not actively discouraged by state policies or actions.

Subcultural theory   A group of theories in which crime is seen as being normal within subcultures that may emerge out of the kind of structural strains associated with *anomie*. It has most often been used in connection with juvenile crime.

Victim surveys   Surveys that ask members of the general or specific population groups about the extent of their criminal victimization.

Victimology   The study of victims of crime and patterns of victimization.

White collar crime   First defined by Sutherland as 'a crime committed by a person of respectability and high social status in the course of his occupation' (Sutherland 1949: 9). Popularly associated with the offences of people of high social status. Its definition has been subject to considerable debate and it has been defined in this book as an abuse of a legitimate occupational role that is regulated by law.

References

Aitken, L. and Griffin, G. (1996) *Gender Issues in Elder Abuse*. London: Sage.

Arnold, T. (1937) *The Folklore of Capitalism*. Westport, CT: Greenwood.

Ashworth, A. (1997) Sentencing, in M. Maguire, R. Morgan and R. Reiner (eds) *The Oxford Handbook of Criminology*, 2nd edn. Oxford: Clarendon Press.

Aubert, V. (1977) White collar crime and social structure, in G. Geis and R. F. Maier (eds) *White Collar Crime: Offences in Business, Politics and the Professions – Classic and Contemporary Views*. New York: Collier and Macmillan.

Audit Commission (1993) *Protecting the Public Purse. Probity in the Public Sector: Combating Fraud and Corruption in Local Government*. London: HMSO.

Audit Commission (1994) *Protecting the Public Purse 2: Ensuring Probity in the NHS*. London: HMSO.

Automobile Association (1994) (in association with the Institute of Trading Standards Administration) *Consumer Protection for Motorists: A Survey of Complaints and Proposals for Action*. London: AA, June 1994.

Barclay, G. and Tavares, C. (1999) *Digest 4: Information on the Criminal Justice System in England and Wales*. Home Office Research, Development and Statistics Directorate. London: HMSO.

BBC news online (1998) http://www.news.bbc.co.uk

BBC news online (2000) http://www.news.bbc.co.uk

Beck, U. (1992) *The Risk Society*. London: Sage.

Benson, M. L. (1985) Denying the guilty mind: accounting for involvement in a white collar crime, *Criminology*, 23(4): 583–604.

Bergman, D. (1992) Corporate sanctions and corporate probation, *New Law Journal*, 144: 1312.

Black, J. (1997) *Rules and Regulators*. Oxford: Clarendon Press.

Block, A. (1993) Defending the Mountaintop: a campaign against environmental crime, in F. Pearce and M. Woodiwiss (eds) *Global Crime Connections: Dynamics and Control*. London: Macmillan.

Bonger, W. (1905 and 1969) *Criminality and Economic Conditions*. Bloomington, IN: Indiana University Press.

Borrie, G., Sir and Diamond, A. L. (1981) *The Consumer, Society and the Law*, 4th edn. Harmondsworth: Penguin.

Bosworth-Davies, R. (1993) An analysis of compliance officers: attitudes towards insider dealing, *Crime, Law and Social Change*, 20: 339–57.

Bottoms, A. (1995) The philosophy and politics of punishment and sentencing, in C. Clarkson and R. Morgan (eds) *The Politics of Sentencing Reform*. Oxford: Oxford University Press.

Box, S. (1983) *Power, Crime and Mystification*. London: Tavistock.

Box, S. (1987) *Recession, Crime and Punishment*. London: Macmillan.

Braithwaite, J. (1979) Transnational corporations and corruption: towards some international solutions, *International Journal of the Sociology of Law*, 7: 143–67.

Braithwaite, J. (1982) Challenging just deserts: punishing white collar criminals, *Journal of Criminal Law and Criminology*, 73(2): 723–63.

Braithwaite, J. (1984) *Corporate Crime in the Pharmaceutical Industry*. London: Routledge and Kegan Paul.

Braithwaite, J. (1985a) White collar crime, *Annual Review of Sociology*, 11: 1–25.

Braithwaite, J. (1985b) *To Punish or Persuade: Enforcement of Coal-mine Safety*. Albany NY: State University of New York Press.

Braithwaite, J. (1989) *Crime, Shame and Re-integration*. Cambridge: Cambridge University Press.

Braithwaite, J. (1992) Poverty, power and white-collar crime: Sutherland and the paradoxes of criminological theory, in K. Schlegel and D. Weisburd (eds) *White Collar Crime Reconsidered*. Boston, MA: Northeastern University Press.

Braithwaite, J. (1995a) Corporate crime and republican criminological praxis, in F. Pearce and L. Snider (eds) *Corporate Crime: Contemporary Debates*. Toronto: University of Toronto Press.

Braithwaite, J. (1995b) Inequality and republican criminology, in J. Hagan and R. D. Peterson (eds) *Crime and Inequality*. Stanford, CA: Stanford University Press.

Braithwaite, J. and Fisse, B. (1987) Self regulation and the control of corporate crime, in C. Shearing and P. Stenning (eds) *Private Policing*. London: Sage.

Braithwaite, J. and Geis, G. (1982) On theory and action for corporate crime control, *Crime and Delinquency*, 28 (April): 292–314.

Braithwaite, J. and Pettit, P. (1990) *Not Just Deserts: A Republican Theory of Justice*. Oxford: Clarendon Press.

Braithwaite, J. and Vale, S. (1985) Law enforcement by Australian Consumer Affairs Agencies, *Australian and New Zealand Journal of Criminology*, 18 (September): 147–63.

Burden, R. (1998) Vulnerable consumer groups: quantification and analysis. Research Paper No. 15, prepared for the Office of Fair Trading. London: Office of Fair Trading.

Cain, M. (1990) Realist philosophy and standpoint epistemologies or feminist criminology as a successor science, in L. Gelsthorpe and A. Morris (eds) *Feminist Perspectives in Criminology*. Buckingham: Open University Press.

Calavita, H. and Pontell, K. (1995) Saving the Savings and Loans?, in F. Pearce and L. Snider (eds) *Corporate Crime: Contemporary Debates*. Toronto: University of Toronto Press.

Cannon, G. and Walker, C. (1985) *The Food Scandal*. London: Unwin Hyman.

Carlen, P. (1976) *Magistrates' Justice*. London: Martin Robertson.

Carlen, P. (1992) Criminal women and criminal justice, in R. Matthews and J. Young (eds) *Issues in Realist Criminology*. London: Sage.

Carson, W. G. (1971) White collar crime and the enforcement of factory legislation, in W. G. Carson and P. Wiles (eds) *Crime and Delinquency in Britain*. London: Martin Robertson.

Carson, W. G. (1974) Symbolic and instrumental dimensions of early factory legislation: a case study in the social origins of criminal law, in R. Hood (ed.) *Crime, Criminology and Public Policy*. London: Heinemann Educational Books.

Carson, W. G. (1979) The conventionalisation of early factory crime, *International Journal of the Sociology of Law*, 7(1): 37–60.

Carson, W. G. (1980) The institutionalisation of ambiguity: early British Factory Acts, in G. Geis and E. Stotland (eds) *White Collar Crime: Theory and Research*. London: Sage.

Carson, W. G. (1981) *The Other Price of British Oil*. London: Martin Robertson.

Clarke, M. (1986) *Regulating the City: Competition, Scandal and Reform*. Milton Keynes: Open University Press.

Clarke, M. (1990) *Business Crime: Its Nature and Control*. Cambridge: Polity Press.

Clarke, M. (1994) EC Fraud, Issues in Sociology and Social Policy: Occasional Paper No. 4. University of Liverpool Department of Sociology, Social Policy and Social Work Studies.

Claybrook, J. (1996) Women in the Marketplace, in E. Szockyj and J. G. Fox (eds) *Corporate Victimization of Women*. Boston, MA: Northeastern University Press.

Clinard, M. B. (1983) *Corporate Ethics and Crime*. Beverly Hills, CA: Sage.

Clinard, M. B. and Yeager, P. C. (1980) *Corporate Crime*. New York: Free Press.

Cohen, S. (1996a) Human rights and crimes of the state: the culture of denial, in J. Muncie, E. McLaughlin and M. Langan (eds) *Criminological Perspectives*. London: Sage.

Cohen, S. (1996b) Crime and politics: spot the difference, *British Journal of Sociology*, 47(1): 1–21.

Coleman, C. and Moynihan, J. (1996) *Understanding Crime Data: Haunted by the Dark Figure*. Buckingham: Open University Press.

Conklin, J. E. (1977) *Illegal but not Criminal*. Englewood Cliffs, NJ: Spectrum.

Cook, D. (1989) *Rich Law, Poor Law: Different Responses to Tax and Supplementary Benefit Fraud*. Milton Keynes: Open University Press.

Cox, G., Sheriff (1998) Determination by Graham L. Cox, QC, Sheriff Principal of South Strathclyde, Dumfries and Galloway into the E. coli 0157 Fatal Accident Inquiry.

Cranston, R. (1979) *Regulating Business*. London: Macmillan.

Cranston, R. (1984) *Consumers and the Law*, 2nd edn. London: Weidenfeld and Nicolson.

Cressey, D. (1986) Why managers commit fraud, *Australian and New Zealand Journal of Criminology*, 19: 195–209.

Cressey, D. (1988) The poverty of theory in corporate crime research, in F. Adler and W. S. Laufer (eds) *Advances in Criminological Theory*. New Brunswick, NJ: Translation.

Crime Concern (1994) *Counting the Cost: A Briefing Paper on Financial Losses Arising From Crime*. Swindon: Crime Concern.

Croall, H. (1987) Crimes against the consumer: an analysis of the nature, extent, regulation and sanctioning of 'trading offences'. Unpublished PhD thesis, University of London.

Croall, H. (1988) Mistakes, accidents and someone else's fault: the trading offender in court, *Journal of Law and Society*, 15(3): 293–315.

Croall, H. (1989) Who is the white collar criminal?, *British Journal of Criminology*, 29(2): 157–74.

Croall, H. (1991) Sentencing the business offender, *Howard Journal of Criminal Justice*, 30(4): 280–92.

Croall, H. (1992) *White Collar Crime*. Buckingham: Open University Press.

Croall, H. (1995) Target women: women's victimisation from white collar crime, in R. Dobash and L. Noaks (eds) *Gender and Crime*. Cardiff: Cardiff University Press.

Croall, H. (1998a) Business, crime and the community, *International Journal of Risk, Security and Crime Prevention*, 3(4): 281–92.

Croall, H. (1998b) Protecting us from powerful interests, *Criminal Justice Matters*, 33(autumn): 23–4.

Croall, H. (1998c) *Crime and Society in Britain*. London: Longman.

Croall, H. (1999a) White collar crime: an overview and discussion, in P. Davies, P. Francis and V. Jupp (eds) *Invisible Crimes: Their Victims and their Regulation*. London: Macmillan.

Croall, H. (1999b) Crime, business and community safety, *Scottish Journal of Criminal Justice Studies*, 5(2): 65–81.

Croall, H. (1999c) Corporate victims, *Criminal Justice Matters*, 36(summer): 4–5.

Croall, H. and Ross, J. (1999) 'Sentencing the corporate offender', unpublished paper given at the International Conference of Sentencing and Society, Strathclyde University, June 1999.

Currie, E. (1997) Market, crime and community: toward a mid-range theory of post-industrial violence, *Theoretical Criminology*, 1(2): 147–72.

Daly, K. (1994) Criminal law and justice system practices as racist, white and racialised, *Washington and Lee Law Review*, 15(2): 431–64.

Davies, M., Croall, H. and Tyrer, J. (1998) *Criminal Justice: An Introduction to the Criminal Justice System in England and Wales*, 2nd edn. London: Longman.

Davies, P. and Jupp, V. (1999) Crime and work connections: exploring the 'invisibility' of workplace crime, in P. Davies, P. Francis and V. Jupp (eds) *Invisible Crimes: Their Victims and their Regulation*. London: Macmillan.

Ditton, J. (1977) *Part Time Crime: An Ethnography of Fiddling and Pilferage*. London: Macmillan.

Doig, A. (1984) *Corruption and Misconduct in Contemporary British Politics*. Harmondsworth: Penguin.

Doig, A. (1995) A fragmented organizational approach to fraud in a European context, *European Journal of Criminal Policy*, 3(2): 48–74.

Doig, A. (1996) From Lynskey to Nolan: the corruption of British politics and public service, *Journal of Law and Society*, 23(1): 36–56.

Downes, D. and Rock, P. (1995) *Understanding Deviance: A Guide to the Sociology of Crime and Rule Breaking*, 2nd edn. Oxford: Clarendon Press.

Durkheim, E. (1897/1979) *Suicide: A Study in Sociology*. London: Routledge and Kegan Paul.

Ericson, R. and Carriere, K. (1996) The fragmentation of criminology, in J. Muncie,

E. McLaughlin and M. Langan (eds) *Criminological Perspectives*. London: Sage.

Etzioni, A. (1993) The US Sentencing Commission on Corporate Crime: a critique, in G. Geis and P. Jesilow (eds) White Collar Crime. Special Issue of the Annals of the American Academy of Political and Social Science, 525(January): 147–56.

Fattah, E. and Sacco, V. (1989) *Crime and Victimisation of the Elderly*. New York: Springer Verlag.

Feeley, M. and Simon, J. (1996) The new penology, in J. Muncie, E. McLaughlin and M. Langan (eds) *Criminological Perspectives*. London: Sage.

Finlay, L. (1996) The pharmaceutical industry and women's reproductive health, in E. Szockyj and J. G. Fox (eds) *Corporate Victimization of Women*. Boston, MA: Northeastern University Press.

Fisse, B. and Braithwaite, J. (1983) *The Impact of Publicity on Corporate Offenders*. Albany, NY: State University of New York Press.

Fisse, B. and Braithwaite, J. (1993) *Corporations, Crime and Accountability*. Cambridge: Cambridge University Press.

Friedrichs, D. O. (1996) *Trusted Criminals: White Collar Crime in Contemporary Society*. Belmont: Wadsworth.

Guardian/Guardian Unlimited http://www.guardianunlimited.co.uk/guardian

Geis, G. (1978) Deterring corporate crime, in R. Ermann and R. Lundman (eds) *Corporate and Governmental Deviance*. New York: Oxford University Press.

Gelsthorpe, L. (1997) Feminism and criminology, in M. Maguire, R. Morgan and R. Reiner (eds) *The Oxford Handbook of Criminology*, 2nd edn. Oxford: Clarendon Press.

Gelsthorpe, L. and Morris, A. (1988) Feminism and criminology in Britain, in P. Rock (ed.) *A History of British Criminology*. Oxford: Clarendon Press.

Gottfredson, M. and Hirschi, T. (1990) *A General Theory of Crime*. Stanford, CA: Stanford University Press.

Gross, E. (1978) Organizations as criminal actors, in J. Braithwaite and P. Wilson (eds) *Two Faces of Deviance: Crimes of the Powerless and the Powerful*. Brisbane: University of Queensland Press.

Habermas, J. (1970) Towards a theory of communicative competence, in H. Dreitzel (ed.) *Recent Sociology*. New York: Macmillan.

Hagan, J. (1988) *Structural Criminology*. Oxford: Polity Press.

Harvey, B. W. (1982) *Law of Consumer Protection and Fair Trading*, 2nd edn. London: Butterworth.

Hawkins, K. (1983) Bargain and bluff – compliance strategy and deterrence in the enforcement of regulation, *Law and Policy Quarterly*, 5(1): 35–73.

Hawkins, K. (1984) *Environment and Enforcement: Regulation and the Social Definition of Pollution*. Oxford: Clarendon Press.

Hawkins, K. (1990) Compliance strategy, prosecution policy and Aunt Sally – a comment on Pearce and Tombs, *British Journal of Criminology*, 30(4): 444–67.

Heidensohn, F. (1992) *Women in Control? The Role of Women in Law Enforcement*. Oxford: Oxford University Press.

Heidensohn, F. (1996) *Women and Crime*, 2nd edn. London: Macmillan.

Herald (1996) http:www.theherald.co.uk

Herald (1998) http:www.theherald.co.uk

Hirschi, T. (1969) *Causes of Delinquency*. Los Angeles, CA: University of California Press.

Hobbs, D. (1995) *Bad Business: Professional Crime in Modern Britain*. Oxford: Oxford University Press.

Hobbs, D. (1997) Professional crime: change, continuity and the enduring myth of the underworld, *Sociology*, 31(1): 57–72.

Hodgkinson, P. (1997) The sociology of corruption – some themes and issues, *Sociology*, 31(1): 17–35.

Hudson, B. (1987) *Justice Through Punishment*. Basingstoke and London: Macmillan.

Hutter, B. (1988) *The Reasonable Arm of the Law?* Oxford: Clarendon Press.

Hutter, B. and Lloyd Bostock, S. (1990) The power of accidents: the social and psychological impact of accidents and the enforcement of safety regulations, *British Journal of Criminology*, 30(4): 409–22.

Jesilow, H., Pontell, H. and Geis, G. (1993) *Prescription for Profit: How Doctors Defraud Medicaid*. Berkeley and Los Angeles, CA: University of California Press.

Kagan, R. and Scholz, J. (1984) The criminology of the corporation and regulatory enforcement strategies, in K. Hawkins and J. Thomas (eds) *Enforcing Regulation*. Boston, MA: Kluwer-Hijhoff.

Kelly, L. (1988) *Surviving Sexual Violence*. Cambridge: Polity Press.

Lacey, N. (1995) Contingency and criminalisation, in I. Loveland (ed.) *Frontiers of Criminality*. London: Sweet & Maxwell.

Langan, M. (1996) Hidden and respectable: crime and the market, in J. Muncie and E. McLaughlin (eds) *The Problem of Crime*. London: Sage.

Law Commission (1996) *Legislating the Criminal Code: Involuntary Manslaughter*. London: HMSO.

Lea, J. and Young, J. (1993) *What is to be Done about Law and Order?*, 2nd edn. London: Pluto Press.

Lees, S. (1996) Unreasonable doubt: the outcomes of rape trials, in M. Hester, L. Kelly and J. Radford (eds) *Women, Violence and Male Power*. Buckingham: Open University Press.

Leigh, D. and Vulliamy, E. (1997) *Sleaze: The Corruption of Parliament*. London: Fourth Estate.

Leonard, W. N. and Weber, M. G. (1977) Auto-makers and dealers: a study of criminogenic market forces, in G. Gies and R. F. Maier (eds) *White Collar Crime: Offences in Business, Politics and the Professions – Classic and Contemporary Views*. New York: Collier and Macmillan.

Lever, L. (1992) *The Barlow Clowes Affair*. London: Macmillan.

Levi, M. (1987a) *The Regulation of Fraud: White Collar Crime and the Criminal Process*. London: Tavistock.

Levi, M. (1987b) Crisis? What crisis? Reactions to commercial fraud in the UK, *Contemporary Crises*, 11: 207–21.

Levi, M. (1988) *The Prevention of Fraud*. Crime Prevention Unit, Paper 17. London: HMSO.

Levi, M. (1989a) Suite justice: sentencing for fraud, *Criminal Law Review*, 420–34.

Levi, M. (1989b) Fraudulent justice? Sentencing the business criminal, in P. Carlen and D. Cook (eds) *Paying for Crime*. Milton Keynes: Open University Press.

Levi, M. (1991) Sentencing white collar crime in the dark?: reflections on the Guinness four, *Howard Journal*, 28(4): 257–79.

Levi, M. (1994) Masculinities and white collar crime, in T. Newburn and E. Stanko (eds) *Just Boys Doing Business?* London: Routledge.

Levi, M. (1995) Serious fraud in Britain, in F. Pearce and L. Snider (eds) *Corporate Crime: Contemporary Debates*. Toronto: University of Toronto Press.

Levi, M. (1997) Violent crime, in M. Maguire, R. Morgan and R. Reiner (eds) *The Oxford Handbook of Criminology*, 2nd edn. Oxford: Clarendon Press.

Levi, M. (1999a) The regulation of fraud revisited, in P. Davies, P. Francis and V. Jupp (eds) *Invisible Crimes: Their Victims and their Regulation*. London: Macmillan.

Levi, M. (1999b) The impact of fraud, *Criminal Justice Matters*, 36(summer): 5–7.

Levi, M. (1999c) White-collar crime in the news. Paper presented at the British Criminology Conference, Liverpool, July 1999.

Levi, M. and Nelken, D. (1996) The corruption of politics and the politics of corruption: an overview, *Journal of Law and Society*, 23(1): 1–17.

Levi, M. and Pithouse, A. (1992) The victims of fraud, in D. Downes (ed.) *Unravelling Criminal Justice*. London: Macmillan.

Levi, M. and Pithouse, A. (forthcoming) *The Victims of Fraud*. Oxford: Oxford University Press.

London Food Commission (1988) *Food Adulteration and How to Beat it*. London: Unwin Paperbacks.

McBarnet, D. (1984) Law and capital: the role of legal form and legal actors, *International Journal of the Sociology of Law*, 12: 231–8.

McBarnet, D. (1988) Law, policy and legal avoidance: can law effectively implement egalitarian strategies?, *Journal of Law and Society*, 15(1).

McCahill, M. and Norris, C. (1999) Watching the workers: crime, CCTV and the workplace, in P. Davies, P. Francis and V. Jupp (eds) *Invisible Crimes: Their Victims and their Regulation*. London: Macmillan.

Maguire, M. (1997) Crime statistics, patterns and trends: changing perceptions and their implications, in M. Maguire, R. Morgan and R. Reiner (eds) *The Oxford Handbook of Criminology*, 2nd edn. Oxford: Clarendon Press.

Maguire, M., Morgan, R. and Reiner, R. (eds) (1997) *The Oxford Handbook of Criminology*, 2nd edn. Oxford: Clarendon Press.

Mann, K. (1985) *Defending White Collar Crime*. New Haven, CT and London: Yale University Press.

Mars, G. (1982) *Cheats at Work, an Anthropology of Workplace Crime*. London: George Allen & Unwin.

Mawby, R. and Walklate, S. (1994) *Critical Victimology: The Victim in International Perspective*. London: Sage.

Merton, R. K. (1938) Social structure and anomie, *American Sociological Review*, 3: 672–82.

Messerschmidt, J. (1993) *Masculinities and Crime: Reconceptualization of Theory*. Lanham, MD: Rowman and Littlefield.

Miller, M. (1985) *Danger! Additives at Work*. London: London Food Commission.

Mills, C. W. (1956) *The Power Elite*. Oxford: Oxford University Press.

Moore, C. A. (1987) Taming the giant corporations? Some cautionary remarks on the deterrability of corporate crime, *Crime and Delinquency*, 33: 379–402.

Morgan, J. and Zedner, L. (1992) *Child Victims: Crime, Impact, and Criminal Justice*. Oxford: Clarendon Press.

Muncie, J. (1996) The construction and deconstruction of crime, in J. Muncie and E. McLaughlin (eds) *The Problem of Crime*. London: Sage.

Muncie, J. (1998) Deconstructing criminology, *Criminal Justice Matters*, 34(winter): 4–5.

Nelken, D. (1983) *The Limits of the Legal Process*. London: Academic Press.

Nelken, D. (ed.) (1994a) *White Collar Crime*. Aldershot: Dartmouth.

Nelken, D. (1994b) Whom can you trust? The future of comparative criminology, in D. Nelken (ed.) *The Futures of Criminology*. London: Sage.

Nelken, D. (1997a) White collar crime, in M. Maguire, R. Morgan and R. Reiner (eds) *The Oxford Handbook of Criminology*, 2nd edn. Oxford: Clarendon Press.

Nelken, D. (1997b) The globalization of crime and criminal justice: prospects and problems, in M. Freeman (ed.) *Law and Opinion and the End of the Twentieth Century*. Oxford: Oxford University Press.

Observer (1999) http://www.observer.co.uk

O'Keefe, J. (1996) *Law of Weights and Measures*. London: Butterworth.

Passas, N. (1990) Anomie and corporate deviance, *Contemporary Crises*, 14: 157–78.

Passas, N. and Nelken, D. (1993) The thin line between legitimate and criminal enterprises: subsidy frauds in the European Community, *Crime, Law and Social Change*, 19: 223–43.

Paulus, I. (1974) *The Search for Pure Food: A Sociology of Legislation in Britain*. London: Martin Robertson.

Pearce, F. (1976) *Crimes of the Powerful*. London: Pluto Press.

Pearce, F. (1992) The contribution of 'left realism' to the study of commercial crime, in B. McLean and J. Lowman (eds) *Realist Criminology: Crime Control and Policing in the 1990s*. Toronto: University of Toronto Press.

Pearce, F. and Tombs, S. (1990) Ideology, hegemony and empiricism: compliance theories and regulation, *British Journal of Criminology*, 30(4): 423–43.

Pearce, F. and Tombs, S. (1997) Hazards, law and class: contextualizing the regulation of corporate crime, *Social and Legal Studies*, 6(1): 79–107.

Pearce, F. and Tombs, S. (1998) *Toxic Capitalism: Corporate Crime and the Chemical Industry*. Aldershot: Ashgate.

Peppin, J. (1995) Feminism, law and the pharmaceutical industry, in F. Pearce and L. Snider (eds) *Corporate Crime: Contemporary Debates*. Toronto: University of Toronto Press.

Pontell, H. and Calavita, K. (1992) Bilking bankers and bad debts: white collar crime and the savings and loan crisis, in K. Schlegel and D. Weisburd (eds) *White Collar Crime Reconsidered*. Boston, MA: Northeastern University Press.

Povey, D. and Prime, J. (1999) *Recorded Crime Statistics, England and Wales, April 1998–March 1999*. London: HMSO.

Punch, M. (1996) *Dirty Business: Exploring Corporate Misconduct*. London: Sage.

Quinney, R. (1977) The study of white collar crime: toward a re-orientation in theory and practice, in G. Geis and R. F. Maier (eds) *White Collar Crime: Offences in Business, Politics and the Professions – Classic and Contemporary Views*. New York: Collier and Macmillan.

Richardson, G., with Ogus, A. and Burrows, P. (1982) *Policing Pollution: A Study of Regulation and Enforcement.* Oxford: Clarendon Press.

Ross, J. (1999) Corporate criminal liability: One form or many forms?, *The Juridical Review*, Part 1: 49–65.

Rothschild, D. and Throne, B. (1976) Criminal consumer fraud – victim oriented analysis, *Michigan Law Review*, March: 661–707.

Ruggiero, V. (1992) Realist criminology: a critique, in R. Matthews and J. Young (eds) *Issues in Realist Criminology.* London: Sage.

Ruggiero, V. (1994) Corruption in Italy: an attempt to identify the victims, *Howard Journal of Criminal Justice*, 33(4): 319–38.

Ruggiero, V. (1996a) *Organized and Corporate Crime in Europe: Offers that Can't be Refused.* Aldershot: Dartmouth.

Ruggiero, V. (1996b) War markets: corporate and organized criminals in Europe, *Social and Legal Studies*, 5: 5–20.

Ruggiero, V. (1997) Trafficking in human beings: slaves in contemporary Europe, *International Journal of the Sociology of Law*, 25: 231–44.

Ruggiero, V. and South, N. (1995) *Eurodrugs: Drug Use, Markets and Trafficking in Europe.* London: University College London Press.

Schlegal, K. and Weisburd, D. (eds) (1992) *White Collar Crime Reconsidered.* Boston, MA: Northeastern University Press.

Schraeger, L. S. and Short, J. F. (1977) Towards a sociology of organisational crime, *Social Problems*, 25: 407–19.

Schwendinger, H. and Schwendinger, J. (1970) Defendants of order or guardians of human rights, *Issues in Criminology*, 7: 72–81.

Scotsman (1999) http://www. Scotsman.com

Scott, C. (1995) Criminalising the trader to protect the consumer: the fragmentation and consolidation of trading standards legislation, in I. Loveland (ed.) *Frontiers of Criminality.* London: Sweet & Maxwell.

Scraton, P. (1999) Denial of truth, pain of injustice, *Criminal Justice Matters*, 35(spring): 18–19.

Shapiro, S. (1990) Collaring the crime, not the criminal: re-considering the concept of white collar crime, *American Sociological Review*, 55: 346–65.

Simon, D. and Eitzen, D. (1993) *Elite Deviance*, 4th edn. Boston, MA: Allyn & Bacon.

Simpson, S. and Elis, L. (1996) Theoretical perspectives on the corporate victimization of women, in E. Szockyj and J. G. Fox (eds) *Corporate Victimization of Women.* Boston, MA: Northeastern University Press.

Sisson, S. and colleagues (1999) Cautions, court proceedings and sentencing: England and Wales 1998, *Home Office Statistical Bulletin, Issue 21/99.* London: Government Statistical Service.

Slapper, G. (1993) Corporate manslaughter: an examination of the determinants of prosecutorial policy, *Social and Legal Studies*, 2: 423–43.

Slapper, G. (1999) *Blood in the Bank: Social and Legal Aspects of Death at Work.* Aldershot: Ashgate.

Slapper, G. and Tombs, S. (1999) *Corporate Crime.* London: Addison Wesley Longman.

Smart, C. (1990) Feminist approaches to criminology or postmodern woman meets atavistic man, in L. Gelsthorpe and A. Morris (eds) *Feminist Perspectives in Criminology.* Buckingham: Open University Press.

Snider, L. (1990) Co-operative models and corporate crime: panacea or cop-out?, *Crime and Delinquency*, 36(3): 373–90.

Snider, L. (1996) Directions for social change and political action, in E. Szockyj and J. G. Fox (eds) *Corporate Victimization of Women*, Boston, MA: Northeastern University Press.

South, N. (1998a) A green field for criminology? A proposal for a perspective, *Theoretical Criminology*, 2(2): 211–34.

South, N. (1998b) Corporate and state crimes against the environment: foundations for a green perspective in European criminology, in V. Ruggiero, N. South and I. Taylor (eds) *The New European Criminology: Crime and Social Order in Europe*. London and New York: Routledge.

Sparks, R. (1997) Recent social theory and the study of crime and punishment, in M. Maguire, R. Morgan and R. Reiner (eds) *The Oxford Handbook of Criminology*, 2nd edn. Oxford: Clarendon Press.

Stanko, E. (1990) *Everyday Violence: How Women and Men Experience Sexual and Physical Danger*. London: Pandora.

Stanley, C. (1992) Serious money: legitimation of deviancy in the financial markets, *International Journal of the Sociology of Law*, 20: 43–60.

Stanley, C. (1994) Speculators: culture, economy and the legitimation of deviance, *Crime, Law and Social Change*, 21: 229–51.

Steffensmeier, D. (1989) On the causes of white collar crime: an assessment of Hirschi and Gottfredson's claims, *Criminology*, 27: 345–58.

Steffensmeier, D. and Allan, E. A. (1995) Age-inequality and property crime: the effects of age-linked stratification and status-attainment processes on patterns of criminality across the life course, in J. Hagan and R. Peterson (eds) *Crime and Inequality*. Stanford, CA: Stanford University Press.

Stephenson-Burton, A. E. (1995) Through the looking glass: public images of white collar crime, in D. Hewitt and R. Osborne (eds) *Crime and the Media: The Postmodern Spectacle*. London: Pluto Press.

Sutherland, E. (1947) *Criminology*. Philadelphia, PA: Lippincott.

Sutherland, E. H. (1949) *White Collar Crime*. New York: Holt, Reinhart & Winston.

Sutton, A. and Wild, R. (1985) Small business: white collar villains or victims?, *International Journal of the Sociology of Law*, 13: 247–59.

Sykes, G. and Matza, D. (1957) Techniques of neutralization: a theory of delinquency, *American Sociological Review*, 22: 664–70.

Szockyj, E. and Fox, J. G. (eds) (1996) *Corporate Victimization of Women*. Boston, MA: Northeastern University Press.

Szockyj, E. and Frank, N. (1996) Introduction, in E. Szockyj and J. G. Fox (eds) *Corporate Victimization of Women*. Boston, MA: Northeastern University Press.

Tappan, P. (1977) Who is the criminal?, in G. Gies and R. F. Maier (eds) *White Collar Crime: Offences in Business, Politics and the Professions – Classic and Contemporary Views*. New York: Collier and Macmillan.

Taylor, I. (1997) Crime and social insecurity, *Criminal Justice Matters*, 27(spring): 3–4.

Taylor, I. (1999) *Crime in Context*. Cambridge: Polity Press.

Thomas, D. A. (1979) *Principles of Sentencing*. London: Heinemann.

Tombs, S. (1995) Corporate crime and new organisational forms, in F. Pearce and L.

Snider (eds) *Corporate Crime: Contemporary Debates*. Toronto: University of Toronto Press.

Tombs, S. (1999) Health and safety crimes: (in)visibility and the problems of 'knowing', in P. Davies, P. Francis and V. Jupp (eds) *Invisible Crimes: Their Victims and their Regulation*. London: Macmillan.

Van Duyne, P. (1993) Organized crime and business crime enterprises in the Netherlands, *Crime, Law and Social Change*, 19(2): 103–42.

Van Swaaningen, R. (1997) *Critical Criminology: Visions from Europe*. London: Sage.

Vaughan, D. and Carlo, G. (1975) The appliance repairman: a study of victim-responsiveness and fraud, *Journal of Research in Crime and Delinquency*, 12: 153–61.

Walklate, S. (1989) *Victimology: The Victim and the Criminal Justice Process*. London: Unwin Hyman.

Walklate, S. (1998) *Understanding Criminology: Current Theoretical Debates*. Buckingham: Open University Press.

Walklate, S. (1999) Can there be a meaningful victimology?, *Criminal Justice Matters*, 35(spring): 5–6.

Weait, M. (1995) The Serious Fraud Office: nightmares (and pipe dreams) on Elm Street, in I. Loveland (ed.) *Frontiers of Criminality*. London: Sweet & Maxwell.

Weisburd, D. and Schlegel, K. (1992) Returning to the mainstream: reflections on past and future white-collar crime study, in K. Schlegel and D. Weisburd (eds) *White Collar Crime Reconsidered*. Boston, MA: Northeastern University Press.

Weisburd, D., Wheeler, S., Waring, E. and Bode, N. (1991) *Crimes of the Middle Classes: White-collar Offenders in the Federal Courts*. New Haven, CT and London: Yale University Press.

Wells, C. (1989) Manslaughter and corporate crime, *New Law Journal*, 7 July: 931–4.

Wells, C. (1993) *Corporations and Criminal Responsibility*. Oxford: Clarendon Press.

Wells, C. (1995) *Negotiating Tragedy: Law and Disasters*. London: Sweet & Maxwell.

Wheeler, S. (1992) The problem of white collar crime motivation, in K. Schlegel and D. Weisburd (eds) *White Collar Crime Reconsidered*. Boston, MA: Northeastern University Press.

Wheeler, S., Mann, K. and Sarat, A. (1988) *Sitting in Judgement: The Sentencing of White Collar Criminals*. New Haven, CT and London: Yale University Press.

Yeager, P. (1995) Law, crime and inequality: the regulatory state, in J. Hagan and R. D. Peterson (eds) *Crime and Inequality*. Stanford, CA: Stanford University Press.

Young, J. (1997) Left realist criminology: radical in its analysis, realist in its policy, in M. Maguire, R. Morgan and R. Reiner (eds) *The Oxford Handbook of Criminology*, 2nd edn. Oxford: Clarendon Press.

Index

Page numbers in **bold** refer to main discussions, *g* denotes a glossary definition.